Real Estate
Valuing, Counseling, Forecasting

Real Estate
Valuing, Counseling, Forecasting

Selected Writings of John Robert White

American Institute of Real Estate Appraisers
of the National Association of Realtors®
430 N. Michigan Avenue
Chicago, Illinois

FOR EDUCATIONAL PURPOSES ONLY

ISBN: 0-911780-72-6

Printed in U.S.A.

Table of Contents

Foreword

When it was suggested that the Appraisal Institute publish a selected group of writings by John Robert White, the response was unanimously and appropriately enthusiastic. John Robert White has been a major contributor to real estate and appraisal thought since the late 1940s. From the beginning, his writings have conveyed his strong commitment to the appraisal profession. In his first articles, he stressed the need for appraisers to view themselves as professionals and to develop a lexicon that would bring their field closer to the greater financial world.

Since that time, John R. White has turned his attention to numerous topics, producing a body of written work of great depth and breadth. Many of his articles have dealt with important appraisal issues and techniques, buttressed by his own experience in appraising, analyzing, financing, and selling real estate, as well as counseling. This experience was gained in working with all types of real estate, including some of the nation's largest megastructures, notably Rockefeller Center, the Pan Am building, and the World Trade Center.

John Robert White has said that much of his success in real estate has largely been due to his appraisal education. In turn, we can say that much of our enrichment has been due to the writings of John Robert White.

Reaves C. Lukens, MAI
1984 President
Appraisal Institute

About the Author

John Robert White is currently chairman and chief executive officer of Landauer Associates (since 1963); president and chief executive officer of Landauer International, Inc. (since 1980). His real estate career began in 1946 with Byrne Bowman & Forshay, Inc. where he became a vice president (1954). He served as senior vice president, director and member of the Executive Committee for Brown, Harris, Stevens, Inc. (1954-1963). He is a director of Landauer Associates (since 1963) and Manhattan Life Insurance Company (since 1969); and a special limited partner of Investment Property Associates (since 1972). He was also a director of Bellemead Development Corporation (1970-1982) and L'Enfant Plaza Properties, Inc. (1976-1983); trustee of ICM Realty, Inc. (1971-1974), Union Dime Savings Bank (1968-1981), and vice chairman and trustee of BT Mortgage Investors (1970-1982).

Mr. White was formerly national president of the American Society of Real Estate Counselors (1969) and president of the New York Metropolitan Chapter of the American Institute of Real Estate Appraisers (1965) and the New York State Appraisal Society (1964); trustee of the Urban Land Institute (1977-1979; 1980-1986); governor of the AIREA Governing Council (1965-

1968), the National Association of Real Estate Investment Trusts (1965-1967), the New York State Appraisal Society (1964-1969), and governor of the Real Estate Board of New York, Inc. (1968-1970; 1976-1978).

Mr. White holds a Bachelor of Arts (B.A.) degree in government from Harvard College (1942) and a Master of Business Administration (M.B.A.) degree in real estate from New York University (1948). From 1948 until 1960, he was first an instructor and then adjunct associate professor of real estate, School of Commerce, New York University.

In addition to writing numerous articles throughout the past 38 years on real estate valuation, economics, and finance, Mr. White contributed to *Selected Readings in Real Estate Appraising* (1953). From 1961 to 1965 he served as chairman of the Editorial Board and editor in chief of *The Appraisal Journal*.

Mr. White is a member of the American Institute of Real Estate Appraisers, holding its MAI designation; the American Society of Real Estate Counselors, holding its CRE designation; the National Association of Certified Mortgage Bankers, holding the DF designation; the New York State Appraisal Society; the Real Estate Board of New York, Inc.; the Regional Plan Association; and the Urban Land Institute.

Preface

The Genesis of a Career

My writing career was inspired by Doctor H.B. Dorau, former chairman of the Public Utilities and Real Estate Department, School of Commerce, Accounts and Finance, New York University. One stormy, sleet-dominated night in the winter of 1948, I was the only student attending Dr. Dorau's graduate seminar in real estate. That evening, Dr. Dorau invited me to teach at the university, which I did for the next 12 years. Also that evening, we discussed the advantages, to both the teacher and the businessman, of writing articles. Little did I realize that I would eventually write 75 or more (I really do not know the precise number).

Dr. Dorau felt strongly about the relative importance of real estate and frequently quoted the industry expression, "Under all is the land." He saw real estate in a light far beyond the commonly accepted version of shelter and family hearth. Dr. Dorau readily saw the proportion of wealth represented by real estate in the capital markets and considered it an investment commodity competitive in all respects with securities and businesses of every sort. These were thrilling concepts to a young Realtor® with a somewhat parochial knowledge of real estate, despite his being located in a urban environment.

Dr. Dorau also recognized the importance of education. I remember how deeply impressed I was by his oft-repeated comment, "The *next* best thing to knowing is knowing how." In other words, some things simply must be learned because direct field experiences are not always possible. One cannot always experience firsthand everything that occurs in the selection, purchase, development, financing, management, and sale of real estate. Surely the appraiser must be doubly conscious of this principle because he or she is more an observer and analyst of the market scene than a direct participant. Thus, education helped to round out the knowledge gained from various experiences early in my career—working as a broker and manager and developing apartment houses—and to equip me to become a real estate consultant and appraiser.

A Career Progresses

From 1947 until 1963, I worked mainly as a broker and manager without a drawing account or expense account or a salary. I instinctively felt the need to have valuation capabilities, probably to relieve my feeling of insecurity about my rather hazardous brokerage existence! I began to perform a number of small appraisal assignments and to devote Friday afternoons to AIREA course study.

Since 1963, my career has been devoted almost exclusively to real estate counseling, including occasional valuation assignments of note. The combination of my early business experiences together with valuation skills enabled me to handle most of the frequent, perplexing problems I encountered. Because our business is essentially an investigative science, I learned early the importance of saying, "I do not know but I will find out." One is respected for maturity and candor and for the willingness to say he or she does not have all the answers.

In retrospect, two activities significantly influenced my career. First, teaching greatly enriched me. The challenges of research, of becoming aware of and understanding market events, and of responding to the great curiosity of my students have affected me deeply. One of my greatest satisfactions has been watching my students mature and prosper in the industry. Teaching also helped cure me of a basic insecurity in addressing groups, which appeared to stem from an unsuccessful attempt at radio broadcasting in my earlier years. Above all, teaching made me acutely conscious once again of the importance of education. I voraciously read business publications because the next best thing to knowing was knowing how.

The second major activity was obtaining the MAI designation. Appraising was never really my main craft. Probably no more than 25% of my time has been spent at it because I was always a generalist at heart. I felt there was a deeper meaning to accreditation. My AIREA training helped me develop a sense of arraying and interpreting figures, which I otherwise would have lacked. I became adept at obtaining both primary and secondary market data. I recognized the need for comparative analysis and for learning how valuation results could be methodologically achieved. I became more sensitive to external causations, such as the effect of the general economy on real estate markets. A deeper perspective on the real estate market was a natural consequence for me.

Undoubtedly the single largest transaction of its type in which I have been involved—the sale of the Pan Am Building—could not have been accomplished without my AIREA training. I needed to call on all my resources to estimate the market value, decide marketing strategy, and negotiate the sale. (*All* details of the sale are revealed for the first time in print in "A Marketing Revolution: The Sale of the Pan Am Building," p.189 of this volume.) I earnestly believe I would not have been able to cope with the complexities of the assignment were it not for my reasonable mastery of the MAI disciplines.

I believe it is absolutely critical for younger persons to undergo the AIREA educational experience. This is no less true for those who do not wish to choose appraising as a professional specialty. Because of the essentially nonhomogeneous and localized nature of real estate as a commodity, the industry is characterized by the need for individual pricing of real estate transactions. Education in market analyses, cost estimations, comparative analyses, income capitalization, and financing are essential to business effectiveness. Without formal training, how can widely divergent real estate of all types, degrees of obsolescence, and location be judged?

Are Collected Readings Worthwhile?

In perusing this book prior to purchase, one can reasonably ask whether much can be gained by reading a compilation of articles that reflect one person's views throughout his career. Would not the potential reader be better served by purchasing the latest books on methodology or the market? In my judgment, collected articles offer an unusual opportunity to appreciate events that are not so apparent at a given moment. For example, it has been fascinating to observe the methodological innovations that have taken place since the simplicity of the early use of the three approaches to value. Frederick Babcock, of Michigan University, was my early god in this respect, to be joined if not replaced by Leon W. Ellwood and James E. Gibbons. In more recent years, refinements in Ellwood's methods have been made by many others in the form of means of discounting future income streams. In my valuation articles, one sees more clearly the evolving nature of the valuation process. There is really no immutable method; change inevitably takes place, sometimes subtly and sometimes not. It is hoped, then, that a sense of perspective will be a major benefit of these articles.

Perhaps a second contribution is the demonstration of the breadth of the valuation process. One can slip easily into a narrow and quite literal interpretation of valuation methods. If nothing else, this slim volume shows how broad a professional practice can be. My most fervent wish is that the reader becomes more confident, even emboldened, about venturing into the mysterious worlds of forecasting future events in a macro and micro sense, and of counseling others on the problems of property ownership. These are natural extensions of the valuation process. They present opportunities for professional enhancement of one's career that are frequently overlooked by the appraiser.

Finally, careful reading of the articles will reveal the fragility of the forecasting process at a given moment. Yet there is no other viable way to estimate the future than to forecast what is likely to happen, property discounted for the time intervals involved. However imperfect the process may be, one must attempt to foresee future events. There can be no shirking of the need. No amount of rationale, for example, can defend successfully those who insist that cash-on-cash returns are the sole or even primary valuation determinant. To believe so makes one appear to be avoiding the consequences of the future.

Wholehearted Acknowledgments

Above all, my wife, Gloria, deserves the most plaudits for furthering my business and writing career. It was her infinite patience, tolerance, and understanding that enabled me to study, teach, and write, sometimes I confess at the expense of time that should have been spent with our growing family. In recent years, as I occasionally faltered in my resolve to keep observing and writing, my second son, Dr. Stuart H. White, geographer and anthropologist, inspired me through the beauty and strength of his own creative and scholarly writings.

In addition to Dr. H.B. Dorau, I have had many mentors and supporters who have aided me in my development. I am particularly fond of and grateful to my father-in-law, J.O. Pedersen, in his time, an apartment developer and investor; to Harry K. Keller, MAI, and S. Edwin Kazdin, MAI, of New York, who were very influential in my early career; and to James D. Landauer and Peter C. Haeffner, who were my predecessors as leaders of Landauer Associates, Inc. A special tribute is due James E. Gibbons who, in my judgment, has had no superior in the practice of real estate valuation and whose contributions to valuation methodology will be recognized for time immemorial. Jim Gibbons has been a very special inspiration in my life and works. Further gratitude and thanks are due to Karla Heuer, AIREA director of External Affairs, for assisting me in binding my disparate writings into a cohesive whole. Finally, Mary H. Smith, my administrative aide, deserves much credit and praise for her editorial assistance and for her shepherding of the publication process.

Part I
Valuing

One of my major philosophical concerns is best expressed in the first article, "This Issue of Professionalism," which I wrote in 1960. In the article, I comment on the standards required to achieve true professional status and ask rhetorically, What is wrong with being considered a business person? Appraisers have since moved closer to professional recognition, but they still lack full credentials in uniform educational requirements and state licensing by rigorous examination. Until we qualify, I do not mind being considered a businessman!

In these articles, and indeed throughout the years I have practiced appraisal, I have attempted to be creative in situations that have allowed a more novel approach than is the case in most appraisal assignments. Occasionally, however, I was a bit restless about the standard methodology of the three approaches to value.

My main contribution to the appraisal profession is usually considered to be expressing a new concept. In "Toward Universally Acceptable Semantics," Peter F. Spies and I sought to move appraisers closer but not identical to the accounting profession by urging the adoption of similar language and format in revenue and expense projections as well as in other areas. In "Land Market

Comparison Techniques in High-Density Urban Areas," R. Gary Barth and I attempted to devise unique methods of land comparison based on land sizes and location. In retrospect, a regression analysis might also have been part of our analysis. For me, the most interesting and rewarding article remains "George Washington Bridge Approach: A Case Study," in which a study was made of the value of air rights over the depressed road beds, and then a modified formula was devised to value air rights. Previously, others, most notably Walter Kuehnle, MAI, had also created air rights formulas. To my knowledge, my modified formula, which can be applied to sales comparison or income capitalization techniques, is still widely used today.

As inflation became more ingrained in our economy in the late 1970s, appraisers increasingly turned to forecasting over a specific time span, usually the expiration period of leases. Initial cash-on-cash returns faded in significance as one peered into the future by constructing rent matrixes and expenses at current levels and then compounding them at estimated growth rates. With the added forecasting and added calculations came the opportunity for abuse. Popularized by the leak of rent projections on the Pan Am Building to the *New York Times,* apparently by a disappointed buyer, the methodology gained widespread use. "Beware the Abusers of IRR Methodology," which I wrote with a former associate, Robert A. Steele, attempts to point out how easy it is to inflate value by excessive compound rent growth rates, underestimation of operating expenses and their growth, and use of indefensibly low internal rates of return or capitalization rates. We were determined to warn the professional appraisal world against abuse. Since 1982, inflation has moderated and oversupply has driven rents down, which together with an 18-month recession has exposed many of the excesses in which some in the industry have indulged.

Another concern has been the inconsistency with which local assessors value private recreational facilities, such as golf courses or tennis and swim clubs, in relatively built-up areas. It is perplexing that such essential open space, serving in many cases as a community decongestant, be taxed for property purposes on its alternate highest and best use, presumably expensive private housing. In "Private Recreational Facilities: Real Estate Tax Policy," suggestions are made for changes in zoning that would enable the local appraiser to value the land as essentially open space. If the open space enhances property values generally, and especially dwellings facing the open space, their assessments should be raised as an alternative.

In looking back, surely the development world has grown bigger. Projects have not only increased in size but have become multipurpose. I have been privileged to have appraised some of the country's largest megastructures. Surely the appraisal techniques differ somewhat from those applying to smaller, single purpose buildings. In "Valuing Megastructures," I have attempted, in a simple way, to explain the differences. Most of these arise out of the impact that such a large structure has on the market. Others involve such matters as increased security and lighting and the difficulty of mortgage financing. All factors illustrate the ever-changing character of the market and the investments in the market. Alertness and responsiveness to progress and change are essential for the practicing appraiser.

1
This Issue of Professionalism

There has been an increasingly strong drive in recent years for professional status and professional recognition among various business groups. A primary motivation appears to be a desire for prestige. Undoubtedly, a further contributing factor is the disposition to feel that professional status will ensure additional income.

The great danger in such a drive is the abuse of the privilege of the term *profession* or *professional*. Many business groups appear to have gone to extreme lengths to attain professional recognition. A recent article in *Business Week* referred to the inclination of public relations counselors and public relations corporate employees to regard themselves as professionals. We are all aware of the desire of the various appraisal societies to achieve true professional status. Concurrently, many brokers performing essentially brokerage functions also have been inclined to regard themselves as professionals.

Traditionally, law, medicine, divinity, and teaching have been regarded as professional occupations. Over the years dentistry, architecture, engineering,

Reprinted from *The Appraisal Journal* (October 1960): 539-41.

and accounting have come to be generally accepted as professional practices. Calling oneself a professional is a privilege which should logically be reserved for those who have been carefully prequalified for the designation.

What are those qualifications that an individual or a group must possess before attaining true professional status? Can standards be devised that would enable real estate practitioners and appraisers to assess more objectively and expertly the qualifications of their field for professional status? The answers can only be derived by comparison with the qualification standards of the recognized professions.

Intellectual capacity.   It is clear that professional status must belong to those engaged in mental as distinguished from manual labor. The demands of intellectual effort must be great and clearly above the level of the intellectual demand in normal business activities.

Significant responsibility and importance.   The business practice must be one in which the practitioner is called upon to exercise a high level of discretionary authority and be depended upon to make decisions and analyses of the highest caliber. It is of vital importance that the authority, decisions, and analyses involve the well-being of the community. It is clear that the appraisal business frequently qualifies in this respect since important decisions concerning buying, selling, financing, and condemning of property are served by an appraisal.

Uniform academic standards.   Professional status may only be attained after the individual has successfully completed the discipline of higher education. This may require a minimum college degree or, as in many fields, one or more advanced degrees. In addition, specialized education is frequently undertaken to ensure a greater mastery of one's professional activity.

Licensing and examinations.   Most professional fields now require that the professional successfully complete an examination given under state auspices. This is true of law, medicine, teaching, architecture, engineering, accounting, and dentistry. These examinations are not minimal, but rather are carefully devised to test the entire range of the examinee's professional competence. Only after successful completion is the individual awarded a license to practice.

Public recognition.   In the final analysis it will be the public who decides whether a particular group or body is truly deserving of professional status and recognition. Only when uniform minimum standards of competence and conduct have been achieved through the discipline of education and group action will the public grant this very essential recognition.

Standards of integrity and conduct.   Every professional group should adhere to a rigorously enforced code of ethical conduct. Personal integrity, exemplary relations with clients and competitors, and conscientious performance of professional duties are the basic elements of a code of ethical conduct.

Social responsibility.   Every professional group has an inherent right to earn income profits. On the other hand, every professional should have a strong sense of social responsibility. This responsibility is best manifest by the contribution of one's services to deserving individuals and groups unable to pay the usual professional fee. This has certainly been characteristic of the medical profession and, in many instances, the legal profession. Both of these professional groups have frequently given their time and competence without fee to aid deserving individuals. Perhaps to a lesser extent, other professional groups are striving to make this type of social contribution.

Formation of professional societies.   Professional practitioners must of necessity ban together for the purpose of expressing their professional view-points, undertaking educational efforts on the group's behalf, accomplishing research to widen their competence and exchanging ideas and experiences.

Assuming that the eight qualifications enumerated above form a sound basis for the determination of true professional status, we may now examine our own practice of appraising with a viewpoint of determining whether we have attained professional standing. There is no question but that we qualify on the basis of intellectual capacity. Certainly we do so on the basis of significant responsibility and importance. Furthermore, we have evolved standards of ethical conduct and have formed many different professional groups for the usual professional purposes. To some extent the public has begun to recognize at least appraising, if not brokerage, as a profession. It cannot be said, however, that complete public recognition of appraising as a profession has yet been received.

In two very important respects we must regretfully say that the appraiser does not yet appear to qualify for professional standing. As yet, no appraisal group requires uniform higher academic standards, although we are increasingly more insistent on the passage of specialized examinations. No qualifications based on academic education as recognized by a college or higher degree have yet been established. It is doubtful that professional status can be achieved until this qualification is accepted by the various appraisal groups. To ensure full recognition, it is also suggested that a state license examination of the highest caliber be devised for appraisers. Unlike the state license examination for salespersons and brokers, this examination should be prepared to determine, in the most comprehensive manner possible, the depth of professional learning and competence of the applicant. The standard of this examination should be such that there will be little doubt about the minimum professional competence of the practitioner after he or she successfully completes it.

Realistically, it will be many years before there is full acceptance in the appraisal business for the need of these two qualifications. Many earnest and competent appraisers feel that a college education and public licensing are not essential prerequisites for professionalism. Although some of us may differ on the meaning of professional status, we are certain that all appraisal groups and all individual appraisers agree that a professional attitude, as distinguished from professional status, is essential in our business. If we continue to base our behavior and conduct on the highest plane of ethics, and if we continue to strive to attain the highest plane of professional competence and learning, our professional attitude will continue to be favorably recognized by the public. Ultimately and inevitably, as more of us agree that we have qualified in every sense for professional standing, the practice of real estate appraising will become a true profession. In the interim, the practicing appraiser has every right to be proud of his or her position as a business person who maintains a professional attitude concerning business activities.

2

Real Estate Appraisals: How They Pay Off for Investors

The highly fragmented and extremely localized real estate market is governed by a dominant factor: the nonduplicative nature of real estate as a commodity. Because no two sites are identically located, these geographical differences can provoke widespread value differentials, even within a physically limited area. When one then considers the multiplicities of use, design, and quality of urban buildings, it is all the more evident that real estate is a nonidentical product. The appraiser thus tends to play a stronger and more influential role in real estate than in products that are readily mass-produced. This is especially the case in pooled real estate investment funds, where a high degree of reliance is placed on valuation experts in recommending properties for purchase and in estimating asset growth over an extended period. The absence of centralized exchanges; the difficulty of tracking down recorded sales data; the problem of getting additional information about the details of sale from the seller—all point to the need to engage a qualified appraiser to supply the market and sales data and offer interpretive opinions on which an intelligent investment decision can be made.

The appraiser is employed for a wide variety of purposes. For example, both government and private users engage him to make condemnation or tax abatement appraisals. He makes estate tax appraisals for attorneys and executors. Mortgagees engage him in connection with prospective financing or refinancing. Our concentration here, however, is on appraisal requirements in connection with real estate investment—either in the acquisition, holding, or disposition of real estate, with special emphasis on how the appraiser serves the institutional investor or commercial bank trust officer.

Questions have been raised in recent years about the relative accuracy of appraisals, as well as the competence of appraisers by investment managers wary of open-end pooled real estate funds. These funds will accept money on a continuing basis to the extent that investment opportunities exist which meet designated criteria. Because these funds are privately operated, investors cannot have a clear idea of market value without annual or biannual appraisals by a disinterested professional appraiser. The appraisers have been criticized variously for inaccuracies, inconsistencies, and for demonstrating a possible bias toward successively higher annual values. Although undoubtedly a small minority of appraisers have been found wanting, there is absolutely no reason for an investor to feel that he may be misled by the use of the annual valuation method of reporting financial performance, or for any other appraisal purpose.

Avoidance of inadequate appraisals starts with the selection process. The client must carefully check out the appraiser's background, experience, and the quality of his clientele. Professional accreditation is only the beginning of his qualifications. It is imperative to determine whether he has appraised real estate similar to that in the portfolio. Consideration also must be given to his experience in multiple property, i.e., multiple location valuation accounts in which a team of experts must be organized, some of whom may be subcontractors of the appraiser.

Importance of Market Analysis

Appraisers traditionally have been weak in market analysis capabilities. Our experience in the past three years of real estate recession has conclusively evidenced the essential role that careful analysis plays in the decision of what and when to build. Marketability and feasibility should be more important to the institutional investor than the precise appraisal amount. Thus, the investor should be insistent that the appraiser be well qualified as a market analyst.

Consistency in the use of valuation techniques will act to lessen errors when many different appraisers are utilized. Uniformity in the reporting format will avoid any misunderstanding of the individual reports by the client. Thus, experience in the organization and management aspects of large-scale portfolio appraising is an all-important qualification.

More effective appraisals also require the client to issue clear and explicit instructions to the appraiser on the appraisal presumptions. Not only must the purpose of the appraisal be made clear, but all other facts bearing on the value must be divulged also. For example, is the appraisal to be made as if the property were free and clear of mortgage debt, or is it to be made subject to any existing mortgages? In a recent instance, a small real estate trust ordered appraisals without specifying them as equity appraisals subject to existing mortgages. The appraiser delivered appraisals as if free of mortgage debt, using an inapplicable Ellwood capitalization method. The results were useless to the client and the work had to be redone.

Generally, but certainly not always, the larger the appraisal company the more assured will be the results where widely scattered properties are involved. The larger companies have more extensive staffs with highly specialized skills, not only in valuation but also in market research and analysis and in computer applications. The larger companies maintain extensive libraries with detailed data on the metropolitan area's economic base and on real estate market conditions. These companies frequently have brokerage, consulting, or development operations as well. The appraisal staff is in a position to draw on the knowledge and skills of other specialists in the solution of appraisal problems. In sum, the thesis that holds the appraisal process as inherently inaccurate or unreliable cannot be accepted. Appraisals made by qualified professionals will reflect the market. If the appraiser's instructions have been provided carefully and thoughtfully for him, the appraisal results can portray market conditions consistently and accurately.

There is a well-known commercial and industrial development company that has a large subordinated note outstanding, held by a group of pension funds. One of the terms of the note requires an annual appraisal. This has now been done for 13 years. In that period, many of the appraised properties have been sold. In the aggregate, the sales have exceeded the appraisals by 3%. This is exceptionally accurate. The development company now has come to rely on the appraisals as reflective of the market and as a basis for sale. The note holders also have a reasonable estimate of the aggregate asset value of the real estate portfolio. Numerous public and private real estate companies have had similar positive experiences with annual valuations.

Annual Appraisal Requirements

Of late, the Securities and Exchange Commission has moved strongly to the concept of annual appraisals by an independent appraiser or appraisal company. Although the real estate investment and development companies do not object in principle, they resist because of the cost. They do agree that the profit and loss statement and book balance sheet in the annual report do not always present the current status of the company accurately. Thus, the idea of an appraised net capital, or appraised net worth, is fast gaining adherents. Only two basic changes are necessary in the balance sheet. First, the net appraised market value of the real estate is substituted for the net book value. Second, a provision is made for capital gains payable in the hypothetical event of sale at the appraised value.

An interesting variation is to have the annual appraisals made by the investment or development company itself. The independent fee appraiser specifies what data must be provided in the company appraisals. The methods employed by the company in arriving at the appraised value also must be approved by the appraiser. The appraisal results then are subjected to review, first for the accuracy of data by the company's auditors, and second, for valuation documentation, rationale, and credibility by the independent appraiser. The appraiser would concur with the company's findings only if his opinion of value were within 10% of the equity value, or within 3% of the free and clear valuation. The definition of concurrence must be spelled out in the appraiser's certification letter, which usually will be included in the annual report.

Trend to Debt-Free Realty Investment

Pension funds generally have been disposed to buy real estate free of mortgage debt to ensure that they will have no unrelated business income tax. An equally compelling reason is the desire of the funds to make only conservative investments. Because the funds seek to avoid income tax liability, it is of no advantage for them to incur tax-deductible mortgage interest. The problem is that pension funds must compete with equity buyers for a scarce supply of available prime properties. Sellers build into the selling price the advantage to equity buyers of good mortgage financing and extensive tax shelter, neither of which has any meaning to the fund. Thus, the fund is paying a premium for investment advantages it cannot use. Additionally, the fund must pay a prepayment penalty that frequently ranges from 2% to 5% if the property has an existing mortgage.

From an appraisal viewpoint, the nondebt-burdened property traditionally has been worth less than a mortgaged property. The general rule is: The greater the cash requirement, the higher the required rate of return. Further, because the property does not have the income tax offset of mortgage interest, it is theoretically liable for large income taxes and is less desirable on an after-tax basis. The obvious compensation for the buyer is to raise the rate of return. The typical noninstitutional investor also seeks to obtain positive leveraging, i.e., a mortgage debt service factor that is less than the free and clear rate of return. This advantage has disappeared of late; leveraging has turned negative as the mortgage factor has exceeded the free and clear rate of return.

However, because the market for debt-free properties is increasingly dominated by tax-free pension fund buyers, the traditional discount for cash is fast disappearing. We are witnessing a condition in which differentials between cash and terms buyers have just about vanished.

Appraisal in Acquisition and Disposition

Real estate acquisitions are being made in increasing numbers by both foreign and domestic institutional buyers without prior experience in the field. Most—especially the insurance companies but also the commercial banks and real estate investment advisers—have relied on investment managers. All the investment managers and advisers have appraisers on their staff who are used to analyzing the market, the property itself, the revenue and expenses, and the anticipated selling price. This staff service is invaluable to the acquisition officers. It avoids errors and helps the managers discriminate in their selection of the available properties. Some buyers have attempted to purchase directly without going through investment managers. If they insist on this approach, they are advised particularly to engage the services of an independent appraiser to assist them in the essential screening process. We have recently witnessed some unbelievably poor acquisitions by institutional buyers acting through brokers, without appraisal or consulting assistance. The costs of such services are minimal when one considers how high the stakes are.

The appraiser also is playing an enlarged role in appraising property in anticipation of sale. The seller in this instance does not require a lengthy or heavily documented report. He needs a range of values with a mean figure representing the most probable selling price. This appraisal should be influenced by the cash requirement and by whether or not any purchase money mortgage financing will be provided by the seller. The appraiser also can offer guidance in setting the asking price, in the probable period of time required to sell, and the most logical type of buyers.

Much time can be wasted by a seller in placing an inordinately high price on a piece of property and expecting the market value to evolve out of offers and negotiations. The seller also runs the risk of damaging the image of his real estate by having it in the market for an extended period of time. He may have missed the market with these tactics. He is served much better by obtaining sound advice on what his real estate logically should sell for and by devising his sales strategy accordingly. Because an extensive report is not required, the appraisal for sale purposes should be obtainable at lesser cost than, for example, appraisals for financing purposes.

Latest Appraisal Techniques

Greater emphasis will be placed on the depth and adequacy of market research and analysis. Especially in new construction, the appraiser must be more effective in analyzing the best site utilization; the style, design, and layout of the space; the obtainable rent; and the period of time required to achieve normal occupancy—commonly referred to as the absorption rate. The allocation to the subject property of its reasonable market share and the timing of receipt of that share is no easy calculation. The truly outstanding appraisers are learning to do this with improved facility.

No arbitrary presumptions will be made hereafter on the vacancy rate. Appraisers once presumed normal occupancy, sometimes on the instructions of their clients, rather than estimate the probable occupancy over a reasonable time span before achieving a stabilized occupancy. Again, increased sensitivity to market conditions will be demanded by appraisers' clientele and hypothetical presumptions that may not bear any resemblance to market realities will be avoided.

Computer Techniques

The computer has become an invaluable appraisal tool in the capitalization process. Techniques have been developed to calculate the pre-tax and after-tax discounted, i.e., internal rate of return over a presumed ownership period. The methodology usually presumes a sale at an estimated price. The internal rate of return is thus an all-inclusive measure of a property's performance. It is now mathematically possible to break out all the components of the return, including net income, tax-free recapture of amortization, tax shelter effect, increases in net income, gain or loss on sale, and costs of the sale. The precise percentage contribution of each component can be identified.

Equally important, the same computer programming permits sensitivity analyses of an advanced character. Any change in presumption which in effect forces other changes is automatically computed. Endless calculating time is saved, and much more can be learned about the prospects for the property. In a recent $38 million acquisition negotiated by a real estate consulting company, the computer was checked for every substantive change in the terms of the transaction in order to preserve a targeted investment goal of a minimum of 10.5% after-tax internal rate of return for the property.

Real Estate Value: A Comparative Process

Another distinct improvement in appraisal technology is found in comparative analysis. Although appraisers have been very efficient in locating raw market data on sales and sales volume, prices, rent levels, occupancy, and construction starts, they have not been as adept in applying this mass of data effectively. Statistical methodology is increasingly finding a place in real estate appraising. For example, regression and linear analysis and probability analysis have become commonplace in analyzing comparable data. More orderly and scientific arraying of data is more evident. The mere random presentation of market data no longer is acceptable. We are more and more appreciative of the fact that real estate value is a comparative process. Real estate, because of its non-duplicative character, best illustrates the theory of relativity: Nothing is absolute, everything is comparative.

Historically, appraisers have had almost a slavish devotion to net income capitalization as the primary and frequently sole method of estimating value. Of late, a new concept of "inherent asset value" is beginning to emerge as an important valuation determinant. This theory holds that value is not solely a function of converting the income stream to a present worth. The value of any existing property also must be influenced by its relationship to the cost of similar but new competitive real estate which presumably embodies all the recent advances in the arts and sciences as expressed in design, functional utility, materials, and equipment. We refer to this relationship as the extent of competitive parity of the existing real estate. In other words, the capacity of the existing real estate to compete against its more modern counterpart is an influencing factor in the valuation, quite aside from its current net income. The higher the degree of competitive parity, the higher the assurance that rents and net income can be increased. Because it has become increasingly more difficult to develop new real estate due to exhaustive regulatory impediments, there is every indication that the existing supply of well-located and well-designed real estate will experience steady increases in net income and value for years to come.

3
Toward Universally Acceptable
Semantics

The appraisal profession has taken quantum strides in developing common parlance appropriate to the methodology of real estate valuation and yet understandable to the financial community. However, further progress is needed. Improved communication and understanding between the appraiser and client and/or client's accountant, banker, and attorney is an important goal. At the base of the problem has been the disposition of the appraiser to adopt a language body that sometimes has a confusing meaning to those using appraisal reports.

In terms of numbers, we are too few to contrive our own lexicon by using inventive phrases; our clients will become misled and frustrated. The American Institute of Real Estate Appraisers (the Appraisal Institute) has approximately 4,000 MAIs, and the Society of Real Estate Appraisers has about 2,200 SREA or SRPA members. Recognizing the prevalence of dual membership, less than 6,200 persons hold a professional designation in the two organiza-

This article was written with Peter F. Spies. Reprinted from *The Appraisal Journal* (January 1978): 67-68.

tions. On the other hand, approximately 700,000 accountants were identified in the 1970 census, and the American Institute of Certified Public Accountants reported a 1974 unofficial membership of about 160,000 CPAs. Furthermore, when financial officers of commercial banks, investment banks, and other lending institutions and corporations are considered, the total number of persons employing a relatively standardized professional investment vocabulary becomes awesome. Even though the appraisal profession has an impact far beyond the size of its membership, we are still too small to establish our own vocabulary. To the extent feasible, we must adopt language in common usage by financial and investment people. Only then can the full intent of the appraisal and/or consulting report be conveyed effectively to the client.

A change to universally recognized semantics has been made doubly necessary because the body of clients seeking appraisal services is assuming new form. For example, national and international financial and corporate organizations are becoming more aware of their large real estate portfolios as a potential for more accurately reporting net worth. For 1976 annual reports, the Securities and Exchange Commission (SEC) has required 100 of the nation's biggest corporations to adopt current value or replacement cost financial statements. Real estate assets on the balance sheets surely will demand professional expertise in deriving reasonable value estimates. Moreover, the major commercial banks who have become unwilling owners of real estate (through either foreclosures on their construction loans or asset swaps with client real estate investment trusts [REITs]) have been directed by the Comptroller of the Currency to obtain professionally prepared independent valuations of their holdings. Recognizing the financial backgrounds of the substantial corporations and institutions, our appraisals can be responsive to their needs only by adopting a common language employed in general financial matters.

A brief history of the appraisal profession's evolution will provide essential background into the nature of the current problem. The Appraisal Institute was founded during the Great Depression of the 1930s. Appraisers appeared to rely mainly on Frederick M. Babcock's classic *Valuation of Real Estate* in establishing a language body. The Appraisal Institute published the first edition of *The Appraisal of Real Estate* in 1951 and subsequently revised the basic text five times (with the sixth edition, third printing, copyrighted in 1977).* Appraising practices experienced dramatic changes when the distinguished L. W. Ellwood introduced his theory in the late 1950s, integrating equity and debt requirements in synthesizing an overall capitalization rate. A new body of terminology was introduced, and the appraisal profession absorbed much new language in describing the far-reaching Ellwood methodology.

For illustrative purposes we have selected several terms and concepts commonly used in appraisal practice and defined in *Real Estate Appraisal Ter-*

---

*The 8th edition of *The Appraisal of Real Estate* was published in 1983.

minology, a glossary of appraisal and related terms jointly sponsored by the Appraisal Institute and the Society of Real Estate Appraisers.[1]

By accounting and financial standards, each term to be discussed is considered either inappropriate, susceptible to misunderstanding, or slang. We shall identify each word or phrase, express our views regarding the ambiguities, and recommend substitute terminology. We offer only a partial list of the most egregious examples in an attempt to elicit discussion; the phrases chosen cannot be construed as all-encompassing. A more formal, comprehensive study undoubtedly will identify additional words or phrases that may be inappropriately used or misunderstood. Painstaking additional research is required to eradicate improper terms from our lexicon and to ensure that our own terminology reflects commonly accepted usage in the accounting and investment fields.

Revenue and Expense Analysis

Quite naturally, the preponderance of terms requiring reexamination are part of the appraiser's revenue and expense projections. (We intentionally have substituted the word *revenue* for the more frequently used *income*; we shall justify our position in a subsequent part of this article.) In establishing essential background, we should recognize that the revenue and expense pro forma taught in Appraisal Institute courses and adopted in general practice is intended basically as an accrual accounting method. Accrual accounting modifies actual cash receipts and disbursements to reflect more stabilized conditions by matching revenues to expenses in the fiscal periods incurred, and is the adopted premise in Generally Acceptable Accounting Practice (GAAP). Conversely, cash basis accounting reflects all revenues received and all expenses incurred in a particular fiscal period, whether or not the events reflect normal circumstances. For example, if a three-year insurance premium were paid in a lump sum, cash basis accounting would take the entire expense in the period paid, while the accrual method would take one-third of the premium for each fiscal year.

The thrust of the appraiser's pro forma is to project stabilized revenues and expenses; hence, this is an accrual accounting vehicle. For example, our gross collections are modified by a vacancy allowance to show levels of most probable revenue receipts. In the case of prepaid rent, the revenues must be projected over the contract period rather than their receipt being recognized at

[1]The authors are indebted to Byrl N. Boyce, compiler and editor of *Real Estate Appraisal Terminology* (Cambridge, Mass.: Ballinger Publishing Co., 1975), and to Eric L. Kohler, author of *A Dictionary for Accountants* (Englewood Cliffs, N.J.: Prentice-Hall, Inc., 1975). Both texts served as the basis for this article.

prepayment. Expenses are adjusted to suggest outflows typically experienced for the fiscal period. Clearly, the recognition of a reserve for replacement fund is an accrual treatment of anticipated capital expenses.

Gross Collections and Revenues

Beginning with the first line of a classic, reconstructed revenue and expense statement, accountants in recent years have tended to prefer the term *revenue* or *gross revenue* in place of *gross income* when reporting sales of goods, services, or rents. Generally, gross collections should be referred to as *revenues,* representing gross receipts before expenses. *Gross potential revenue* should include scheduled rentals, escalations, percentage rents, concessions, electric payments, tenant charges, and other revenues (unless their respective expenses have been netted out). Following the same thought, *effective gross income* actually should be *effective gross revenue.* The reference to *income* should be associated with *net income,* i.e., gross revenue less all expenses. The following paragraphs will further clarify our suggestions concerning the various levels of net income.

Expenses

Proceeding into the expense categories, the traditional discipline requires an allocation into fixed, operating, and reserves for replacement expenses. Although these three primary expenditure classifications permit an orderly presentation, the allocation is entirely unique to the appraisal field and has been unable to attract other financial reporters to follow suit. By itself, the above reason is insufficient to prompt a change. Unfortunately, the three-tier distinction causes confusion. The investment community identifies all normal recurring expenses as *operating expenses.* When the appraiser reports a certain level of operating expenses (v. fixed expenses or reserves), the client tends to confuse the estimate with the total amount of annual recurring outflows. Compounding the problem is the appraiser's use of an operating expense ratio. The Appraisal Institute teaches that an operating expense ratio is total operating expenses (including fixed, reserves, and operating) divided by either *gross or effective gross revenues.* In one instance, *operating expenses* implies only one of three basic expense classifications, while in another situation the same label means all recurring outflows. The obvious inconsistencies demand correction. A revised revenue and expense format with appropriate nomenclature will be suggested in a subsequent section of this presentation. Fixed expenses and reserves simply should be part of a normal operating expense budget.

Net Operating Income or Net Income before Recapture

The next pitfall on the reconstructed statement is net operating income or net income before recapture. We'll discuss the terms in reverse order.

Appraisers have devoted many hours of course lectures and reams of literature to describing the methods of recapturing the initial capital investment; this has been an important area of concern. However, the larger financial community rarely introduces terminology intimating levels of income before or after capital recapture. In fact, the word *recapture* is used most often to indicate that portion of a capital gain attributable to accelerated depreciation deductions during the period of ownership.

Before Ellwood introduced his theories highlighting capital recapture of the equity position and focusing upon the significance of financing, net operating income generally was attributed to a property held on a free and clear basis. Presuming capitalization with straight line recapture, the capitalization rate used to convert net income imputable to the building into a present value incorporated a provision for a loss in value (and a related decline in income) attributed to the improvements, thought of as wasting assets. Consequently, net income free and clear was sometimes identified as *net income before depreciation.* With the recognition and acceptance of mortgage-equity concepts, the phrase was changed to *net income before recapture,* emphasizing *return of* investment was not necessarily accounted for through a depreciation allowance. However, when an investment is acquired on an all-cash basis (as many foreign investors and large commingled pension funds have a penchant for doing), net income before depreciation is germane. Furthermore, *depreciation* is universally acceptable and suggests a loss in value. Establishing a depreciation allowance effectively permits recouping invested capital in a wasting asset. *Net income before recapture* should be eliminated; the term is inhibiting and not readily understood. When the appraiser wants to use methodology requiring identification of net income before provision for capital return, it is best to express it as a net income before depreciation. We will make further specific suggestions incorporating these thoughts in subsequent paragraphs.

Recognizing the reconstructed revenue and expense statement as an accrual method of accounting for various inflows and outflows, net operating income is an invalid label when subtracting all expenses from *effective gross revenue.* The phrase should be altered to clarify misconceptions because many questions are left unanswered. Is the net operating income before or after federal, state, and/or local income taxes? Have principal and/or interest payments been deducted? Has depreciation been expensed? These honest inquiries are asked frequently by financial and accounting professionals reading appraisal reports.

Conciseness is a virtue when appropriate, but descriptive nomenclature clarifies ambiguities and tends to avoid investment decisions founded on erroneous presumptions. Consequently, we would like to see net operating income and net income before recapture replaced with *pre-tax net income before debt service or depreciation*. Admittedly, the long descriptive phrase is cumbersome, but it is precise and immediately will convey the proper message to financial and accounting executives.

Remember, *pre-tax net income before debt service or depreciation* is a presumed typical sum; the actual dollars received for the year under study almost certainly will vary from the carefully derived estimate. The accounting and financial communities understand the methods used in income forecasting and readily accept a bottom line premised on an accrual system.

Equity Dividend

Now the semantic problem multiplies. Subtracting principal and interest payments from *pre-tax net income before debt service or depreciation* leaves an amount attributable to the equity that is commonly identified as either an *equity dividend* or a *pre-tax cash flow*. Both terms are inaccurate.

Equity dividend is part of the nomenclature resulting directly from Ellwood's outstanding mathematical contributions. The accounting field avoids distinguishing between an equity dividend and any other type of dividend; most dividends paid by corporations are drawn from after-tax earnings. (Of course, the obvious exceptions are the REITs, which may avoid the incidence of federal taxation by distributing 90% or more of their pre-tax earnings to their shareholders.) An equity is an interest in real estate subject to the claims of creditors, if any; the monetary return on equity is net income or net earnings and is not a dividend. Furthermore, the corporate dividend is usually only a part of corporate after-tax earnings, and after-tax earnings are computed by GAAP methods that expense both depreciation and interest on debt but exclude debt repayment. Principal repayment of long-term debt (known as amortization) is a savings because it reduces an outstanding liability and hence is not treated as an expense, even though it is an outflow. Because dividends flow from corporate earnings that connote an after-tax position and that expense depreciation while not deducting amortization payments, any attempt to draw valid parallels to standard financial terminology by adopting the phrase *equity dividend* becomes highly improper. Additionally, the term *dividend* implies a corporate form of ownership, while in actuality real property ownership is effected in a variety of other ways including individual proprietorships, partnerships, or joint ventures.

The use of equity dividend is inaccurate and raises so many issues that it must be discarded as a description of any portion of *pre-tax net income before debt service or depreciation*. Use of the phrase *equity dividend* has been peculiar to the appraisal field and has inhibited effective communication with the financial community.

The Problem of Cash Flow

Pre-tax cash flow is also an inappropriate substitution for equity dividend because it intimates cash basis accounting, or actual cash receipts and disbursements. Corporate financial statements usually refer to cash positions in terms of *source and application of funds* or *changes in financial position.* Many credit analysts and accountants feel cash flow statements provide a helpful perspective regarding a financial position and are useful for planning and budgeting. As we have clearly defined above, the portion left of the *pre-tax net income before debt service or depreciation* after making principal and interest payments on the outstanding debt is premised on accrual accounting; identifying that portion of the income as a pre-tax cash flow is a practice that potentially could cause a client to make an investment decision based on an erroneous presumption.

Cash flow is simply cash in and cash out. Unlike cash accounting, cash flow consolidates revenues from capital sources such as equity or loan proceeds together with rents and other miscellaneous revenue. Similarly, it provides an outgo picture that includes both capital and operating outlays.

As a matter of procedure, businesses maintain two sets of books; one for reporting earnings and the other for Internal Revenue Service purposes. The appraisal profession may be approaching the era when two statements are appropriate, including both a reconstructed profit and loss statement based on accrual accounting, and a source and application of funds projection, i.e., cash flow presentation. For example, for an office building requiring extensive capital improvements in a near-term time framework (perhaps for tenant installations with either older leases approaching termination or for a new structure still experiencing initial leasing activity), a traditional revenue and expense statement based upon averaging recurring expenses would be necessary and proper in establishing asset value. Equally as important would be a true cash-flow statement comparing expected revenues with the large capital expenditures anticipated in the early years. Armed with the anticipated chronology of income shortfalls, prudent financial planning will be able to make effective preparations to alleviate cash shortages in the investment.

Pre-Tax Net Income before Depreciation

Accepting equity dividend as misleading, and acknowledging pre-tax cash flow as inaccurate (because the cash flow presumption is violated), we offer a simple substitute. The portion of the *pre-tax net income before debt service or depreciation* remaining after making principal and amortization payments could best be described as *pre-tax net income before depreciation.* The term clearly identifies a before-tax status, and deleting the *debt service* reference indicates principal and interest payments have been deducted.

We are tempted to suggest the phrase *pre-tax earnings* to designate this income. Nevertheless, the reference to *earnings* is disorienting because (1) earnings are on an after-tax basis in most cases, with the most obvious exception relating to REITs already mentioned; (2) they are computed by expensing depreciation; and (3) earnings make no deductions for mortgage amortization payments (because the amortization payment is applied toward reducing debt and hence contributes to net worth in the balance sheet). Too much confusion would arise and too lengthy an explanation would be required to overcome the traditional concepts triggered by introducing the concepts underlying an *earnings* position.

We have misgivings about perpetuating the use of debt service, inclusive of amortization, as a subtraction from pre-tax net operating income. We all recognize that amortization is not an expense. Someday, perhaps, our profession and its investors will move to a recognition that interest only should be subtracted. However, because the use of debt service as an expense is so deeply entrenched in the methodology of the investment process, we are constrained to accept its popular use even though it is technically questionable.

After-Tax Cash Flows

Quite naturally, we also have problems with after-tax cash flows, defined in *Real Estate Appraisal Terminology* as before-tax cash flow less personal or corporate (depending upon the owning entity) income-tax liabilities. Recognizing the major problems inherent in using a before-tax cash flow basis (discussed above), we would have the same complaints and disagreements with an after-tax cash flow label. Appraisers frequently err by combining elements of accrual and cash flow statements into one. The most common error is to use the *pre-tax net income before debt service or depreciation* (estimated on an accrual basis) and subtract debt service and federal income taxes, labeling the result after-tax cash flow. It most certainly is not! It may be thought of only as after-tax net income. Even thought *net income* suggests an after-tax status, because of the confusion associated with the various income levels over the years we recommend including an *after-tax* label for emphasis.

To summarize the above, the Table 3.1 is offered as a proper format for presenting revenue and expense statements.

Absorption or Initial Rent Period

Real Estate Appraisal Terminology omits any reference to an absorption period. One of the basic weaknesses throughout the Institute's and Society's educational courses is the lack of emphasis in analyzing income-producing poten-

Table 3.1   Revenue and Expense Projection Accrual Basis

Gross potential revenues			
Rents @ 100% occupancy	$_____		
Other	$_____		
Subtotal		$_____	
Vacancy & credit loss		$_____	
Effective gross revenue			$_____
Estimated operating expenses			
Real property taxes	$_____		
Insurance	$_____		
Utilities	$_____		
Reserves	$_____		
Etc.	$_____		
Subtotal			$_____
Pre-tax net income before debt service			
or depreciation			$_____
Annual debt service			$_____
Pre-tax net income before depreciation			$_____

In computing after-tax net income, the following format would be appropriate:

Pre-tax net income before debt service			
or depreciation			$_____
Depreciation	$_____		
Interest on debt	$_____		$_____
Taxable income			$_____
Less: tax @_____%			$_____
After-tax income			$_____
Plus: depreciation	$_____		
Less: amortization	$_____		$_____
After-tax net income			$_____

tials of properties that are planned or contemplated, or that are already completed but have not achieved normal occupancy levels. Exacerbating the unfortunate experience of the REIT industry was the work of many appraisers. Usually acting on lender's instructions, valuations on yet-to-be-built developments were premised on the property having achieved normal occupancy levels at projected rent rates. Clearly, converting a not-yet realized level of *pre-tax net income before debt service or depreciation* into a capital value provides a hypothetical estimate that may or may not be reached even when the presumptions eventually have been achieved. If the capitalized value indeed represents a market value, that market value would be appropriate only at a future date when the presumptions regarding occupancy and rental rates were attained. In any event, the market value of the property as of the date of appraisal is something substantially less than what the appraiser presented and is largely a function of the time required to achieve normal occupancy at then-market rates, as well as a function of appropriate risk rates needed to attract equity and debt capital. We would suggest including either *absorption period* or *initial rent period* in *Real Estate Appraisal Terminology.* A general definition appropriate to both may be as follows:

> *The period of time required to either rent all available space to normal occupancy at estimated market levels, or to sell all available units at market prices. The absorption period will be a function of supply and demand forces in the market and cannot be estimated properly until complete research is conducted and a comprehensive understanding is obtained regarding all relevant economic, demographic, and marketing information.*

The methodology and concept associated with scheduling anticipated rental or sales receipts over a period of years and discounting bottom line numbers to a present worth are vitally important if we are to serve the investment community as professional appraisers and consultants.

Losses

Another omission in *Real Estate Appraisal Terminology* is the word *loss.* The term relates to any item of expense, whether recurrent or nonrecurrent, such as in a profit and loss statement. It also can mean an involuntary expense or irrecoverable cost of a capital asset. For example, a loss in value of a building from external market conditions resulting in excessive vacancies can be manifest both as an operating loss and a capital loss. The term is used too loosely by appraisers who frequently do not specify the operating or capital nature of the loss.

Equity Appreciation

Equity buildup, although an inappropriate slang term, is properly defined in *Real Estate Appraisal Terminology* as the "increase in the equity investor's share of total property value resulting from gradual debt reduction through periodic repayment of principal on a mortgage loan and/or increase in total property value,"[2] but it often is misused by practicing appraisers. Perhaps a more precise phrase would be *equity appreciation.* Our clients would more readily understand the concept conveyed by this terminology. Too frequently, equity appreciation is attributed solely to amortizing a mortgage on a dollar

---

[2]*Real Estate Appraisal Terminology, op. cit.,* p. 78.

for dollar basis. As correctly defined, equity appreciation is an increase in the equity interest dependent on both loan amortization and property value at the end of the investment term. The amortization feature and the property value are independent phenomena but are integral parts in the equity appreciation calculation. If property value declines, equity appreciation is experienced only if amortization exceeds the loss in value. If the property value increases, equity appreciation is a combination of amortization and higher property values. Equity appreciation cannot be automatically presumed. Recently, many properties have fallen in value at a rate exceeding the extent of mortgage amortization.

Maximum Site Utilization

Highest and best use, a hallmark in appraisal terminology, is one of the basic principles affecting all valuation problems and is defined as follows: "That use, from among reasonably probable and legal alternative uses, found to be physically possible, appropriately supported, financially feasible, and which results in highest land value."[3]

Elementary to the appraisal premise is the presumption of a property use that will allow the greatest residual profit to the land, subject to zoning constraints, whether the profit will be measured in tangible monetary returns or intangible amenities. Understanding the significance of *highest and best use,* the phrase itself seems nondescriptive. All investment officers and financial analysts acknowledge the goal of maximizing returns, and they appreciate the need of directing the use of available assets into the proper mode to achieve investment objectives. Generally, these concepts are referred to as maximizing yield, seeking upside potentials, or meeting optimum goals. The financial and accounting literature rarely (if ever) uses the superlatives *highest* or *best,* probably because the words are somewhat vague. We would like to see the profession adopt terminology that would be more recognizable. The phrases *maximum site utilization* or *optimum site utilization* might be better suited. The related financial communities already are oriented toward maximizing profits, and the imagery triggered by *maximum site utilization* or *optimum site utilization* would compare favorably with the Institute's definition of highest and best use.

Market Value versus Book Value

On the positive side of the ledger, and more specifically within the appraiser's domain, are the concepts associated with a definition of market value. The ac-

[3]*Ibid.,* p. 107.

counting field until very recently has relied upon valuing an asset for balance sheet purposes by presuming an extremely conservative treatment.

The reported book value generally was computed by taking the original acquisition price or cost and subtracting book depreciation already taken. As a result of the recent SEC directive to 100 of the nation's biggest corporations, current value or replacement cost accounting is being tested. The attempt is to provide a more realistic barometer of asset worth. As applied to real estate, the initial procedures suggested applying current replacement costs and subtracting a reasonable estimate of all accrued depreciation. A forward step has been achieved with the publication of The Rouse Company annual report for the year ending May 31, 1976. The Rouse Company is one of the nation's largest publicly held real estate companies, with the majority of their holdings represented by income-producing properties. Permission was granted by the SEC to alternatively value their investment properties by analyzing the income-producing capacities of each asset. The entire valuation project was conducted by in-house staff, and the studies and results were reviewed by a national real estate consulting firm retained as valuation consultants by Peat, Marwick, Mitchell & Co., company auditors. Here is an example where the appraisal professional has guided the larger financial field; the methods adopted by The Rouse Company, with the appraiser's guidance, incorporated (with minimum modification) many traditional capitalization and/or discounting techniques taught in our appraisal courses. More importantly, the values in the May 1976 annual report embody the principles adopted in the Institute's definition of market value; i.e., the estimates reflect reasonable amounts knowledgeable buyers and sellers ultimately would negotiate, presuming a proper marketing period and the absence of undue constraints. The appraisal profession has been the standard-bearer. Understanding the intricacies and implications of market value, a precisely stated, time-tested definition apparently is gaining applicability in the financial reporting arena.

Summary and Conclusions

In providing real property consulting services, a major segment of our prospective clientele is oriented toward the accounting and finance fields. In order for our analyses to be responsive to their needs, we must adopt an identifiable terminology. Misusing references to *cash flow,* contriving the term *equity dividend,* and abusing other phrases discussed above tend to undermine our credibility. The recommendations discussed here are intended as constructive criticisms and are proffered with the intent of stimulating discussion, aiding the educational process, and provoking further study to achieve a greater professionalism in our work.

4

How Does the Real Estate Market Determine Value?

In the absence of centralized exchanges similar to the New York Stock Exchange, where the views of securities analysts, investors, and financial institutions are synthesized into a market price per share, how does the highly fragmented and disjointed real estate market place a value on a particular real estate parcel? The process seems especially perplexing and evasive to the newcomer in real estate. Even for the seasoned, professional investor, the selection and valuation procedure is assuming even greater importance in a market beset by oversupply, demand cutbacks, high interest charges, and cost overruns. The process starts with a recognition of the fact that real estate is a nonduplicated commodity. Geographical locations can provoke widespread value differences since no two sites are exactly alike or identically located. When the multiplicity of urban building types is added, it becomes even more a nonidentical product. It follows that each real estate deal must in a sense involve a separate, custom pricing process. Since we are not an assembly-line business, the appraiser assumes more importance in real estate than in other products. He is employed

Reprinted from *Real Estate Forum,* May 1975.

by government or by owners for real estate tax and condemnation requirements, by financial institutions making mortgages, and by investors buying or
selling.

Real estate value is a comparative process. It consists of ascertaining all
the competitive land prices, building rents, construction costs, and selling
prices. *Competitive,* of course, means comparative. The greater the market
knowledge, the easier it becomes to place a value on a property. Surely real estate is the best illustration of the theory of relativity; nothing is absolute,
everything is relative or comparative.

Yet, the process defies completely scientific quantification. The traditional "feel" for value still is an important factor. Imagination, innovation,
and courage play important roles. These attributes are uniformly possessed by
the Helmsleys, the Zeckendorfs, the Roses, and by the Fred Browns of a bygone era. The appraisers, orderly and calculating by nature, tend to have a
more methodical approach. The galaxy of developers and buyers, on the other
hand, put more heart into the decision-making process. Individual motivations also play a strong role. It is not unusual for decisions to purchase to be
made on sentiment, on personal social philosophy or even convenience. For
example, it is said that C. Russell Feldman, then chairman of National Union
Electric Corp., purchased the old McGraw Hill Building on West 42nd Street,
New York, in 1970 for $15 million, at least partially because his first job as a
youth of 16 was a tightener of leather belts for belt-driven machinery in a shop
only a block away from the sight. Perhaps the board chairman of CNA was
motivated by his boyhood upbringing in the state in his approval of the purchase for resort development of the Queechee Lakes tract in Vermont. The appraiser tries to sort out transactions that seem to be representative of the general pattern of sales in order to arrive at what the real estate should sell for,
rather than what it did sell for.

Rates of return in real estate are quoted on a cash-on-cash basis. This
means that net income is calculated as the cash income after real estate taxes,
operating expenses, mortgage interest, and amortization. The rate of return is
the cash income divided by the cash investment. Of course, amortization is not
deductible for income tax purposes because the reduction or payment of a debt
reduces one's liabilities and thus constitutes a savings. When the term *cash
flow return* is used, it means the net dollar income after interest, amortization,
and federal income taxes, if any. Most real estate investors attempt to shelter
their income from federal taxation by using as large depreciation allowances as
the IRS allows. The excess of depreciation (a non-cash expense) over mortgage
amortization in each year is the amount of cash income sheltered from income
taxation. Wall Street financial analysts, on the other hand, are oriented to
after-tax earnings and are less impressed by cash flow. As a result, real estate
lacks favor with some investors who typically stress after-tax income.

The goal in real estate is to finance or refinance income property at a lower debt service constant factor than the overall rate of return, free and clear of mortgage. Thus, if a property is financed at 10% constant, and the free and clear rate is 12%, the equity (cash) return will jump to 15% or more. This is called *positive leveraging.* In recent years, due to sharp increases in interest rates, the debt service factor is frequently higher than the overall rate of return, thus producing *negative leveraging* with a consequent disproportionate reduction in the equity return to the 6%-to-8% range.

The availability of money also sharply affects the volume of construction and values. At the moment, we are witnessing the most severe downturn in housing since the 1930s. Activity in office buildings and, to a lesser extent, in shopping centers has also been greatly reduced. The shortage of money coupled with a significant demand retrenchment and cost overruns have produced crisis situations for many developers. Land prices particularly have fallen under the competitive pressures. Prices of improved and operating real estate may decline somewhat as the relative shortage of money continues.

Generally speaking, the higher the tax shelter, the lower will be the cash-on-cash rate of return. The converse is certainly true as well. Investors want real estate that qualifies for accelerated depreciation, has a high proportion of depreciable building value to total value, and is highly leveraged with tax deductible interest charges. Frequently, a deal can be bought, especially development properties, where there is little or no income taxes to be paid for as long as 12 to 15 years. Under these conditions, investors are willing to accept a negligible or modest cash-on-cash return in the early years, provided they have confidence the cash income will grow through rent increases over a reasonable time period. This has surely been the history for most well-located and designed real estate.

However, our double digit inflation is reshaping the way investors look at real estate. Disenchantment in long-term net-leased property at fixed rents has become very evident because investors are chary about the erosive effects of a continuing decline in the purchasing power of the dollar. We have seen good net-leased deals in recent months returning as much as 12% or more on cash equity. Who wants to be locked in to a fixed rate of return with economic conditions as unsettled as they now are? Many of these deals are being sweetened by shortening the rent term or providing for graduations during the rent periods.

Increased Risk

A second consequence of double digit inflation is the greatly increased risk in development. Extraordinary capital costs and material shortages, together with ecological hindrances and cautious consumer attitudes, have made recent new construction projects relatively unattractive to investors, public and private. The tribulations of Kassuba, Klingbeil, and others have been well publicized. The plight of the construction and development loan REITs has also focused attention on the hazards of development projects. Foreclosures and bankruptcies are fairly commonplace today.

The inevitable result is the increasing favor with which investors view the existing inventory of completed projects, especially those with a proven record of performance. After all, the investor reasons, someone else has been through the headaches of development and the risk factor has declined markedly. Why not pay a profit under these circumstances, especially since the price is apt to be substantially under current replacement costs?

Investors also instinctively feel that real estate represents the best hedge against inflation in a world beset by monetary instability, currency maladjustments, and balance of payment problems. This assumption, of course, is only true in markets that are not oversupplied. In some sections, such as New York, Los Angeles, Miami, Phoenix, and Atlanta, real estate has shown pronounced weakness in rents and values despite inflation, because of oversupply. On the other hand, where a reasonable supply-demand equilibrium exits, real estate does act as an important inflation hedge and probably is the best of the tangible assets.

Houston Project Proves Point

As an example, we purchased for clients 1,000 apartments in Houston, Texas, in 1969-1970 at a time when vacancies were about 7%. Today, there are virtually no vacancies and because there is no current oversupply, rents have increased faster than expenses, thus assuring substantial income gains. This is apt to happen in all types of existing real estate, provided they are well located and functionally modern.

Much has been made of the English, North European, and Arab interests in American real estate. Certainly, this interest appears to be at its highest level today. Foreigners regard American real estate as being relatively underpriced in this inflated world. They also tend to discount or ignore depreciation as a real expense, believing instead that it will be more than canceled out by inflationary increases in net income. Foreign investors tend to consider amortization as an addition to the rate of return, even if on a deferred basis, since the benefits can only be achieved on refinancing or resale. American capital, on the other hand, traditionally has said that market or actual depreciation should be regarded as being about equal to amortization and the two wash out. This in recent years has come to be regarded as a more conservative view than warranted by events. Probably the answer between the two extremes lies somewhere in the middle.

Foreign capital also attaches a greater premium to location and to quality of the buildings than American capital. Foreigners will accept a very modest return on the best real estate yet want a very high return on less desirable property. Their range of return is far more extensive than American investors and they tend to be more selective.

Appraisers use three different methods of arriving at value and then correlate the results into a final valuation estimate. They rely principally on market comparison techniques on sales, rents, and costs. Appraisers have special access to market information which frequently gives them a more sound basis for value judgments. For rental properties, appraisers use an income capitalization approach in which they capitalize, i.e. convert, the expected net income before mortgage debt into a capital value. The overall capitalization rate selected should reflect the relative risk, money market conditions, real estate supply-demand conditions, income tax shelter, and inflation.

The third approach, the replacement cost approach, is intended to estimate the cost of replacing the real estate at today's prices for labor and material. It is a useful estimate because the difference between replacement cost and market value, arrived at either by comparison or by capitalization, is the true and only measure of accrued depreciation, or loss in value, the real estate has sustained since it was built. Also, the cost approach puts a ceiling on how much an investor would be willing to pay for the property. The point is that no experienced investor prudently would pay more for a property than its replacement cost.

Absence of Pattern

Investors and developers in their analyses of individual properties make the market for real estate. Because real estate is highly localized and nonhomogeneous, and because accurate market data is often difficult to obtain, it is sometimes hard to see a pattern of value emerge. Transactions are frequently made on what appears to be a nonrational basis. Appraisers, on the other hand, are interpreters of the market. They do not set market prices. They are not market leaders but may be thought of as economic observers of the market scene. They tend to be far more rational and consistent than the market. They are also less finance- and income tax-oriented than investors and developers.

The most successful investors and developers possess common characteristics. First, they see the investment within the essential framework of the national economic and local real estate market scene. This sense of perspective is all important. Second, they have gathered more comprehensively and more accurately all market facts and have analyzed them for their application to a prospective investment. Appraisers and market analysts render a considerable service to investors in providing this information. Third, these successful investors have unusual financing acumen. This enables them to structure a deal to result in the highest possible equity return. This is accomplished not only by obtaining superior mortgage terms but by a wide variety of devices, including ground leasing and coventuring on a favorable basis to the managing partner.

5

Values and Valuation Techniques in the Seventies

The last half of the 1960s began with the severe credit squeeze of April 1966 and ended in late 1969 with the onset of a little-understood recession. An accelerated inflation arose in 1966 and continued through 1971. Cost of living indexes indicated annual increases of 5% and 7%, and in construction, costs rose from 8% to 10% annually. In the last five years of the 1960s, commercial rents rose 50% and land values doubled.

The psychology of inflation was rampant. Lenders demanded higher interest as compensation for the expected erosion of the long-term purchasing power of their money. Producers priced their goods on a cost basis and tended to lose their competitive edge in adjusting their costs to market demands. Real estate was the principal beneficiary of this inflationary binge. As monetary conditions deteriorated and as the growth of corporate profits flattened, investors turned increasingly to real estate. A significant diversion of capital funds into real estate as the best tangible asset was evident. Strong demand drove up prices and reduced rates of return. This fueled added production at

Reprinted from *The Appraisal Journal* (October 1972): 545-55.

high capital costs and necessitated extraordinary rents, while sowing the seeds of an eventual serious oversupply.

Will Inflation Ebb?

A combination of the recession of 1969-1971 and the President's wage and price control policy as a means of mitigating cost-push inflation has cooled inflationary fires significantly. Considerable controversy exists over the extent of this cooling process. However, inflation, in the author's opinion, will stay well banked for the foreseeable future. Although the nation will not return to the relative tranquillity of the late 1960-1965 period, in which costs of living and rents simultaneously rose less than 2% annually, it does seem likely that the 6% annual inflation rate of the late 1960s can be at least halved.

A public awareness and concern regarding runaway inflation is growing as increases in income are more than matched by continuous price increases. Perhaps a more serious issue is the recurrence of sharply competitive conditions, a factor that is most evident in the real estate market. Labor, to an extent, has become more productive and technological advances are partially offsetting wage increases. An ample supply of all types of real estate ensures more competitive pricing of the product and, to a similar degree, of all other commodities.

Counterbalancing forces, of course, are also at work. The most significant of these forces is the extensive and inflationary federal debt the nation is now facing. A second factor concerns market attitudes—the conviction that inflationary forces are so strong and pervasive that no real abatement may be anticipated. This in turn produces such adverse effects as permissiveness regarding labor wage increases in excess of productivity, the compulsion to hold interest rates at higher levels, and the belief that prices should be related solely to production costs rather than being governed by the market.

What does this mean to the appraiser? Undoubtedly the selection of a capitalization rate will be profoundly influenced by personal convictions concerning the rate of future inflation. Generally, a stable or competitive economy will provoke a market demand for higher rates of return. On the other hand, an inflation-riddled market will settle for a low rate of return, assuming rents, net income, and prices continue to rise. Rates of return are currently still relatively low, but may be expected to increase if the investor gains confidence in the containment of inflation.

The Resumption of Rises in Effective Disposable Personal Income

The cooling of inflation should produce a climate in which the wage and salary earner will *effectively* increase his or her income on a continuing basis, the term *effective* implying wage increases in excess of the rate of inflation. The author foresees an era in which the consumer will find prosperity, relative economic stability, and constant net increases in purchasing power. Additional leisure time, brought about by the reduction in the average work week and the experimental four-day week, will be combined with more effective income to produce an active but changing real estate market for the balance of the decade.

This new and improved economic climate will undoubtedly increase the obsolescence of marginal housing as the upgraded primary housing accommodations accelerates. The amount of substandard housing will decline sharply. Further, extensive rehabilitation of existing housing on a private basis will increase as homeowners and investors find rehabilitation more viable than new construction at high capital cost.

As incomes rise, the average family will seek a fresh and radically improved environment, thus intensifying development in outlying areas. Families will demand the newest and most innovative housing with such amenities as swimming pools, tennis courts, and club houses. Although these amenities have traditionally been more characteristic of apartment or condominium development, they are now foreseen as integral to a conventional one-family housing project.

The Leisure Market

The well-publicized and frequently oversupplied leisure time market should really come into its own in the balance of the 1970s. A sharp increase in second-home living is anticipated as families satisfy their vacation and weekend requirements with lakeside cottages, ski chalets, or oceanside condominiums. The market to date has been a disappointment to such large industrial corporations as International Paper Company, Boise Cascade, and Chrysler Corporation. Demand simply did not reach the expected levels in the 1960s and in fact reduced considerably during the recession.

The leisure market was also hurt by inadequate market analysis.[1] Developers tended to produce housing in a price range far beyond the financial capacity of the mass of possible buyers, thus precipitating a disappointingly low sales volume. Families are seeking more modest accommodations, often preferring to save costs by performing in part their own labor. Designs should also provide simply and economically for future expansion. It is essential that real estate research companies improve their microanalytic capacity to determine precisely what families are seeking.

[1]See John B. Bailey, "Market Analysis—Fundamental to Defensible Valuation," *The Appraisal Journal,* October 1972, pp. 644-49.

Interestingly, the leisure time market has achieved an astounding volume in lot sales. Although their housing has been far less successful, subdividers of resort and recreational land have had extraordinarily profitable land subdivision operations—as many as 20 lots are sold for each completed house. Regarding a lot purchase as a long-term investment, families buy on the installment plan in anticipation of building after the lot is fully paid for. Others consider a lot purchase an inflation hedge or an investment that can be profitably resold. Some disappointments will inevitably occur and both the appraiser and the market analyst must watch for possible changes in prices and sales volume arising from a realization that lot purchases are frequently a poor investment.

Changing Land-Use Patterns

The balance of the 1970s will witness a continuation of the diminishing role and declining relative dominance of the central city. This is not to imply that the commercial center of the metropolitan area will ever be effectively replaced. Rather, the nation is experiencing a growing tendency to spread out, to develop land more extensively and less intensively at the core.

Countless reasons underlie this trend, some interrelated and others seemingly independent. Frequently, this expansion outward is simply due to continuing metropolitan population growth, which spills over to less expensive areas where land exists for development. The primary deterrent to metropolitan growth is the high cost of housing and commerce in central city areas. Business concerns and families frequently share a common reluctance to financially overextend themselves for the convenience of city living. A more positive reason is the desire to flee the congestion and abrasions of the central city—with its weight of numbers, endless queues, congested thoroughfares, polluted air, and the continual threat of violence. Further, deteriorating schools pose a seemingly insoluble problem, while the fiscal plight of the city, which finds its most direct expression in an escalating tax rate, is in many cases the crowning blow.

The central city plight has been further complicated by an extensive oversupply of commercial space, especially offices. Urban renewal has helped considerably in combating inner city deterioration. Probably the financial institutions deserve the most recognition for preserving the central city through their sponsorship and construction of imposing new bank and office structures. Large department stores have also aided in the renewal of the central city by modernizing their existing space or creating new stores. Further, parking and access to central city areas has improved significantly.

In contrast to the smaller, more vulnerable cities, the larger the metropolitan area, the less difficult it will be for the center city area to survive the competition from outlying office buildings and shopping centers. Nevertheless, it is probable that central city land values will not increase perceptibly over the balance of the decade. In fact, values may very well decline and in special circumstances adjust to new and lower levels than those prevailing in the 1969 peak, such as a serious oversupply of office space or an inadequate system as experienced in New York.

From the standpoint of valuation, lower capitalization rates are obviously justified in the expanding outlying sections of the metropolitan area. Correspondingly, land values in outlying areas should increase and appraisers must attempt to sense the rate of increase rather than to rely exclusively on the historical record. On the other hand, the uncertainties of central city areas should merit the application of higher capitalization rates for typical urban real estate in the core area.

Housing in the Seventies

Subsidized housing in one form or another now constitutes about 28% of our current annual housing supply. This is the principal message of the balance of the 1970s in housing. The federal government is making a massive effort to relieve the relative shortage of housing through numerous rehabilitation and new construction programs. Although some mortgage defaults and foreclosures, inadequate construction, and poor management practices will invariably mar government efforts, overall they will provide a substantial contribution to the needs of the nation's low- and moderate-income families.

The inability of the federal government to concentrate a sufficient amount of this housing in central city areas in or near the ghettos has been a glaring deficiency. This problem is largely created by the unavailability of land in fully built-up areas and is compounded by (1) the disposition of sponsors to seek inexpensive sites in less socially complicated outlying areas where problems in tenant relations are expected to cause less difficulties, and (2) the natural attempt to produce a better mix of housing permitted by highly economically stratified suburban sections.

Feasibility and marketability studies are indispensable prerequisites to these programs. The appraiser can make a special contribution by an evaluation of the location and housing design, correctly predicting the required mix of unit sizes, the rent level, the period required to attain normal occupancy, and the occupancy rate. Although it may seem unusual that subsidized housing programs require market analysis, the fact is, such analyses are sorely needed. For example, the high locational standards applicable to conventionally financed, fully taxpaying housing must be compromised when housing subsidies are involved—but to what extent? Further, is it certain that the distribution of units is comparable to the size of families for this type of housing?

Estimating Values of Condominiums

The trend to construct a substantially higher proportion of condominium, cluster housing units as an effective alternative to renting at extremely high rental rates is rapidly growing. A similar conversion of rental units to condominiums is expected as tenants grow increasingly concerned and annoyed by the continuation of high rents, especially those required by recent high construction and land costs.

The prospect of income tax deduction on real estate taxes and mortgage interest significantly influences the condominium purchaser who might otherwise be a renter. Further, the prospective purchaser may anticipate the recapture of some or all of the amortization and indeed even experience a capital gain. This is an inviting alternative when compared with the endless rent receipts of the tenant.

The appraiser as yet has failed to develop adequate valuation procedures regarding condominiums. Mortgage lenders as well have not dealt effectively with the need for a new valuation approach. When a sponsor plans condominium units, the architect designs them as homes, not as rental units. It logically follows, therefore, that they must be appraised as homes. How can this be accomplished? First, if there are sufficient sales of comparable units, the primary valuation approach should be market comparison. Secondly, if there is an insufficient sales market, the appraiser may hypothetically estimate rental values. But the realities preclude obtaining rents sufficiently high to produce an adequate return on investment under normal investment circumstances. The only feasible technique in this case is to reduce drastically the capitalization rate. There is no place in condominium appraising for an 8%, 9%, or 10% overall capitalization rate; rather, the indicated rate should reflect the basic nature of the units as homes. The appraisal must minimize or ignore depreciation and bear a rate similar to what a homeowner expects on his or her local savings account, say 5% to 6%.

Recently the author reviewed an appraisal report on a condominium project in which the appraiser found to his dismay that the value by market comparison, i.e., the pricing of the units, could not be supported by the capitalization of the hypothetical net income at an overall investment capitalization rate of 9%. To close the gap, he chose a 20% "entrepreneurial factor," which he added to the capitalized value. Naturally, the lender objected and based his loan on the value without the 20% factor.

What neither the lender nor appraiser appreciated was that the home concept should have prevailed in their consideration of value. If one were to mathematize the differential between the home value and the income value, i.e., the additional 20% home value, it may be said to reflect two basic factors: (1) the introduction of amenities not found in rental units and which the renter cannot or will not pay for, and (2) the capitalization of the expected income tax savings into the purchase price. The increment to ascribe to each factor is a matter for the appraiser to decide.

The Mobile Home as a Housing Factor

The contribution of the mobile home to our housing needs has been enormous. It has successfully brought the price of housing down to an affordable level for countless millions of households. It has permitted a job mobility that otherwise would have been impossible for the seasonal or relocated worker. In southern climates the mobile home provided housing for the retired and for the second homeowner. Currently over 500,000 of these units are produced annually, but are not even included in our basic housing statistics.

If the mobile home is securely anchored on a concrete foundation and is attached to water, electric, and sanitary sewer systems, it should be evaluated as a permanent home. Logically, it follows that the mobile unit should be both appraised and financed as a home, admittedly with a shorter life, which conceivably could stretch to 15 or 20 years. If under these circumstances the mobile could be financed as real estate rather than in a manner similar to discount auto financing, the carrying charges would be effectively reduced and the opportunities for improved housing could be broadened to include countless thousands of households of modest income.

Commercial Real Estate in the Seventies

It is quite evident that the peak of central city office development has passed. An unusual conspiracy of circumstances will relegate office construction to a secondary role for the balance of the decade: the oversupply glutting many if not most central city markets, the reordering of corporate priorities arising out of the recession of 1967-1971, the consignment of office expansion to a lower priority ranking, and the diversion of demand to outlying areas at the expense of the central city. While the central city area will always play the most important role in commerce, the resumption of construction will not occur in force until the very last part of this decade.

The bulk of further office construction will take place in outlying or suburban areas and the keynote will be ease of vehicular access. Many companies will no longer feel the same compulsion to congregate within a very small geographic range. With the improvements in communication systems and the ease of surface and air travel, a reasonable and continuing amount of office decentralization may be anticipated.

The character of location criteria visualized in the 1970s will differ from that experienced in the 1960s. First, there will be a diminishing interest in the solitary, single company office building with a sylvan campus setting in a relatively remote area, perhaps best exemplified by the American Can home office complex in Greenwich, Connecticut. Although environmentally attractive and pleasant, such locations are insular and hence mentally debilitating for key executives who need to relate to customers, suppliers, consultants, attorneys, and bankers. The difficulty of obtaining suitable rezoning, as RCA found out in Darien, Connecticut, is a further deterrent to this campus type of office development in many metropolitan areas.

Second, a distinct growth is expected of office submarkets within central locations. These submarkets will be located close to mass transit and interstate highways in commercial hubs in the outlying sections of the major metropolitan areas. For example, General Telephone and Electronics has decided to relocate from mid-Manhattan to an urban renewal site in the heart of Stamford, Connecticut, a city of approximately 110,000 people about 35 miles from New York. Located directly on Interstate 95 and opposite the railroad station, GTE expects to have the best of both worlds. It will be located in a vibrant small city with all the urban conveniences and characteristics, including a population and income mix. Yet Stamford is of a manageable scale and unlike New York will not overpower its workers and residents. Neither will GTE executives experience the insularity of a remote location; its key personnel will soon be able to reach the center of Manhattan in 40 minutes in new, high-speed trains. One can work in comfort en route, thus avoiding the frustration, fatigue, and high cost of driving into the city.

Another natural evolution will be the increase in planned office parks catering primarily to the smaller space user, but also to accommodate the larger company. The office user is assured of an attractive setting through the establishment and enforcement of strict planning rules relating to floor area, ratios, building design, landscaping, and parking. The user can eat in the public restaurants on the premises as well as shop. Many of these office parks will be contiguous to major shopping centers and will offer a wide variety of retail, entertainment, hotel, and professional services to the office force, in contrast to the free-standing highway office structure on a discordant, nonhomogeneous strip development.

The most successful park will have the highest land development criteria. For example, it will not tolerate front parking except for visitors, with the bulk of parking underground or in parking decks. An overall landscaping plan will be required, and a centrality of supporting services will be established. Street graphics will be artistic and sensitive, not garish or inharmonious, and all architectural plans must be approved. Similar to industrial park development, land may be sold in small parcels for improvement, subject to the master plan, or a package deal may be arranged whereby the developer will build to the tenant's specifications.

Estimating Values of Central Business Districts

It is essential that the appraiser master new techniques to appraise office parks. As a primary approach the appraiser must learn to (1) project the probable annual land sale and lease package development rate on a 5- to 10-year basis, (2) estimate the costs against the sales and leasing revenue, and (3) strike a pre-tax and after-tax discounted net income for capitalization. If, in the appraiser's judgment, the tract is too large to be fully absorbed within the 5- to 10-year projection period, the remaining land should be valued at that point and discounted to the present time. Where a park is under active development, use of the market comparison approach alone, discounted over the absorption period, may produce an unduly low valuation result. Some element of going concern value must find expression in the valuation process when the office park atmosphere begins to take form and substance and when a good record of performance has been achieved.

The office park concept is, to some extent, part of the trend to create in effect a new, carefully planned central business district in outlying sections. Indeed, the large regional shopping center of the future will in fact be a regional business center and will provide retail, business, hotel, professional, entertainment, government, and service space of a completely integrated and coordinated nature.

The smaller city will become increasingly vulnerable to the threat of this new type of business district. An outstanding example of this is the success of the Belden Village Shopping Center, in Canton, Ohio. Approximately 400 acres of surrounding land was assembled by the principal tenant, Higbee's Department Store, in conjunction with local investors. The center was master planned for a wide variety of supportive uses, including offices, service establishments, added retail, motels, and housing. As a result, it has sapped the vitality of downtown Canton, despite heroic efforts to hold commerce in the central city through an imaginative urban renewal program and the efforts of local business groups. Today, Belden Village is attracting a market as far as 30 miles away, including a surprising number of Akron residents 20 miles distant.

This rapid growth of central business districts in outlying areas creates distinct and almost insoluble appraisal problems in valuing central city land. The historical record frequently will not provide sufficient clues as to the extent of the downturn in land values. How then can the new price level be accurately estimated? No simple answer exists. A related problem involves the evaluation of the potential possible foreshortening of the economic life of central city buildings and the extent of the additional functional and economic obsolescence sustained as a result of the intensified outlying competition.

Evolving Valuation Techniques

Today, the most compelling need of appraisers is to adopt, in collaboration with the accountants and the financial and market analysts, a uniform glossary of terms in which a common body of semantics may be used. An understanding of valuation issues is frequently lost simply because appraisal terminology is foreign and confusing to accountants or security analysts. It is essential that appraisers move closer to the position of the financial world and abandon terms such as *recapture rate, equity cash income,* and *net income before debt service,* which have little meaning or appreciation outside the appraisal profession.

Further, the professional appraiser must take greater cognizance of the income tax implications of real estate investment. The disposition of appraisers to value income real estate on a cash basis is becoming as outmoded as grandmother's proverbial bustle. Eventually market value will be estimated on the basis of after-tax earnings estimates, perhaps tailored to the client's tax status or that of the typical purchaser.

Heretofore, many appraisers minimized if not ignored the income tax aspects of an investment, assuming that the ownership could be any one of many different legal entities, each maintaining a different tax status. Secondly, it was felt that the personal income tax status of investors varied so widely that it was impossible to reflect effectively the tax advantages or disadvantages. Today, this of course is no longer felt to be the case.

Tax Consciousness

A greater tax consciousness can be valued in two ways. First, the after-tax earnings can be capitalized, after mortgage interest and depreciation. Income tax losses have a positive benefit to the investor and assuming a certain tax rate, the after-tax benefits may be capitalized to determine their value. Consideration must also be given to the cash flow, that is, the cash income after interest, amortization, and federal income taxes, if any. The appropriate income tax rate to be hypothetically applied would largely depend on the size of the property and the typical financial structuring of the ownership and the mortgage debt. A second technique is to recognize the income tax implications by adjusting the overall or direct capitalization rate to reflect the tax benefits of the property.

It might be successfully argued that the influence of tax shelter is expressed in the earnings-price ratios of comparable sale properties. If this is the case, the appraiser need only apply the appropriate rate, i.e., net income ÷ sales price = overall rate.

The problem is to find sufficiently precise evidence of comparability. So many variances exist in land and building ratios, location, debt financing, probable economic life, operating ratios, and the like, that a custom estimation of value will frequently be required, with the comparables at best serving as an essential market framework. In any event, if the appraiser does not develop a sense of income tax consciousness, his or her values may be indefensibly conservative. Today numerous transactions are made on a virtual break-even basis, i.e., without any pre-tax income, that sell for substantial sums over the mortgage because the investor recognizes the value of the income tax shelter represented by the excess of allowable depreciation for tax purposes over mortgage amortization.

Equity Considerations

Another trend in real estate valuation that finds support in the Ellwood system of investment analysis is the recognition that the mortgage contract is part of the capital structure and must be accepted by the appraiser as an element in the value. The author foresees a widespread increase in equity valuations. In the case of appraisals for mortgage loan purposes, the equity will be the value over the proposed loan or a hypothetical loan deemed appropriate by the appraiser.

If a mortgage contains onerous prepayment provisions and the owner is effectively locked in, the appraiser must recognize these terms and value the equity accordingly. If the appraiser assumes a refinancing on improved terms, he or she must charge the real estate the prepayment penalty. In any event, *the appraiser must become more finance-oriented and more tax conscious,* altering valuation techniques accordingly.

Computer Techniques

Finally, it is important to take note of the appraiser's increasing fascination and preoccupation with mathematical techniques, as best exemplified by the use of computers. The computer unquestionably plays a crucial role in the valuation process. At the very least, the computer substantially reduces labor costs, while at best it provides the most sophisticated answers involving an infinite and otherwise unworkable number of variables. In fact, no large-scale investment appraisal practice can afford to be without it.

However, the appraiser's fascination with *form* has produced a distinct problem. The appraiser has dangerously minimized his or her main function—the importance of *substance* as opposed to form—represented by the collection of hard market data. The systematic amassing and analysis of rents, vacancies, prices, construction and sales volume, operating expenses, cost data, and rates of return is considerably more important to the valuation process than slick mathematical and computer techniques.

The truly professional appraiser will maintain an essential balance between the collection of market facts and the use and application of techniques, and will not sacrifice substance for form. On the other hand, the appraiser will apply these techniques at the highest possible level when they are of benefit to the client. It is essential that the appraiser develop a constant awareness of secular trends and a sense of perspective regarding fundamental changes in investment thinking, and thereby be better equipped to alter valuation techniques accordingly.

6

Land Market Comparison Techniques in High-Density Urban Areas

The market comparison techniques set forth in this article were actually used by the authors, in conjunction with other valuation approaches, to estimate the value of 11.7 acres of midtown Manhattan land underlying Rockefeller Center. Mr. White, in addition to appraising the land, represented Rockefeller Center, Inc., in negotiating the new ground rent agreement with the fee owner, Columbia University. The ultimate agreement calls for a rental of $9 million in the first year, increasing annually by $200,000 so that the average annual rental during the 21-year renewal period will be $11 million.

In addition to the graduated rental, Rockefeller Center agreed to pay a lump sum of $4 million to Columbia. This lump sum and a substantial portion of the graduated rentals were considered payment for the university's agreement to make sweeping revisions in the ground lease, which offered the center the opportunity to mortgage, sublease, or sell the leasehold with minimal restrictions.

This article was written with R. Gary Barth. Reprinted from *The Appraisal Journal* (October 1974): 494–517.

Unique factors characteristic of high-density central city areas compel additional consideration of the methodologies employed in comparative sales analysis. Unlike land sales in outlying, suburban, or rural sections, land for urban development frequently must be painstakingly assembled by purchasing several contiguous parcels in order to ensure the improvement of the site in the most economical manner. Thus, questions of assemblage factors, or plottage, will arise. In many cases, the land is burdened with obsolete structures that must be demolished at the purchaser's expense. Similarly, although the buildings on the land may be worthless, these improvements may be encumbered by a lease or leases of varying lengths which might force the need to buy out the leases as a means of obtaining earlier possession. Locational factors must be analyzed more carefully because a distance of just a few hundred feet can make as much as a 50% difference in land value; this type of sharp locational differential is rarely found in outlying areas.

Case History Illustration

A deeper understanding and appreciation of urban, high-density land sales analysis is achieved by the presentation of an actual case history made in the fall of 1972, in which a substantial number of verified sales were analyzed and subjected to all comparative land value techniques. In the process, the methodologies, adjustment factors, and, indeed, laws and regulations applicable to high-density, heavily urbanized areas are highlighted. The area selected for study is easily the most valuable high-density urban section in the world, known as Rockefeller Center.

A special, very comprehensive comparable land sale study was made which used the portion of the land under Rockefeller Center in New York City owned by Columbia University as the subject property under appraisal to apply the required adjustment factors to the land sales. The Rockefeller Center land owned by Columbia comprises the bulk of three city blocks, totaling 510,000 square feet, or 11.7 acres. It is bounded by Fifth Avenue and Avenue of the Americas, from West 48th to West 51st Streets, New York City. The Rockefeller Center complex was erected by John D. Rockefeller, Jr., between 1928 and 1933; it consists of 10 buildings with over 6 million square feet of commercial space. Some 45 years after the original ground lease was signed, it still is considered the premier example of urban land-use planning in the United States. The initial ground lease terminated in 1973, and thus the purpose of the study was to estimate a land value, presuming the land is vacant, unencumbered, and unrestricted, in connection with the renewal of the ground lease for an additional 21 years.

Method 1: Use of Adjustment Factors

The major technique for the estimation of value is the use of comparable sales.

Because land is a nonhomogeneous commodity, and because market conditions are subject to continuing change, the analysis of sales requires the use of certain adjustment factors that seek to equate the price of each comparable sale with the value of the property under appraisal. Initially in our study, some 380 sales were analyzed in an area bounded by 45th and 54th Streets, from Third Avenue to Seventh Avenue. This area was subsequently broadened to ensure that all relevant assemblages were included in the analysis. About 500 sales were analyzed. Particular attention was given to those sales that could be identified as part of assemblages for the purpose of erecting office buildings. Sales of adequately utilized sites where the improvements had obvious value were disregarded. The zoning for the comparable sales area was for the most part the same, permitting a base commercial building of 15 times the lot area, with a floor area bonus of three for the observance of setback, plaza, or arcade areas.

Twenty-seven such assemblages dating from 1964 to 1972 were analyzed (Table 6.1), after having been identified (Figure 6.1) from the individual sales. The individual sales that made up these assemblages were not separately analyzed because the examination of assembled, that is, total, office building sites enables an appraiser to apply a much more logical approach, involving adjustment factors applied to buildable plots that are comparable to the property being appraised. The techniques used in developing the adjustment factors depicted in Table 6.1 will first be described; the results of this study will then be analyzed.

The assemblages are made up of sales that in almost all cases were verified on the public record. Sales that were in essence an integral part of financing vehicles (such as some sale-leasebacks of major properties in this period) were disregarded if their sales prices were then not reflective of true property value. Sales in which information was incomplete or not specifically verifiable were excluded.

Market Conditions

The period from 1964 to 1972 was selected for sales analysis. Based on a comprehensive analysis of all sales, the sales price trends occurring over this extended period of time have been expressed in percentages as a Market Sales Trend Index (Table 6.2). The year 1965 was selected as the base year, or 100%, because this marked the year before the onset of the intensive and wild inflationary episode that originated in 1966 and continued through 1970, followed by what appeared to be a decline in land values.

The period from 1961 to 1965 was one of relative economic tranquillity, following the mild recession of 1960-1961. The Consumer Price Index during this five-year period rose less than 2% annually. Office and retail rents in midtown Manhattan were almost completely stable, rising less than 2% a year.

Table 6.1　Comparable Sales Analysis

Sale No.	Location & Address (for Completed Building)	Block	Size (Sq. Ft.)	Average Purchase Year	Price/ Sq. Ft. ($)	Time Factor	Size Factor	Location Factor		Adjusted Price/Sq. Ft. ($)	New Bldg. Size (Sq. Ft.)	New Bldg. Completion Date (Year)	Prime Tenant
1	Madison Ave; 49th-50th; 437 Madison Ave.	1285	40,182	1964	$187	1.33	.78	1.07	=	$221	712,000	1967	I.T.T. Americas
2	Ave. of Amer. 49th-50th; 1251 Ave. of Amer.	1002	98,175	1965	272	1.20	.93	1.07	=	326	2,100,000	1971	Exxon
3	52nd-53rd near 5th; 10 E. 53rd	1288	17,078	1965	148	1.20	.78	1.25	=	182	350,000	1972	Harper & Row
4	Broadway; 44th-45th; 1515 Bway (1 Astor Plaza)	1016	65,764	1966	160	1.04	.88	1.50	=	227	1,417,000	1971	W. T. Grant
5	Ave. of Amer. 48th-49th; 1221 Ave. of Amer.	1001	102,937	1966	197	1.04	1.00	1.07	=	219	2,200,000	1972	McGraw-Hill
6	5th Ave. & 52nd; 650 5th	1267	13,490	1966	430	1.04	.78	.83	=	280	300,000	1974 +	
7	Bway to 7th Ave.; 52nd to 53rd; 810 7th Ave.	1024	31,439	1967	213	.92	.70	1.67	=	275	601,000	1970	First Natl. City Bank
8	Ave. of Amer.; 47th-48th; 1205 Ave. of Amer.	1000	80,852	1967	199	.92	.93	1.25	=	219	1,800,000	1973	Celanese
9	57th-58th near 5th; 9 W. 57th	1273	39,462	1967	184	.92	.78	1.36	=	195	1,500,000	1972	Avon Products
10	Park & 57th; 450 Park Ave.	1292	13,437	1967	324	.92	.78	.94	=	207	258,000	1972	Franklin Natl. Bank

No.	Location												
11	3rd Ave; 49th-50th; 800 3rd Ave.	1304	24,063	1967	155	.92	.70	1.15	=	119	500,000	1972	Seagram
12	Broadway; 45th-46th	1017	58,206	1968	196	.80	.78	1.50	=	212	NA	NA	NA
13	Broadway; 44th-45th	997	73,655	1968	186	.80	.88	1.36	=	193	NA	NA	NA
14	Ave. of Amer.; 41st-42nd; 1095 Ave. of Amer.	994	56,840	1968	190	.80	.78	1.36	=	179	1,200,000	1972	N.Y. Tele. Co.
15	56th-57th near Ave. of Amer.; 40 W. 57th St.	1272	32,637	1968	227	.80	.70	1.50	=	227	551,000	1972	Squibb
16	Madison Ave.; 56th-57th	1292	45,105	1968	395	.80	.78	1.07	=	257	NA	NA	NA
17	Lexington Ave. & 50th	1305	17,338	1968	490	.80	.78	1.15	=	358	NA	NA	NA
18	3rd Ave. & 57th; 950 3rd	1311	12,163	1968	258	.80	.78	1.25	=	214	270,000	1971	Greenwich Sav. Bank
19	46th-47th near Ave. of Amer.	999	29,500	1969	131	.63	.70	2.14	=	193	NA	NA	NA
20	Ave. of Amer.; 45th-46th; 1166 Ave. of Amer.	1261	58,077	1969	349	.63	.78	1.36	=	269	1,460,000	1973	NA
21	Madison Ave. & 55th	1291	22,994	1969	389	.63	.70	1.36	=	268	NA	NA	NA
22	Madison Ave.; 53rd-54th	1289	34,250	1969	344	.63	.70	1.25	=	200	NA	NA	NA
23	52nd-53rd betw. Mad. & Park	1288	25,712	1969	297	.63	.70	1.25	=	172	NA	NA	NA
24	Lex. to 3rd; 53rd-54th	1308	66,817	1970	383	.60	.88	1.36	=	322	NA	NA	NA
25	3rd Ave; 46th-47th; 747 3rd	1320	21,000	1970	398	.60	.70	1.15	=	179	370,000	1972	NA
26	3rd Ave.; 48th-49th	1303	19,250	1970	347	.60	.78	1.15	=	184	NA	NA	NA
27	3rd Ave.; 52nd-53rd	1326	25,520	1970	309	.60	.70	1.25	=	170	NA	NA	NA

Figure 6.1 Location of 27 Comparable Assemblage Sales
(Subway stations: IRT = ●, IND = ⊗, BMT = ◑)

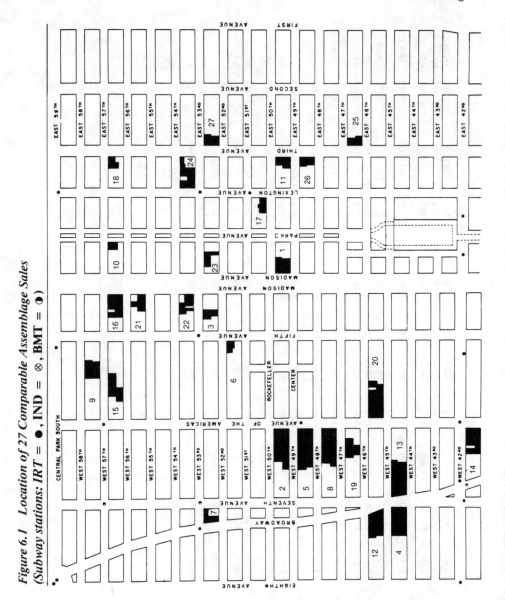

Thus, 1965 was selected as an appropriate base year because it marked the end of an era and preceded the serious inflation of the second half of the 1960s.

Table 6.2   Market Sales Trend Index

Year	Index
1963	90%
1964	90%
1965 (base year)	100%
1966	115%
1967	130%
1968	150%
1969	190%
1970	200%
1971	165%
1972	130%
1973	120%
1974	120%
1975	130%
1976	140%
1977	150%

In early 1966, somewhat coincidentally with the first severe credit squeeze in April of that year, there commenced an intensification of sales activity as well as sharply escalating prices. Speculative fervor gripped the market. In the ensuing five-year period, land sales prices were estimated to have doubled, reaching a peak in 1970. On the other hand, 1971 and 1972 witnessed a sharp decline in activity and inferentially a decline in land values. We estimated that the bottom of this decline would be reached in 1974 before a moderate-scale recovery might ensue. Prices at the bottom, in our judgment, would have declined from the 200% peak in 1970 to 120% of the 1965 base year (100%).

In the construction of the Market Sales Trend Index, we expressed in percentages the annual rate of appreciation in land sales through 1970. We then charted a four-year drop before commencement of a market recovery in 1975, leveling off by 1977 to a relatively stable plateau estimated to be 150% of the 1965 prices and about 75% of the 1970 peak. These annual price-level factors were used in our analysis of assemblage sales. The purpose of this was to bring, theoretically, each sale current with market conditions prevailing as of the presumed appraisal date.

Volume of Sales Activity

The extent of the decline since 1970 may be estimated in several ways. The first is to examine the volume of sales activity over an extended period. Table 6.3

shows the number of individual sales by year. The purpose of each such sale was the assemblage of an office building site. The assembled site was either developed with an office building or held for development until the market improved to the point where development activity resumed.

Table 6.3   Midtown Assemblage Sales

Year	No. of Sales
1964	24
1965	22
1966	31
1967	25
1968	38
1969	46
1970	42
1971	10
1972	6

Note from Table 6.3 that assemblage sales activity intensified at the same time as inflationary psychology began to pervade the market in 1966. The number of sales reached a peak in 1969, held with only a minor reduction in volume in 1970, and thereafter declined precipitously in 1971 and 1972. By early 1973 it could truly be said that there was virtually no land sales activity in Manhattan, except isolated sales to complete assemblages long since started.

There was ample market evidence of the oversupplied state of the office market in the number of assemblages that had been abandoned or halted. Listed below is the current status of several of these assemblages, most of which form a part of the comparable sales analysis. It is significant to note that these abandoned assemblages are all in the more marginal locations, with one exception.

(1) An investor has given up the deed to a hotel on West 43rd Street between Broadway and Avenue of the Americas. He owns several other contiguous properties and was attempting to assemble the balance of the midblock area.

(2) An owner had executed a ground lease with a prominent builder to build an 800,000-square foot office building on the Broadway blockfront between 52nd and 53rd Streets. This builder has returned the property to the owner and dropped his security deposit. The owner also has assembled a plot of approximately 35,000 square feet at the southeast corner of Broadway and 62nd Street, which has been available for construction for over two years.

(3) A developer has assembled, with possession, a plot of 62,000 square

   feet on the Broadway blockfront, 51st to 52nd Streets. There are no
   current development plans for the site.

(4) An investor had a long-term lease on the blockfront, 49th to 50th
    Streets, on the east side of Third Avenue. The lease was returned to
    the owner and the investor lost approximately $500,000 in option
    money.

(5) An investor owns the Buchanan Apartments on the westerly block-
    front of Third Avenue between 47th and 48th Streets and has aban-
    doned, for the time being at least, any attempt to construct an office
    building.

(6) A developer owns the westerly blockfront on Third Avenue between
    54th and 55th Streets and is not proceeding with the development of
    this site.

(7) A development company attempted to assemble a site between 53rd
    and 54th Streets at Fifth Avenue and purchased nearly 40,000 square
    feet of land. Further attempts to complete this assemblage were aban-
    doned, and one parcel of the property was sold last year.

(8) Developers contracted to purchase Cathedral High School, at the
    northwest corner of 50th Street and Lexington Avenue, from the
    Archdiocese of New York, but have recently relinquished their op-
    tion. The parcel is now for sale.

Rent-Level Trends

A second way of estimating the trend in prices is through the decline in rents
from the 1969-1970 peak (for full-floor occupancy, as an average, of a typical
new building in a prime location) of $12 per rentable square foot down to $10
in 1973. All other factors being equal, simplified Table 6.4, on the following
page, dramatically portrays how a drop of 50¢ per rentable square foot in rent
can provoke a decline of as much as $100 per square foot in land value. Al-
though exactly proportionate drops probably do not occur, it is fair to state
that land values must decline to some extent under the pressures of rent
reduction.

   It seemed evident from the study that Manhattan land values would not
readily recover to 1969 levels; it was concluded that a long-term moderate deflation in Manhattan land values had occurred, evidenced by the severe rent
decline, and that the recovery would lag behind the recovery from the 1969-
1971 recession. The extent of the decline in rents can best be documented by
using a particular building. Two major office buildings were selected as factual
illustrations of the decline in rents (Tables 6.5 and 6.6). Although it is conceded
that rent trends are not a perfect substitute for sales data, they do provide a
very effective alternative where land market activity has halted or reduced to
the point where comparative sales analysis is ineffectual.

Table 6.4   *Required Rent at Varying Land Values* [a]

Land values per sq. ft. of land area	$200	$300	$400	$500	$600	$700
Capital costs per sq. ft. of building area						
Building	$ 45	$ 45	$ 45	$ 45	$ 45	$ 45
Land [b]	11	17	22	28	33	39
	$ 56	$ 62	$ 67	$ 73	$ 78	$ 84
Net return on capital cost at 9%	$5.04	$ 5.58	$ 6.03	$ 6.57	$ 7.02	$ 7.56
Real estate taxes, operating expenses, and vacancies	+ 4.50	+ 4.50	+ 4.50	+ 4.50	+ 4.50	+ 4.50
Required gross rent per sq. ft.	$9.54	$10.08	$10.53	$11.07	$11.52	$12.06

[a]J. R. White, "Central City Land Values," *The Appraisal Journal,* July 1972, p. 353.

[b]Land value expressed in square feet of permissible building area, presuming a floor area ratio of 18 times the lot size.

Effective rental rate information for the second major building (Table 6.6) also dramatically shows the drop from the 1969-1970 market peak. Effective rental rates take into account not only the gross reported rent, but also the concessions made by landlords, including completing work, rent abatements, lease takeovers, and payment of brokerage commissions to a greater extent than was the practice prior to the market downturn. Due to these concessions, the real decline in rental rates can be measured better if comparisons are made from the market peak of 1969-1970 to the present through the use of effective rental rates.

Table 6.5   *Pattern of Rent Levels (1968-1972)*

Building 1
Actual Leases

Lease Number	Floor	Sq. Ft.	Year	Term (Yrs.)	Gross Rent (Incl. Elec.)	Comments
1	22	23,435	1968	10	$11.23	—
2	29	10.794	1968	5	12.50	As is
3	43	22,590	1969	10	16.50	As is
4	53	4,938	1970	7	18.50	—
5	31, 32, 33	100,000	1972	10	10.25	As is
6	37	12,700	1972	10	9.25	Adjusted for tenant improvements
7	6, 7	104,524	1972	5	8.00	As is

Table 6.6   Decline in Effective Rental Rates (1970-1973)

Building 2

Time Period	Effective Rental Rate	% Decrease from Previous Period
5/1/70-4/30/71	$11.09	
5/1/71-4/30/72	9.06	18%
5/1/72-9/14/72	7.87	13%
9/15/72-1/11/73	7.22	8%

Table 6.6 shows the decline in effective rental rates for all leases over a 2½-year period for large new deals (5,000 square feet and more) made during specific time periods. Since the indicated time frames, some improvement in rental rates has been reported by the building owner.

Individual Sales

A third and most direct way of estimating the trend in prices is to study individual sales levels. Because of the drop in sales volume, direct current evidence was sparse, but to a limited extent did exist. Most assemblages are now in relatively strong hands, and owners are attempting to hold through the recession in real estate activity. We have been able, nevertheless, to infer current land values by adjusting the historic record of sales in accordance with changes in past and present market conditions on the basis of techniques previously discussed.

Individual nonadjusted sales prices of small parcels within completed assemblages were $500 to $1,000 or more per square foot. These sales prices are very misleading and tend to provide an incorrect conclusion that the entire tract is currently worth on a square-foot basis what was formerly paid for an individual parcel. The record clearly demonstrates this is not the case.

The appraiser must attempt to develop a sense of perspective and a sense of anticipation about land values. The historic record, although voluminous, does not always provide sufficient clues. An ability to value land demands a capacity to see cyclical real estate market and economic trends and to apply this knowledge to the valuation problem. In this instance, value must be inferred not only from direct evidence represented by sales levels, but also from sales volume, rent levels, vacancies, construction volume, and absorption of new office space. While the recent cessation of sales activity made our adjustment process more difficult, it did not invalidate the use of a comparable sales analysis technique as one of several value indicators.

The Market Sales Trend Index (Table 6.2) is, in part, judgmental and cannot be considered mathematically precise. It is a form of discipline that enables the appraiser to compare different sites with the subject site on a more orderly

and systematic basis. The purpose is to bring all past sales to the current time
by applying the indicated time adjustment factor.

Location

Locational quality was estimated on a percentage basis for the area from 42nd
Street north to 59th Street, from Broadway to Second Avenue (Figure 6.2).
The bases for the rating system consist of the following factors: vacancies, intensity of use, rents and land values, convenience to transit, convenience to retail and service facilities, and character and use of the building.

    As Figure 6.2 indicates, the area on Park Avenue from 45th Street to 50th
Street is regarded as the premium land location and is rated 100%. The subject
property has an overall locational rating of 75%; this is a composite factor resulting from a 95% rating for the Fifth Avenue blockfronts, 80% for Avenue
of the Americas, and 60% for the large amount of interior space on the side
streets.

    To illustrate the use of the locational rating in adjusting land value, pre-
sume, for example, a sale of land in the 100% area. The sales price would be
adjusted by dividing 75% by 100% and applying the resulting location factor
of .75, thereby reducing by 25% the land value per square foot of the comparable property to obtain a more accurate idea of what the comparable value
for the subject parcel may be. We also emphasize that the midblock percentage
of 60% would be no more than 50% were it not for the sole ownership of virtually all of three blocks. In other words, with the usual plot configurations
and with fragmented ownership, the side street value ratios would decline
sharply.

Plot Size

An important element in land valuation is the effect of size on value. Generally
speaking, plots between 20,000 and 40,000 square feet command the highest
square foot values. Over 40,000 square feet in size, the price per square foot
for the assembled land tends to decline gradually (Table 6.7). This is due to the
lower prices commanded by interior, side street plots. Price also is influenced
by the problems that added plot size provokes, namely, higher unit building
costs with very large buildings (e.g., say, greater than 1.5 million square feet),
more speculation on the absorption of the space by the market, higher capital
investment requirements, and higher proportionate carrying charges. Many
developers have assembled plots between 20,000 and 40,000 square feet, with
the option, certainly, of continuing to assemble contiguous parcels to create a
larger building site, but have chosen to keep the smaller plot and thus the eventual office building to a size that would not create these problems.

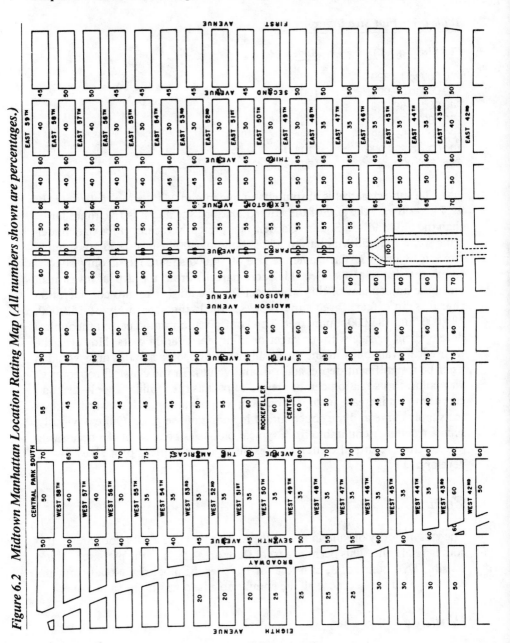

Figure 6.2   Midtown Manhattan Location Rating Map (All numbers shown are percentages.)

Table 6.7   Plot Size Index

Plot Size (Sq. Ft.)	Index
10,000 to 19,999	90%
20,000 to 39,999	100%
40,000 to 59,999	90%
60,000 to 79,999	80%
80,000 to 99,999	75%
100,000 to 299,999	70%
Over 300,000	65%

The subject parcel is absolutely unique in mid-Manhattan real estate. Its 11.7 acres dwarf the size of the United Nations site and it is five times larger than the old Madison Square Garden site, presently vacant. (Plot sizes underlying some 145 mid-Manhattan office buildings built since 1950 are summarized in Figure 6.3. Their average size of 34,000 square feet is only one-fifteenth the size of the subject 11.7-acre parcel.) From a practical investment view, the adjustment of this large tract for size must take into consideration that it is, in effect, three superblocks, consisting separately of 142,000, 183,000, and 185,000 square feet. This configuration would permit theoretical development or sale without street or utility installation costs. However, the theoretical availability in one ownership of this huge tract at this time would in itself be a significant depressant on land values. In the classical economist's viewpoint, this situation can be viewed in part as the familiar supply-demand curve with an increase in supply causing a rightward and downward shift of the supply curve and the concomitant lowering of the price. Quite obviously, such a tract is discountable from typical plot sizes because of the necessarily longer time required either for resale in more typical plot sizes or for development.

Zoning

The vast majority of land in the midtown area is in a 15 FAR (floor area ratio) commercial zone. This permits a total floor area 15 times the plot area, plus a possible FAR bonus of 3, or a total of 18 times the plot area. No adjustments were required here because all the comparable land was in the same zone.

Plottage

No adjustment for a so-called plottage increment has been made in the comparable sales analysis for several reasons. First, because most of the sales occurred in the wildly inflationary period of the late 1960s, prices in most cases

Figure 6.3   Midtown Manhattan Office Building Plot Sizes

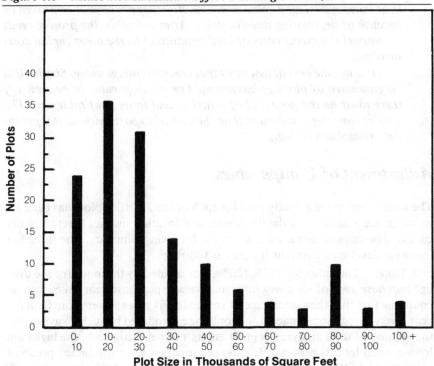

included the hypothetical plottage increment, due to the excessive amounts paid for individual parcels within the assemblage. Second, plottage is not a prize that automatically attaches to a completed assemblage; the market is the only arbiter of an assemblage increment. Third, we regard the plottage increment as part of the entrepreneurial reward or profit that the developer will receive, provided all events occur as required. The extent of the profit will depend on the residual net income to land upon successful completion of the building. As we have discussed in connection with plot size adjustments, plottage can be a negative factor when the tract under appraisal is larger than the optimum configuration for the prevailing pattern of site utilization.

The official textbook of the American Institute of Real Estate Appraisers, *The Appraisal of Real Estate,* has this to say about plottage:

> *Plottage value is defined as the increase in unit value resulting from improved utility where smaller plots are combined to form a larger one. To accommodate a substantial building development, small plots may need to be assembled, often from different owners. This procedure usually en-*

tails extra costs, and key parcels may need to be purchased for more than their independent land value either because they are already improved or because of negotiating disadvantage. After assembly, the project needs to support the excess costs of land in addition to the other capital costs involved. . . .

It is not the cost of assembly that creates plottage value. Size itself is no guarantee of plottage increment. For plottage value to be realized, there must be the potential of a higher and more profitable use. The whole cannot be worth more than the sum of its parts without this potential.[1] (Emphasis added.)

Adjustment of Comparables

The square foot price actually paid for each of the 27 office plots has been adjusted in accordance with the time, size, and location indexes heretofore discussed. The calculations are shown in the following summary. The three factors were developed from the indexes as follows:

Time.   The index for 1973, 120%, was divided by the index for the *average purchase year* of each assemblage. Average purchase year takes into account the fact that the assemblage of some plots is spread over more than one year. Even though some inaccuracy could be engendered by such an averaging, the volume of sales analyzed is great enough to net statistically the highs and lows created by this process. Because the analyses were conducted predominantly in early 1973, the index of 120% was used. The 120% shown for 1973 does not mean to indicate a precise and immediate drop of 10% on the first day of 1973, but rather our feeling of the value level that the index would eventually approximate during that year. It is not possible for the appraiser to quantify such judgments to the nearest integer in this case, and thus we have used 120% in actuality to mean 120% plus or minus some 5%, this being true, of course, with all the other indexes as well.

Size.   The index for 100,000 to 299,999 square feet of 70% was divided by the index for each assemblage. This index is in all cases less than one (except for the site of the McGraw-Hill building, where it is equal to one). Thus, its application served to adjust the actual sales prices downward in accordance with the previous discussion of the problems provoked by excessive plot size.

Location.   The index for Rockefeller Center is a composite of the three values for Fifth Avenue, Avenue of the Americas, and interior plottage. This composite value of 75% was then divided by the index for each assemblage.

Table 6.8 lists the adjusted square foot prices for all assembled plots in as-

[1]*The Appraisal of Real Estate,* 6th ed., American Institute of Real Estate Appraisers, National Association of Realtors®, 1973, p. 127.

Table 6.8   Adjusted Square Foot Prices

1st Quartile	2nd Quartile	3rd Quartile	4th Quartile
$119	$193	$219	$268
170	193	219	269
172	195	221	275
179	200	227	280
179	207	227	322
182	212	227	326
184	214	257	358

cending order, broken down into quartiles, each quartile containing one-fourth of the total number of variables.

These adjusted prices also have been placed in Figure 6.4 to form a somewhat regular normal (or bell-shaped) curve. The median (the value that divides all the variables into two halves—in this case 13 above and 13 below) of this distribution is $214, while the mean (more commonly known as the arithmetic average) is $225. The range of values, from $119 to $358, is $239, a rather meaningless measurement because so few values lie at the extremes of the dis-

Figure 6.4   Frequency Distribution of Prices

(27 Comparable Assemblage Sales)

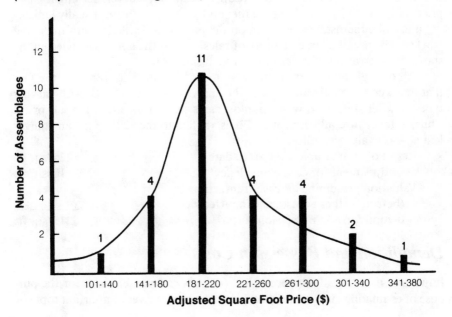

tribution. To avoid these extremes, which occur due to sales that are counter-market or to an appraiser's errors in adjustments (which is exacerbated by the relatively small number of sales), the two middle quartiles are examined.

The range of the second and third quartiles, from $193 to $257, is $64 and somewhat more representative of the variation that is acceptable to an ap-praiser in placing a value on any property. Thus, using the mean of $225, as depicted by this market data approach, in conjunction with a total spread of $64, is identical to saying that the value is $225 ± 14%, a tight enough range around the mean value to use it as a result of the market analysis.

Construction of a distribution curve for the 27 assemblages prior to ad-justment reveals no such close range of prices; indeed, such a curve does not even approach any meaningful pattern as does the post-adjustment distribu-tion. The greatly differing nature of these sales—in time, location, and size—causes a widely spread, nonuniform distribution. What an appraiser must do through the adjustment process is translate these assemblage prices into a value for the subject property in a manner that produces a meaningful result, as shown in Figure 6.4.

Of course, the ideal situation for an appraiser would be that in which a consistent adjustment process produces the same or nearly the same value for each adjusted sale. The many variables involved in each developer's assem-blage of a building plot, including inconsistency of judgment and knowledge by the purchasers, make such a result virtually unobtainable.

Because of circumstances unknown to the appraiser, or if known, not nec-essarily applicable or germane to a proper valuation, a developer might pay a price for land totally out of line—either above or below (below usually indicat-ing unusual circumstances existing on the part of the seller)—with the going market. The use of a large quantity of sales enables the appraiser to lessen the statistical aberrations that result from such situations.

An overall judgmental factor also must be employed to reflect the fact that many comparable sales used in the analysis are encumbered with varying types of seller financing, which in most cases serves to increase the sale price. Thus, a downward adjustment of 5% is applied to the $225 to get an equiva-lent all-cash value, as follows:

Result of comparable analysis to date	$225/sq. ft.
5% adjustment for cash equivalency	− 10/sq. ft.
Valuation presuming all-cash transaction (before further adjustment for effects of demolition and possession costs)	$215/sq. ft.

Demolition and Possession Costs

Important to a valuation process that analyzes comparable sales for the pur-pose of estimating land value is a consideration of the very important topic of demolition and lease buyout costs. Procedures for the addition of such costs as a positive adjustment to a determined fee value often are fraught with divergent views over the exact meaning of any adjustment made, its relevancy to the valuation under consideration, and its magnitude.

However, because the subject land is considered for valuation purposes to be "vacant, unencumbered, and unrestricted," adjustments have been made to the results of the comparable sales analysis so that the estimated market value can be considered equivalent to vacant, unencumbered land. In essence, a developer will pay only up to a certain price for land assemblage if he or she must buy out leases and demolish structures prior to the development of the site. The higher the anticipated costs of obtaining possession through lease buyouts, the lower the land price the developer will pay. The total cost of both is the governing factor comprising the total land value.

To illustrate, let us presume the existence of two contiguous parcels of identical size, shape, and suitability for development. One of the parcels is vacant while the other is encumbered with an improvement and associated leasehold; the fee interest in both is for sale. A developer interested in this location for a new office building finds an encumbered fee available for $100 per square foot of land. The developer also knows that he or she can buy out the leasehold interests and demolish the improvements for an after-tax price, which equates to $20 per square foot of land. The contiguous, vacant parcel can be purchased for $110 per square foot. Thus, of the two comparable building sites, the developer chooses the vacant fee, which yields a cheaper total purchase price by virtue of its unencumbered state.

The same concept causes the appraiser to adjust encumbered, comparable sales to bring them to a presumed vacant, unencumbered, and unrestricted state. In the analysis of the 27 land assemblages (Table 6.1), the land purchase prices were confirmed and verified. It was impossible, however, to obtain uniformly accurate and comprehensive data on the lease buyout costs. Information gathered was fragmentary and somewhat incomplete.

In any event, the cost of lease buyouts varied widely with such influencing factors as remaining lease term, profitability of the business, awareness by the lessee of the assemblage, and market conditions. When the lessee learns of the assemblage, holdout costs invariably result. But can these be considered value? To what extent is the ability and capacity of the assembler a factor? Finally, if land is available with possession, what would a developer pay to obtain possession of a similar plot? These are the variables that the appraiser must consider in a valuation analysis.

Demolition Costs

Demolition costs under Internal Revenue Service Regulations are capitalized and added to the land basis where the objective is to improve the land with a new building. The costs may not be expensed for tax purposes, nor may they be capitalized and then amortized or depreciated with the building. It was impossible for us to determine what demolition costs have been for all properties. However, actual demolition costs for improvements similar to many of those included in the comparable sales analysis were available. These data were used as a basis for adjustment in the comparable sales analysis to bring all sales to a theoretically vacant state.

Possession Costs

Under established case law for income tax purposes, the cost of obtaining possession, commonly referred to as lease buyouts, is now generally added to the building cost of the new improvements and depreciated over the economic life. In some cases, these costs have been separately capitalized and amortized over the remaining lease terms. However, the recent tax court decision of *Houston Chronicle* v. *U.S.* clearly affirms that lease acquisition costs must be amortized over the useful life of the new building. The actual impact of this accounting provision is to penalize land value because most assemblers will attempt to scale down their land purchase prices to reflect the cost of lease buyouts. This again is a reflection of the residual nature of land value. Thus, all comparable land sales before adjustments are net of lease buyouts.

The significant valuation factor in most of the 27 land assemblages is that some unknown amount of money was or will be paid by the developers to accelerate the time at which they gain possession for the purpose of starting construction. How much a developer pays for land largely depends on the estimate of how much he or she must pay a lessee to get possession. These figures generally are not available from developers, yet an appraiser must make an effort to reflect total land costs, regardless of how they are handled for IRS purposes. Thus, to bring all comparable sales to a theoretically vacant state (the same as the subject property), a further upward adjustment in the comparable sales was made to depict accurately total land costs.

A further complication in the consideration of demolition and lease buyout costs as an element in land valuation is the fact that there are income tax benefits to the fee owner in his or her right to amortize the cost of lease buyouts over either the term of the leases or the life of improvements. Thus, the after-tax cost of obtaining possession is the applicable figure, not the gross lease buyout costs.

The amount paid by developers to buy out leases is a very difficult figure to obtain. Unlike the sales price of fee interest, possession costs are in no way a part of the public record. Developers often are reluctant to disclose the actual costs involved. Access to various confidential sources, including some of the developers who have assembled the parcels in this comparable sales analysis, was possible. What is clear from all sources is the unwillingness to pay now an amount anywhere near what would have been paid only three years ago. Many of these sources are just permitting leases to expire on assembled sites. In the present oversupplied market, there is little or no disposition to pay inflated prices to buy out leases, except perhaps to complete an assemblage long since started. There are countless assemblages today where possession is already obtainable. Who would start an assemblage in an oversupplied market and encounter these costs unnecessarily when available plots may be purchased with possession at attractive prices and terms? Thus, actual lease buyout costs for the period covered by the sales analysis must be adjusted as were the sales themselves.

Summary of Demolition and Possession Costs

Demolition and possession costs gathered from confidential sources and adjusted as described above yield the following sums, which must be added to the previously developed figure for land value net of demolition and lease buyouts of $215 per square foot, or

	$109,600,000
Demolition @ $10/sq. ft. of land area	5,100,000
Lease buyouts @ $50/sq. ft. of land area	25,500,000
Total value by market comparison approach ($275/sq. ft.)	$140,200,000

Method 2: Land Subdivision Technique

A second and supplementary technique of market comparison has been employed as a check on the results of the valuation employing the adjustment factors. The large size of the tract compels analysis on the basis of a presumed subdivision or parcelization of the land into plot sizes that are more reflective of typical plot assemblages and existing plot configurations. The theoretical marketability of the land as one parcel, or indeed as three parcels in one ownership, is badly impaired because of the unique 11.7-acre size. There are only six office buildings north of 42nd Street that are built on entire blocks; all these are the small 200′ × 400′ or 80,000-square foot blocks. The Rockefeller Center blocks average 2.1 times larger. The probabilities are that the land must be subdivided substantially to sell or develop it. This obviously affects the valuation process and the selection of valuation techniques.

The presumed plot subdivision also must take into consideration the fact that the blockfront properties will command substantially higher prices than the interior portions of these extraordinarily long Rockefeller Center blocks of 920 feet. We are presuming that as many as 12, and as few as 6, sales of the land will take place over a six-year sales period. These plots could be as small as 25,000, or as large as 100,000, square feet. In total, the zoning would allow

about 10 million square feet of commercial space. The difficulties of marketing such a large amount of space compel consideration of the land on a wholesale basis. It has been presumed that no sales will take place the first year, and
that the first group of sales will not occur until the end of the second year because of current recessionary real estate conditions. The oversupply of mid-
Manhattan office space—now at some 20 million square feet—is so great in
relation to demand (only 4 million square feet of new space in both the mid-
and lower-Manhattan markets were leased in 1973) that there is absolutely no
assemblage activity. At the time of the study, no midtown assemblages had recently been started to our knowledge. Ultimately, construction activity will resume, but the availability of so many sites will slow the sales or development
pace. Thus, it is estimated that it would take six full years to market this
amount of land successfully at full "retail" prices.

     Also forecast over the six-year period has been a recovery in land prices to
levels at about 80% of the prior peak, but not necessarily to 1969-1970 peak
levels. This is foreseen as a gradual and moderate improvement starting probably around 1976 from what we believe to be a current trough in land prices.
For valuation purposes, however, the presumed ascending prices have been
averaged. Very importantly, this method also presumes that the owner-subdi-
vider is recapturing to the extent that the market will allow the cost of demolition and lease buyouts out of the so-called retail prices of the land at the time
of sale over the presumed six-year development period.

     The aggregate presumed selling prices to be realized over the six-year pe-
riod were allocated to the avenue frontages and interior parcels (Table 6.9).
These prices are indicative of what we ascertain to be realistic retail land values
for a somewhat stabilized mid-Manhattan office building market. Frontage
on each of the avenues has been taken to include 250 feet of depth, with the
middle 420 feet being defined as interior. As mentioned earlier, the midblock
area can support such a high value only because of the existence of sole ownership, which would offer an owner extreme flexibility in development plans.

Table 6.9   Subdivision Technique: Allocation of Presumed Selling Prices

Frontage	Sq. Ft. Area	Price per Sq. Ft.	Market Value
Fifth Avenue	100,000	$500	$ 50,000,000
Avenue of Americas	150,000	400	60,000,000
Interior side streets	260,000	285	74,100,000
Total value after subdivision and marketing over six-year period			$184,100,000

     The total selling price then has been divided into five equal amounts, and
a 9% discount factor applied to each year to reflect the interest lost on the in-

vestment during the marketing period (Table 6.10). We have used 9% because it tends to compensate for other expenses that are in excess of revenue during the holding period. For example, parking revenue will not cover the cost of real estate taxes and liability insurance during the holding period. The discounted value is considered to be the amount at which substantial investment interest in purchasing would be attracted.

Table 6.10   *Market Value of Land after Discounting at 9% for 6 Years*

Year of Sale	Sale Proceeds	Discount Factor	Present Value
End of 1973			
End of 1974	$36,820,000	.8417	$ 30,991,000
End of 1975	$36,820,000	.7722	28,432,000
End of 1976	$36,820,000	.7084	26,083,000
End of 1977	$36,820,000	.6499	23,929,000
End of 1978	$36,820,000	.5963	21,956,000
Total market value by the subdivision technique ($260/sq. ft.)			$131,400,000

Summary of Market Value by Market Comparison

This case study has analyzed what are considered to be the relevant mid-Manhattan sales by two very distinct techniques. The first technique—the use of adjustment factors applied to assembled plots to infer a value for the very large parcel—was made difficult by the near cessation of comparable sales activity in the last two years. An adjustment factor for time was, therefore, an important ingredient in the valuation process. Perhaps the most significant adjustment figure was for plot size. Emphasis cannot be made sufficiently for the discount applicable to such a large land mass in a market dominated by plots ranging from 15,000 square feet to 100,000 square feet, with an average plot size for mid-Manhattan office buildings of some 34,000 square feet.

Another significant adjustment was for lease buyouts. Of necessity, this is a controversial subject. The frenzied pace of buyouts in the late 1960s is not likely to be repeated for the foreseeable future. The first element in land value to fall under the downward pressure of a pronounced oversupply is lease buyouts. No developer will pay a high price for them. Instead, if there is to be any assemblage activity it will occur first on those plots that have no possession problems. Thus, a heavy discount has been applied to the average after-tax cost of obtaining possession as an element in vacant land valuation.

The vacant land subdivision technique was used because of the extraordinary tract size. Little or no prospect for sale as one parcel was foreseen, except at the discounted value level. The length of the marketing period became a somewhat speculative estimate because there was no assurance that the market would recover to the extent prophesied. At the time of the study, in late 1972, the effects of the energy crisis on central city development could not have been foreseen. Generally, the severe gas shortage of the winter of 1973-1974 has had a buoying effect on urban land values. Nevertheless, the method has excellent applicability because it is a practical and realistic way of approaching the problem of handling a sale of this magnitude.

Conclusions

What results can be cited of the use and application of comparable sales techniques in high-density urban areas? What lessons have been learned from this study of 27 assemblages and over 500 individual sales?

First, it was obvious that individual prices paid for small parcels within the assemblage were misleading and offered inaccurate evidence of the value of the assembled plot. The range of prices varied widely and without rational meaning. Generally, the prices paid for small parcels rose as the assemblage neared completion, and the traditional holdout received the highest price.

It was clear that in fully built-up, high-density core areas, the costs of demolition and lease buyouts had not been accounted for fully by appraisers as essential adjustment factors. This was particularly the case when the land to be appraised was either vacant or presumed to be vacant. It was also our experience that the prices paid for lease buyouts were extremely volatile, with notably higher and lower cyclical extremes. In the period from 1966 through 1970, extremely high prices paid for acceleration of possession were common. Since then, the willingness of assemblers to pay for possession has declined far more markedly than land prices. When completed assemblages are available in abundance, there obviously is no incentive to incur these extra costs unnecessarily. This has been more than confirmed over a 10-year study period in which the market hit cyclical extremes.

The study indicated that appraisers must devote more time and attention to the effect of plot size on value. Heretofore, in high-density urban areas, it was almost automatically presumed that the larger the plot, the higher the unit land value. A plottage factor was presumed and applied almost universally. This was not borne out by the statistics. After the sales were arrayed by size and price, it was apparent that there was an optimum price within a certain plot size range. Beyond this point the unit land value tended to decline. The economic law of diminishing returns could be applied easily where statistical study revealed what the local metropolitan area considered to be the optimum plot size in a given area.

Locational adjustments in high-density urban areas were found to be far more significant than appraisers generally were willing to recognize. Land value changes within limited linear footages were extremely varied. Appraisers and developers were found to attach in many cases too much importance to interior contiguous parcels merely because they were part of an assemblage. In other cases, the subtlety of change in land value from one block to another was not fully appreciated.

Ultimately, it was found extremely helpful to use the discipline of mathematical techniques on each of the adjustment factors of size, location, and time. It was not enough to "feel" a value for the subject tract, based wholly on a mental comparison of the comparable sale with the subject property. A much greater sense of order developed from the use of the mathematical techniques. It was true that subjective judgments were required, nevertheless, in the multiplicity of judgments involved, but a more scientific result inevitably was achieved.

Although the statistical techniques of regression analysis were considered, the relatively small population size in conjunction with the use of three independent variables (time, location, and size) produced results with a very low degree of statistical reliability. Nevertheless, the logic and orderliness required by regression analysis, wherein subjective, qualitative judgments are to a substantial extent eliminated, were also an overriding consideration in this study.

Another unique consequence of the case study was the need to account for the complete cessation, except in isolated cases, of land sales activity. How was the appraiser to account for such a sharp decline in the volume of sales? The best device was to chart the change in rent levels and vacancies as a means of inferring the hypothetical decline in land values. Table 6.4 shows the relationship between rent levels and land values under certain reasonable presumptions. It provides the best possible guide to urban land values when there is a dearth of sales.

7
George Washington Bridge Approach:
A Case Study[1]

The sale or leasing of air rights over rail yards, depressed highways, and bridge approaches has increasingly captured our attention as the shortage in the last decade of large open land areas in convenient urban locations has become evi-

[1]Although the author was not engaged by the City of New York, the Port Authority of New York, or the Kratter Corporation to make an appraisal of the market value of the air rights, Landauer Associates undertook an air rights feasibility study for the Port Authority in 1956, prior to the author's association with the company. The case study presented here is based on facts made available through various private, government, and published sources. It is purely a demonstration study, which hypothetically assumes the need for the appraisal in August 1961, prior to actual construction. The estimates of rents, taxes, and operating expenses are solely the author's and may not correspond precisely to collections or expenses subsequent to the assumed appraisal date. Although every effort has been made to provide wholly accurate facts and circumstances, the accuracy thereof cannot be warranted. The market value for the air rights suggested herein is the author's personal judgment and does not imply that the purchase price was too high.

Reprinted from *Case Studies in Air Rights and Subsurface Tunnel Road Easements,* (Chicago, 1965) 29-39. Copyright ©1965 by the American Institute of Real Estate Appraisers.

dent. It is prohibitively costly for private enterprise to assemble large land masses in urban centers without resorting to the devices employed under the various housing acts relating to urban renewal. Where assemblage can be successfully achieved on a private basis, the land cost is frequently so high that an adequate return on the investment becomes a matter questionable at best and impossible at worst.

The situation in New York City is even more complicated and difficult because a stringent and incomprehensible rent control law still exists. This holds rents to abnormally low levels and imposes regulations on builders and investors who wish to sponsor new construction. These make it tedious and costly to obtain possession for demolition of ancient and obsolete residential structures. Rent control in turn stultifies the market and creates pressures for new construction. In 1961, Governor Nelson Rockefeller proposed that air rights transactions be encouraged over such public facilities as parkways, tracks, tunnel entrances, bridge approaches, and piers. The proposal was probably sparked by the transaction that is the subject of this study, which took place prior to the governor's announcement.

All metropolitan areas feel the rising interest in air rights development because it minimizes or eliminates the perplexing and often costly problem of obtaining possession. It allows for essential urban construction in core areas that otherwise might have deserted the city itself in favor of relatively inexpensive outlying land. Certainly, when public improvements on the air rights are contemplated, it reduces the tendency for government to compete with private enterprise for the admittedly scarce supply of well-located central city land.

Thus, all appraisers in the medium and large metropolitan areas must consider the techniques and devices that can be applied in the valuation of air rights. Undoubtedly, our members will be expected to provide the expert guidance required to make these valuations. It is with this knowledge that this case study is offered as one of the many possible ways of determining a supportable market value.

Air Rights Defined

Just what are air rights? They may be defined as the interest one may purchase or lease in the air space within delineated boundaries over a certain elevation. These rights may be obtained over private or public land areas. They do not necessarily start at grade level; there are instances in which the rights commenced some 60 feet or more above grade. For example, in the United Nations North Complex, in New York City, a 34-story cooperative apartment house is being built by Alcoa Properties, Inc., over a six-story office building. In another instance, the air rights over a rapid transit marshaling yard have been created at an elevation about 12 feet above the principal abutting street. It is true, however, that in many cases the fee owner desires use only of the area below grade, as for a depressed expressway, and wishes to dispose of his or her interest in the air space above grade for another use that will in no way impair the subsurface functioning.

Perhaps the most significant factor to remember about air rights is that their value depends on a relative scarcity of suitable land for similar development. As a general proposition, it may be said that air rights attain value when the capital cost of creating them is less than the value of available and similar land. This is surely true of the Park Avenue area, in New York, north of Grand Central Terminal. Air rights leases have been made here at rents that indicate a capital value for the air rights of $250 per square foot.

The Problem

Our prime purpose is to value the air rights subject to a New York state- and city-subsidized housing project development plan, as will be shortly described. An incidental consideration is the estimate of the market value of the fee (subsurface) interest. This is usually defined as the difference between the unencumbered land value and the air rights value. The air rights value must be estimated within the framework of the existing zoning ordinance. Another qualifying matter is any restriction imposed by the seller on the type or intensity of utilization.

Historical Background

In 1956, the Port Authority of New York asked Landauer Associates to investigate the feasibility of developing through the air rights over the two blocks bounded by 178th and 179th Streets, between Wadsworth and Audubon Avenues, in the open-cut expressway proposed between the George Washington Bridge and the Bruckner Expressway. This east-west route provides an essential link between the west side of Manhattan and the expressways to Long Island, Westchester, and Connecticut. At the subject site, the expressway was planned to be 12 lanes wide. The Port Authority further proposed to erect an interstate commuter bus terminal in the contiguous area to the west, bounded by 178th and 179th Streets, Fort Washington Avenue to Wadsworth Avenue.

As part of the expressway construction, the Port Authority was willing to install, at an estimated cost of $200,000, beam-bearing seats in the retaining walls on each side and column footings between the traffic lanes so that the air space could be utilized by tall buildings. The Port Authority also agreed to install lighting equipment and required ventilation below the overhead structures. Most important, at that time it was also willing to quit claim without consideration the air rights to the city of New York for disposition. All utilities, sewers, water, gas, and electric, were available in abutting streets.

In this previous study, we concluded that residential apartments were feasible. The best use was preferably cooperatives, provided that special tax consideration be given the project by the city and that mortgage financing at preferential interest rates be made available under either state or federal housing laws. It was also our conviction that unless some credit against the extraordinary decking or platform cost be given by the seller, economic feasibility would be lacking. Our reasoning was that the age, plus the obsolete and declining nature of the surrounding neighborhood, prevented successful development at economic rents. In 1960, the city of New York offered the air rights for sale at public auction. Many prominent builders were present. The bidding was won by the Kratter Corporation, a public real estate company, at a price of $1,065,000.

The Ultimate Utilization

Eventually the Kratter Corporation built four 32-story apartment buildings without stores. They contained a total of 960 units and 5,040 rooms, plus 204 parking spaces. The units were built under the Limited Profit Housing Companies Law of New York State, by which the state provides 90% of the $19.3 million cost at a constant debt service factor of .0505. The city also agreed to provide a 40% tax abatement. This resulted in an assessed valuation at 40% of total project cost. The sponsor was limited to a 5% return on his equity investment.

As a result of the low debt service factor, the tax abatement, and a room count that is substantially inflated over that of standard rental room counts, the rents per room were projected at about $28 per month. This was $2 per room under the administrative ceiling of $30 imposed by the state.

None of the previous planning or studies had apparently visualized as many apartment units on a plot, which was ultimately set at 130,000 square feet, or three acres. It would appear that the decision to increase the density to 960 units, or 320 units per acre, may have been influenced by the air rights purchase price. The effect of the increased density was to reduce the purchase price to $1,110 per proposed dwelling unit. This is considered to be well within the ceiling of land value for moderate-income housing projects. The true cost for air rights, however, is the purchase price, plus the net cost of abnormal construction and other costs necessary to build on air rights.

Valuation: The Comparative Approach

Two approaches can be employed. The first relies as a starting point on the market value of land in fee simple, unencumbered by any air rights agreement. From this must be subtracted any impairment to the value of air rights development as a result of the lease or sale of these rights. In the subject case, there were certain possible losses of value as a result of the inability of the developer to use fully the subsurface for parking, storage, and building facilities. The noise and odor from open air venting of vehicular exhaust from the depressed expressway also had to be calculated in some manner. Certainly the latter is a good illustration of economic obsolescence; it was at least partially the reason why full market rents could not be obtained here. Still another consideration is any lack of accessibility arising from the elevation at which the air rights start, in relationship to the abutting street grade.

Other subtractions from the air rights value are the extraordinary or abnormal costs involved in decking or platforming the depressed road bed and in installing columns to support the deck and superstructures. A final factor is the extra time involved in the construction process as a result of the abnormal costs. Conceivably this could affect somewhat the pricing of the project construction by subcontractors. The extra time means interest and carrying expenses incurred, as well. All must be accounted for.

There are increments or additions to the air rights value, which are offset against the extraordinary costs; these, too, must be considered. They include the savings to the developer in erecting the usual load-bearing foundation walls and footings. Surely further savings arise from the elimination of excavation, demolition, tenant relocation, and losses on the investment during this period.

A suggested formula follows:

A = Air rights value
V^c = Land value by comparison in fee simple, vacant but improved with all utilities at lot line
X = Loss of residual value from functional or economic obsolescence arising from creation of the air rights
C = Added capital improvement costs to air rights purchaser or lessee in construction of building
D = Savings to air rights purchaser or lessee in excavation and foundation costs, demolition, tenant relocation, and income losses during relocation and demolition
I = Added interest and carrying charges as a result of added capital improvement costs in C
R = Residual value of fee interest
Thus: $V^c - [X + (C - D)] - I = A$
Also: $V^c - A = R$

Comparable Land Sales (V^c)

In this instance, no comparable land sales took place in the vicinity. For a considerable surrounding distance, the neighborhood was subdivided into small lots ranging from 37.6 by 100 to 200 by 100, with some exceptions. Improvements consisted of tenements built between 1901 and 1929, stores and offices, and a few modern apartment houses. To some extent, the site area could overcome the declining character of the neighborhood because it was large enough to create—at least in part—its own self-sufficient atmosphere. It also had the advantage of excellent rapid transit to job centers and was convenient to expressways and highways. A similar land plot with similar conveniences and outstanding views would sell for as much as $15 per square foot, or $1,950,000.

Functional and Economic Obsolescence (X)

After a study of the proposed plans, it was felt that there was no loss of value due to impaired access or as a result of the decking. The plans called for a suspended deck below the ground level deck to accommodate most of the building mechanical equipment.

There was no functional obsolescence resulting from the loss of income because of the decking of the depressed roadbed. The proposed plan represented a far more intensive utilization than the land use pattern in the neighborhood; hence, no penalty could be attributed.

Probably a developer would be resistant to the prospect of noise and exhaust odors from the open portions of the depressed roadway. (About 90,000 square feet of the total 130,000 square feet was covered by a concrete platform. The difference was used for open air venting.) Surely, the tenant would pay less rent. The investment analyst could calculate this by capitalizing the net rent loss. Another technique is to estimate subjectively the discount which a purchaser would expect. This figure was determined to be $1 per square foot of air rights area, or $130,000.

Abnormal Capital Costs (C)

From studies made by consulting engineers and cost estimates by the purchaser, it was determined that the abnormal cost for erecting a concrete platform or deck on reinforced concrete columns into bearing seats provided by the Port Authority would be $1.5 million, or about $11.50 per square foot of land area. This was about 8% of total improvement costs, a considerable figure when the objective was to provide moderate-income families with lowest possible rents.

Savings to Air Rights Owners (D)

The market analyst estimated that the savings in demolition of the structures taken for that portion of the expressway, excavation and foundation costs, tenant relocation, and income losses amounted to about $750,000. This figure is significant and is frequently overlooked or minimized by appraisers. Its effect is to offset by 50% the abnormal costs and reduce them to only 4% of total improvement costs. In turn, it reduces the pressures on the rent necessary to qualify for moderate-income occupancy.

Extraordinary Interest and Carrying Charges (I)

The proposed project would take an estimated 24 months to complete and could have applicable interest and carrying expenses of $1.4 million during this period. If it were not for the delays encountered in the deck construction, it was estimated the project could have been finished in 21 months. This 12½% of $1.4 million, or $175,000, must be subtracted from the land value.

Substituting the actual figures, the results are

$1,950,000 − [$130,000 + ($1,500,000 − $750,000)] − $175,000 = (say) $900,000

This is about 85% of the price paid by the purchaser. The appraised value itself is only warranted because the unencumbered land value of $1,950,000, established as a matter of judgment by the investment analyst, was favorably influenced by the knowledge that the highly desirable low-interest New York State mortgage and City tax abatement was assured. Since the appraisal is subject to the housing project plan and financing, both the presumed land value and the air rights value subsequently found through the above formula were deemed to be higher than ordinarily may have been the case. Another factor influencing the value was the extraordinarily high density. It was felt that density in a typical new housing project in the area generally would be limited to about 160 families per acre. The fact that the plan for 320 families per acre had been approved and low-cost financing assured provoked an unusual situation. The residual air rights value was out of proportion (after adjustments) to the level of land values in the section as much as the proposed buildings were out of keeping with the general character of land utilization.

Land value and air rights values basically stem from the character of utilization. The intensity, quality, and function of the utilization must affect residual values despite the pattern of far less intensive and obsolete residential utilization that existed in the area. This would not be the case, however, if at the time of appraisal no formal plan had been conceived and approved, and financing obtained. In that instance we would be dealing with a hypothetical improvement in which residual values are speculative at best. Had these circumstances existed, only the market comparison approach would have been used.

Valuation: Residual Capitalization Approach

When comparable land values cannot be found or when a special character of land utilization is contemplated, such as the state-financed, tax-subsidized housing erected on the subject site, residual capitalization may very well be required. This is especially the case when a building plan has been drawn and financing has been arranged. No longer need we speculate hypothetically about the type and size of the improvements to be erected; we are now able to work from certain assured facts and conditions.

The key judgment factor is in the selection of apartment rent level. In this process, one must weigh the possible functional and economic obsolescence that affects rent values. The other important consideration is the adjustments to improvement costs, arising from abnormal column or decking costs as well as the savings from the items previously discussed, and lost interest. The loss from functional and economic obsolescence must be calculated in the selection of the level of gross rent, and hence, is eliminated from the formula.

Our analysis is shown in Table 7.1.

As that example illustrates, if the symbol V^R represents the hypothetical or real residual land value, the formula may be restated as

$$V^R - (C - D) - I = A$$

when the estimation of X is a function of the selection of gross rent.

The extremely low overall rate of return may well be questioned. Similarly, employing a cash flow band-of-investment method of synthesizing the overall rate of return may not be understood. The low overall rate of return stems from the low interest rate on the mortgage, about $4\frac{1}{8}\%$, the long 40-year amortization period, and the 5% equity return to the sponsor. The cash flow method substitutes a sinking fund mortgage amortization for the anticipated depreciation. It is felt that the amortization generally will cover the depreciation, especially since a replacement reserve for short-term depreciable equipment has been included as an operating expense. Furthermore, the so-called "tax shelter" on projects of this type leaves them tax-free for several years since 95% of development cost is depreciable on an accelerated basis.

Correlation

The comparative approach in this case study is vulnerable because the estimate of land value established by comparison was almost wholly a judgment calculation by the investment analyst. This was necessary because there were no land sales at the time that were remotely comparable to the subject area. The land value employed in the formula of $1,950,000 was on the basis of $2,000 per proposed dwelling unit. It represented an informed estimate; however, it could not be well-supported by comparable sales data.

The residual capitalization approach had special applicability because a housing project that was state-financed, city tax-subsidized, and privately sponsored, already had been approved at the time of the assumed appraisal.

Table 7.1   Residual Capitalization Approach

Gross revenue at 100% occupancy		
5,040 rooms at $348 per room annually		$ 1,753,920
204 garage spaces at $360		+73,440
		$ 1,827,360
Allowance for vacancies and collection losses		−55,360
Effective gross revenue		$ 1,772,000
Estimated expenses		
Taxes ($8,000,000)	$ 340,000	
Operation	412,000	
Replacements	35,000	
	$ 787,000	−787,000
Net income before debt service or depreciation		$ 985,000
Direct capitalization		
Overall rate of return: 5%		
Mortgage: 90% of .0505		
Equity: 10% of .0509		
Indicated capital value		$19,700,000
Less building cost (without abnormal costs)		−17,825,000
Residual land value, before creation		
of air rights		$ 1,875,000
Less: Abnormal costs	$1,500,000	
Savings	−750,000	
	$ 750,000	
Interest and carrying	−175,000	
	$ 925,000	−925,000
Residual air rights value		$ 950,000

All the essential elements were known—the rent ceiling of $30 per room per month; the plans and specifications; the probable taxes; the mortgage and equity terms. It was relatively easy, then, to find a residual air rights value. True, a vulnerable element was the evaluation of the effect of any functional or economic obsolescence on the rent structure. It was concluded that this was not a serious element when dealing with below-market rents.

It was the judgment of the investment analyst that the air rights had a market value, as of August 1961, of $950,000, assuming the proposed development plan.

8

Private Recreational Facilities: Real Estate Tax Policy

The private club is facing a deepening fiscal crisis that threatens its very existence and has brought it in many instances to the verge of extinction. The significant inflation experienced since 1966 has adversely affected the operation of private recreational facilities and contributed to their severe current fiscal problems. One result of this inflation has been sharply accelerating real estate tax rates and/or assessed valuations. Since real estate taxes are a major item in the expense budget, a reexamination is required regarding the relationship of these recreational facilities to the community and the environment, and their capacity to pay real estate taxes.

A *private recreational facility* may be defined as any privately owned profit or nonprofit entity, operated either on a private club plan or open public plan, occupying five or more acres of ground, and providing on basically open space either active or passive sporting facilities, such as golfing, tennis, swimming, riding, boating, skiing, shooting, and lawn games. This article focuses on the club in which golfing is the major sport, frequently with supporting swimming and tennis facilities.

Reprinted from *The Appraisal Journal* (January 1972): 26-31.

The majority of private country clubs are operated on a nonprofit basis, that is, the objective is to raise sufficient revenue from their members to cover operating expenses and depreciation of their plant and equipment. Despite the adoption of austerity budgets, most clubs are finding it difficult or impossible to break even. Some clubs have been forced to use depreciation reserves to meet current operating expenses, and most have instituted special surcharges and dues increases. Their deficit position has been aggravated both by declining membership and declining use of club facilities. It is quite evident that some means must be found to decrease operating and fixed costs for country clubs. A developing resistance is growing among members to any further increases in dues and other charges as a means of coping with rising costs, thereby making it imperative to obtain real estate tax relief.

The Club and the Community

The existence of a country club has significant positive effects on community land use and values. A country club creates a desirable atmosphere, which in turn is translated into higher residential and commercial property values than would otherwise be the case. Significant real estate tax increases are obtained at no added cost to the community.

However, the private country club cannot afford the assessments its presence creates for the rest of the community. The effect of a high assessed value on a club is to force its sale for other private uses and provoke an irretrievable loss to the community. Stated differently, the inherent attraction of a large greenbelt area is reflected in the creation of large homes in the community, especially those within a reasonable range of the parklike atmosphere and vistas of the country club. These homes not only pay higher taxes but demand far less municipal services. Thus, the cost per person of municipal services is significantly lower in communities with country clubs.

Although a private club cannot operate in the manner of a public park, there are innumerable times when nonmembers have the benefit of this vital open space. Bird watchers, strollers, joggers, cyclists, tobogganists, skiers, and sledders use club facilities at times when it does not interfere with golfing play. The course is frequently made available by agreement to civil service and other city employees at designated times without charge. On a limited basis, the clubs make their facilities available to nonmember guests for civic and social affairs. In short, the country club has been and will continue to be a good neighbor and a vital social and civic force in the community.

The country club also makes a reasonable contribution to the economic base of the community. The club employs a substantial number of people on a year-round basis and provides wholesome outdoor summer employment to high school and college students as caddies or in its tennis or swimming programs.

The Club and the Environment

Despite the private nature of the country club, it serves a vital public function in its maintenance, at no direct cost to the community, of a widespread greenbelt area. This large open space in turn has significant ecological and land use implications. Further, this greenbelt buffers and protects the community from the more harmful effects of the urbanizing process.

The creation and continuance of an appropriate ecological balance rests primarily in population control and dispersal. The ecological balance is defined as the ideal relationship among all forms of life species, man included, and the natural and physical environment in which they live. Dispersal is ideally achieved, and congestion and crowding minimized where greenbelt areas are interspersed amid population and commerce. Further, our diminishing wildlife's existence depends on these natural oases.

The cost has made it prohibitive for government to acquire under eminent domain sufficient land areas in the older metropolitan areas to provide this essential ecological balance. The country club can and does provide a compelling natural and physical function and purpose without cost to the community by maintaining open space, reducing crowding, and providing scenic beauty.

The loss of this open space to a housing subdivision, for example, is an irretrievable disaster to the community not only for ecological reasons, but because of the high municipal costs that inevitably are required for municipal services. These greenbelt areas also reduce vehicle traffic and hence automobile pollution. Since the auto produces 60% of our air pollution, any private land use that reduces automotive concentration renders a positive community contribution. Traffic reduction in turn means less congestion, less municipal costs, and less road maintenance, as well as a cleaner atmosphere.

A Suggested Tax Assessment Approach

It is clear that all privately operated recreational facilities provide an essential public service, which must be recognized in assessment practices and procedures. One recommended concept is of a private recreational land use designation, perhaps formalized by a modification of the existing zoning ordinance to create a special private recreational zone. This concept would achieve a positive result since it would rule out consideration of the value of these private lands on the basis of their alternate highest profitable site use or uses. In many cases the private recreational zone would undoubtedly be for private dwelling use. In addition, the community may consider certain portions of a golf course to be alternately suited for commercial use, which is potentially ruinous to a club when used as a basis for a real estate tax increase.

Many assessors have unwittingly further penalized country clubs in valuing the land as though it were to be subdivided into building lots by adding to that value the cost of constructing the golf course itself, i.e., the fairways, tees, greens, hazards, earth moving, and sprinkler system. This procedure is highly improper since none of these golf course improvements has any value if the valuation approach is to consider the land in its alternative best private use. These improvements must be demolished to make way for the hypothetical housing development. In fact, the absence of trees as well as the clubhouse detracts from the use of the land for subdivision because of the denuded look. Moreover, what possible use is the clubhouse on the assumption of a residential development?

Legal Precedent

The private recreational land use, zoning, and real estate tax concept is not without legal precedent. For example, Chapter 193 of the Florida real property statutes was amended on September 1, 1967, to provide that "outdoor recreational or park lands" be assessed as such on an acreage basis, provided the private owners would agree to a convenant that the land would not be used for any other purpose for a minimum period of 10 years. The statute in part says, "In valuing such land for tax purposes, an assessor or any taxing agency shall consider no factors other than those relative to its value for the present use. . . ."

The language of the preamble to this Florida statute is particularly appropriate and describes clearly the contribution club grounds provide for the community:

> WHEREAS, there is a need for open spaces, parks and greenery in the communities of this state; and
>
> WHEREAS, savings are realized by the public through the development and maintenance by private interests of outdoor recreational and park lands containing landscaped areas; and
>
> WHEREAS, lands surrounding and in the vicinity of outdoor recreational or park lands are enhanced in taxable value because of the existence of such outdoor recreational or park lands; and
>
> WHEREAS, privately owned outdoor recreational and park lands provide recreational facilities which otherwise would have to be provided by governmental authority and would, therefore, not be subject to real estate taxes; and
>
> WHEREAS, outdoor recreational and park lands require and make little or no demand upon governmental authority for governmental services; and
>
> WHEREAS, it is the intent of the legislature to encourage the estab-

lishment and maintenance of privately owned outdoor recreational and park facilities. . . .

Minnesota has an Open Space Property Tax Law, which states, in part,

The present general system of ad valorem property taxation does not provide an equitable basis for the taxation of certain private outdoor recreational open space and park land property and has resulted in excessive taxes in some of these lands.

The statute provides that the value be determined solely with reference to its appropriate private outdoor, recreational, open space, and park land classification and value.

In determining such value for ad valorem tax purposes, the assessor shall not consider the value such real estate would have if it were converted to commercial, industrial, residential . . . use.

Section 247 of the General Municipal Law of New York provides that any county, city, town, or village may acquire interests or rights in real property for the preservation of open spaces and areas, recognizing that such acquisition constitutes a public purpose. Open space is defined as

(1) natural scenic beauty or (2) whose existing openness, natural condition, or present state of use, if retained, would enhance the present or potential value of abutting or surrounding urban development, or would maintain and enhance the conservation of natural or scenic resources.

Scenic Easements

It is important to stress that such property rights may take the form of a scenic easement in which title and use remain with the private recreational facility and the easement is held by the municipality or county. By contract, the country club could agree not to erect any new buildings or additional physical improvements on the land. Since the scenic easement limits the use and development of the land, the assessed valuation may be reduced because the country club must be contained in its present use for the life of the agreement. A 1969 amendment to the law specifies that after acquisition of the property right, the assessed valuation placed on such open space should take into account and be limited by the future use of the land.

Thus, the municipality or the county is free to negotiate the tax reduction as it sees fit. At least one such scenic easement has been negotiated wherein the assessed value was reduced. The agreement provided that the country club could cancel the easement on paying the difference between the agreed assessment and what it would have been without the easement, plus 6% interest. One difficulty in applying Section 247 might be the reluctance of mortgagees to lend money on a country club burdened with an encumbrance such as a scenic easement. This requires careful investigation.

Reducing Assessed Valuations

The Florida and Minnesota state laws cited earlier may not have specific legal relevance in each state. However, they indicate a distinct trend toward the acceptance of the concept of private recreational land and the public necessity to keep real estate taxes very low on these facilities. The New York State law, on the other hand, provides an alternate, through which assessed valuations may be reduced. When assessed valuations are inequitably high, consideration should be given to developing a real estate tax agreement under similarly devised state statutes.

The now generally discredited appraisal approach to open space, such as a golf course, was to visualize its value for the alternate highest profitable use, and most clubs could not obtain the added revenues to pay such a tax. Sale of the land to a developer for subdivision as a housing tract would not only eliminate a lovely natural area, but would bring substantial added costs to the community in sewer, water, and road installations, and school and other municipal expense increases, thereby creating higher taxes for all while losing the benefit of the open space.

Conclusions

Country clubs as areas of natural scenic beauty enhance not only the value of adjacent real estate but contribute immeasurably to the desirability of the community. Far from being a negative fiscal contributor, the country club can pay a modest real estate tax while serving as a major generator of other net tax ratables, i.e., quality tax revenue at relatively low cost to the community.

The greenbelt area of the country club is a bastion which protects the community from the rapid urbanization of the countryside, with its attendant destruction of nature and its prospects for insensitive real estate development. An ideal ecological balance can only be achieved with lower population density. A country club's acreage achieves this population dispersal and reduces the noxious effects of automotive pollution by its decongesting effect.

Real estate taxing procedures must recognize the importance of these private recreational facilities, as they reduce acreage values to an affordable level by accepting the present land use rather than some vague and hypothetical alternate use as the basis for the assessed value. If this approach is unavailing, the scenic easement approach must be employed as a basis for obtaining a reduction.

9

The Fallacy of Gross Income Stabilization

The use by appraisers of the technique of gross income stabilization at an income level substantially lower than that prevailing under short-term leases has created the impression that an incontrovertible valuation doctrine and dogma exists requiring the identical treatment of all short-term gross income. It is suspected that the doctrine has arisen because the appraiser believes that he or she must identify with conservative valuation practice. This is unfortunate because undue conservatism does not professionally serve the appraiser's clientele or require any outstanding knowledge or ability. It is easy to be conservative!

What is meant by gross income stabilization? An appraiser sometimes does not properly consider cyclical market conditions, neighborhood and district characteristics, and the relative desirability of the improvement, and thus lowers the gross income either to an average of what he or she believes to be reasonably anticipated or the level to which the income may immediately or ultimately fall. The danger of this technique as well as its impracticality has never been fully realized.

Reprinted from *The Appraisal Journal* (July 1956): 348-50.

How does the appraiser determine the level to which the income should be lowered? Shall it be 10%, 20%, or 30% of the current level obtainable? If the appraiser relies on past levels of income or dollar worth (that is, base points), he or she may be completely unrealistic since economic history clearly demonstrates that each successive real estate cycle brings us to higher price plateaus. What currently seems like excessive gross income often subsequently proves to be relatively moderate. Even if the appraiser is convinced that an absolute cyclical peak has been reached and that a decline in income is impending, it is still difficult, if not impossible, to estimate the level to which the income should be lowered. This is particularly true since our economy is now supported by "built-in" stabilizers in the form of old age insurance, unemployment insurance, pensions, stronger unionism—buttressing factors that did not exist in the 1930s.

The impracticality and unrealistic results of this improbable and scarcely scientific approach are frequently compounded by the selection of a thoroughly inappropriate capitalization rate. Many appraisers apply the same rate to stabilized rentals as to current market levels. This practice will yield indefensibly conservative results. If we insist on establishing stabilized rentals, we must also stabilize the capitalization rate. But which rate is to be selected? How may a selection be proved?

Another disturbing facet of gross income stabilization is the casual disregard of that portion of the income stream that has the most valuation significance—the immediate years when income is not so heavily discountable. McMichael once said, "Present money commands a premium over future money. That money, remote in time, when subjected to a present money statement, suffers in the perspective of desire very much as things distant in space suffer in the visual perspective. One is disposed to pay less for that which is to be enjoyed in the future than for that which is to be enjoyed at present."

Alternatives

Which alternatives exist to this concept of gross income forecasting? First, let us return to fundamentals. Income has three characteristics—quantity, stability, and futurity—on which the appraiser must reflect in projecting an income flow.

Quantity.   If relatively long leases exist, say for three or more years, the appraiser must accept that level at least for the term of the leases. To do otherwise would seem to be ethically dubious unless the appraiser would separately capitalize the excess income for a limited time. In those instances in which the appraiser cannot draw any precise conclusions as to how long these admittedly high rentals may be sustained, he or she has little or no recourse but to accept that level.

Stability.   The risk in sustaining gross income over the economic life of a property may be capable of evaluation by the appraiser through investigation of the rent levels of comparable realty, market conditions, terms of the leases, credit and character standing of the tenancy, the relative locational desirability, and competitive utility of the improvement. These factors should be considered in light of current market earnings-price ratios. They may warrant a departure from established market ratios.

Futurity.   The remaining economic life must be forecast. This has pertinence since it is generally recognized that the longer the economic life, the greater the possibility of sustaining the level of the gross income.

One solution appears to rest in an increasing awareness and development of a greater sensitivity to the selection of the proper capitalization rates. Current overall rates of return—the ratio of net income, free of mortgage indebtedness to the selling price—are demonstrable economic facts. They are economic indicators of the tone and outlook of the market. They form a base from which the appraiser may draw conclusions of value. Gone would be the necessity of groping in the abyss of a hypothetical level of income or fretting over the selection of the capitalization rate in our efforts to seek the all-too-elusive concept of normality. Market activity, however, is a wonderful source of information from which the appraiser may draw. Further, the market is continually and increasingly better educated and informed, and its conclusions of value should be respected, although the appraiser's detachment and impartiality may lead to a different valuation conclusion.

Vacuum Appraising

Many cases illustrate the thesis presented here. To take just one example, let us consider the attached brownstone dwellings, 20- and 25-feet wide, which are characteristic of Manhattan's East and West sides and can also be found in many older cities such as Boston, Philadelphia, Chicago, and Baltimore. Following World War II, many of these handsome New York dwellings were converted to modern apartment houses, with eight to ten small apartment units Gross annual incomes of $600 to $800 per room were obtainable because of the residential shortage. Many appraisers stabilized this income at $400 to $500 per room and groped for a so-called "stabilized value," arrived at by capitalization at a standard rate of 6% plus an allowance for depreciation. At that time, several sales were recorded which indicated that the ratio of actual net income, free and clear of mortgage, to the selling price was as high as 12% to 13%. Equity returns ranged from 25% to 30%, depending on mortgage terms. Obviously, the market was also concerned at the prospect of sustaining these high rentals and demanded a high return on its investment. Here were facts on which appraisers could actually "hang their hats" but were nevertheless largely ignored. Many similar instances have occurred, particularly in regard to new construction where it has become a fetish to stabilize rents at less than what the market is willing to pay. This is appraising in a vacuum without a realistic regard for what exists.

What is the solution? The appraiser's principal valuation problem is to measure the degree of risk in a particular property. Risk cannot be solved by the utilization of artificial and theoretical valuation concepts that are direct-opinioned rather than analytical. It seems unwise to appraise in an ivory tower while significant market activity whirls around the appraiser's head.

Why not use existing market data? Accept income as it actually exists and find appropriate earnings-price ratios in current sales. Believing that market prices are too high, an appraiser may adjust his or her final value estimate, but only provided the appraisal report contains an explanation of the reasons for the appraiser's departure from market prices. This involves a knowledgeable perspective of real estate cycles and market conditions so that the differential between market price and market value may be more readily estimated and explained.

For lenders who seek to estimate value on a conservative stabilized basis for mortgage purposes, it is suggested that more attention be devoted to actual market facts and that market value be more realistically appraised. If a lender feels that a decline in gross income, and hence values, is not only impending but imminent, loan value ratios should be adjusted in accordance with the risk involved in sustaining the income. And to all appraisers, it is suggested that market value be objectively appraised, no matter what the purpose of the appraisal may be, by a realistic treatment of gross income.

10
Selection of the Capitalization Rate

In real estate valuation, the selection of the capitalization rate is perhaps the most important element. *Capitalization rate* is defined as a rate of interest used for converting a series of net income payments into capital value. The proper process of rate selection and correct procedural technique are most imperative. A high degree of skill and judgment may have been used to estimate the anticipated income and expenses, to analyze neighborhood trends, and to make a painstaking physical inspection of the property; but none of these elements assumes the prominence that should be accorded the judicious and well-documented selection of the proper capitalization rate. Yet little consideration has been given to a scientific analysis of the reasons for its selection.

It has been the author's experience to hear real estate valuation experts, as they testified in certiorari and condemnation proceedings, fail repeatedly to substantiate in a logical and intelligent manner the rate selected. The usual answers are: "It's the prevalent return on investments of this character," or "My thirty years of experience indicates this to be the current market rate." Fortunately for the real estate experts, the corporation counsels of the local munici-

Reprinted from *The Appraisal Journal* (October 1949): 478-89.

palities are not much better informed, and that particular line of questioning terminates since neither expert nor counsel can contribute any information of value on the subject.

It appears that undue emphasis has been placed on phases of the valuation process that require mechanical rather than intellectual ability. It is relatively easy to determine typical expense figures for all types of buildings, to describe the physical appearance of the realty and the neighborhood, or to figure the cost of reproduction from data published by many organizations. The *interpretation* of these factors, however, and their incorporation into the selection of the rate is perhaps a more vital aspect. Judgment and experience play a major role in the process of rate selection, it is true, but much remains to be accomplished in substantiating in a scholarly and scientific manner the rate utilized.

Interest

A study of capitalization rates requires a knowledge of the phenomenon of interest. The appraiser recognizes interest as the premium or charge made for the privilege of hiring capital.

When an investor commits funds to an investment in real estate, he or she expects a premium in the form of income as compensation for the sacrifice of foregoing immediate use *of* capital for the risk and hazard of an uncertain future return *on* capital. The amount of the premium, in relation to the capital investment, varies with the investor's inclinations concerning the degree of risk involved.

In the real estate economy, interest assumes the form of money income collectable at stated intervals. To determine the unknown quantity, the capital value, it becomes necessary to convert the interest payments, that is, the net income, into capital value by a simple mathematical process. The procedural techniques in capitalization are not the subject here; rather, the discussion will be confined to the selection of the rate itself.

Components of Interest

The three commonly recognized components of interest are pure interest, management of the financial investment, and risk. Occasionally, a fourth component, nonliquidity, is added. Pure interest is the safe or prevailing long-term government rate of interest, which at present is regarded as 2.50%. Theoretically at this amount, neither risk nor servicing is required to obtain the interest return. Management of the financial investment encompasses the policy decisions made concerning the investment as to sale, servicing, and holding, as well as the considerations involved in the initial purchase for investment. This component is usually accorded a rate of 1.00% on income-producing real estate and perhaps .75% on private dwellings.

These two components are relatively fixed in amount and remain reasonably constant except under the impact of revolutionary changes in interest rates. They apply equally to all classes of property, ranging from the most efficient realty to that with submarginal characteristics. Therefore, the appraiser can find that portion of the capitalization rate attributable to these components since the percentage amount they contribute to the total interest rate results from general business and political conditions not inherent in the realty under appraisal.

The third component risk is the great variable. The measurement of risk involved is the real estate enigma that must be solved and with which we are presently concerned. The degree of variance in the risk factor often is as great as 6% alone, as in comparing the interest rate for a ground lease under a long-term leasehold to a AAA-1 company with that of an old law tenement on the lower east side of New York.

Contrary to beliefs held by many in the real estate field, the capitalization rate is not a standardized, arbitrary amount used indiscriminately for all types of real estate, nor is it confined to a very narrow range, as many assert. Others hold that the only permissible variance in the capitalization rate results from the manner in which a provision is made for the recapture of the capital investment in the building asset, which is recognized as depreciable and having limited economic utility. In other words, interest and its components are confused by adding a percentage amount that is designed to recoup the building investment over a certain period of years.

The risk factor, as contrasted with other components of interest, varies according to the type, style, age, utility, location, desirability, and condition of the improvement and the character of the tenancy as measured by the amount, stability, and futurity of net income. Thus, in determining the proper capitalization rate, the appraiser's ingenuity is tested in the measurement of risk attached to the purchase.

A preliminary conclusion, later to be proved, may be stated first. Capitalization rates should be accorded the sensitivity that the market characteristics and the particular site justify. Real estate is a highly localized nonhomogeneous commodity and the rate tends to vary widely.

The remainder of this article will be a study of the economic forces that influence and determine the capitalization rate, and create impelling reasons for variances. If the reader considers that any error of one point, say from 4% to 5%, in the selection of the capitalization rate will make a 20% difference in the capital value, perhaps he or she will realize the importance of the selective process.

Of the data that will be analyzed to assist in making the correct decision, one type reflects general economic and business conditions outside the real estate economy; the other reflects the real estate market and its characteristics that influence and determine the rate.

Effects of General Economic Conditions

In the long run, variations in interest rates are rarely ever confined to real estate alone. Real estate, even though it characteristically lags behind the general business cycle, is sensitive to general business conditions and is influenced by significant changes in interest rates. In a given locality, factors of supply, demand, and cost, not characteristic of general conditions, may indicate a capitalization rate pattern that runs counter to the basic trends in interest rates; but over a period of time, business conditions sharply affect realty. If national income and volume of employment decline, inevitably there is a lesser rate of family formation and less people per family unit. This undoubtedly would affect the ownership and investment in real estate since it would increase the risk and hazard involved and thus increase the general rate because of anticipated decreases in occupancy.

The influence of business and financial conditions on realty is basic, of course, and affects all classes and types of structures. None are spared, and the increase or decrease in the capitalization rate applies, although not necessarily in the same proportion, no matter what the class or character of the realty may be.

Stock and Bond Market

The stock and bond market is the pulse of the business world, sensitive to the slightest changes in the physiology of business, and immediately reflects changes in interest rates. The precipitous decline in market prices of stocks in the latter part of 1947 indicated a lack of confidence by the investing public in the future of business, together with a mounting concern over foreign affairs. These factors sought and found expression in the willingness of the market to buy stocks only if the yield were greatly increased, in recompense for the increased risk and speculation involved in uncertain future business conditions.

The study of daily market transactions and quotations together with current articles on business and financial affairs are helpful. There is an abundance of valuable data in Moody's Indexes, the Amott Baker index of real estate bond prices, *Federal Reserve Bank Bulletin, Business Week* magazine, and Department of Commerce publications. Analyses of these data will enable the appraiser to become acquainted with the interpretations of events concerning interest rates and economic trends by experts in the fields. Then the effect of significant trends in money cost on the real estate capitalization rate must be measured.

An analysis has been made of the comparative yields on public utility bonds of different risk characteristics. The lower rated bonds were unable to withstand the constrictions of severely depressed business conditions during the early 1930s and sold at such a heavy discount in open market sales that BAA bonds in 1932 commanded a yield of almost 11%. This provides a strong contrast to AAA bonds, which even during the height of the depression never sold to yield more than 5%. With the general economic recovery that followed, the yields tended to vary in inverse proportion to the trend of business conditions, and as they improved the price of the bonds gradually rose. The yields, of course, declined in the same proportion as the price increased. In 1945, AAA bonds were yielding 2.6%, while BAA issues were returning 3.5%.

What parallel can be adduced from this information that can assist the real estate appraiser in determining the proper capitalization rate? It is safe to conclude that marginal realty suffers the most during the low points in the real estate cycle, as does BAA and A bond issues. This in itself indicates that risks in real estate vary widely, as do other forms of wealth such as stocks and bonds. Obsolete or inadequate real estate must be compensated during the high point in the real estate cycle since this type of realty is the first to feel the competitive effects of more adequate, better-situated realty. Any relative amount of oversupply or constriction in the demand for space will adversely affect property of this type and consequently lessen its capital value in a disproportionate ratio to the more desirable realty.

Thus, as with public utility bonds, real estate of a more speculative and hazardous nature, about which forecasts are difficult concerning the stability, amount, and futurity of the income flow, should command a higher rate of return. There is a lesson here for every member of the real estate profession— the prevalent attitude that seeks to ascribe an arbitrary rate of capitalization to all types of real estate is basically unsound and contrary to business and economic fundamentals.

Stock and bond market prices are nothing more than the valuation by a consensus of investors of the present capital worth of the anticipated income, together with an adjustment concerning the probabilities of incremental gain, and the basic fundamentals, if not specifically, may be generally integrated with the real estate market. Significant developments in stock and bond prices would most certainly affect the rate of return on real estate, especially since a revolutionary variation has a psychological effect on all classes of investors and all investment channels.

Perhaps the best example of the influence of stock and bond trends on the real estate economy may be found in the revolutionary changes in interest rates that commenced in the latter part of 1946 and have continued to date. There is a mass of available material on the subject from which the professional appraiser can draw conclusions. As an illustration, in the November 15, 1947, issue of *Business Week,* it was reported that weakness in new bond issues has had a direct competitive influence on preferred stock issues. As a result, cumulative dividend rates of 3.50% and 3.75% are no longer attractive and the de-mand now is for 4% preferreds. On the heels of this development, the *New York Times,* on November 25, 1947, reported that the Federal Reserve System and the Federal Deposit Insurance Corporation had warned banks to curtail all loans for speculative securities, commodities, and real estate. The *Wall Street Journal,* on January 2, 1948, predicted ". . . [the] new twist will be a sharp upward climb in the cost of credit. This inflation in interest rates will tend to discourage a deflation in other things by raising the cost of making and selling goods." The article also predicted a 2% rate for prime commercial paper and a general tightening in real estate loans. At the same time, the majority of trust companies in New York were raising their short-term loan rate from 1½% to 2%.

Other signs pointed to a significant change in the cost of money. As a further example, the May 1945 and the October and December 1947 issues of the *Federal Reserve Bulletin* demonstrate the relationship of AAA public utility bonds with long-term taxable government bonds. The excess of public utility issues over government bonds in 1942 averaged around .25%. During 1943 and 1944, the excess decreased to .18%. However, a gradual upward trend commenced, and by December 1947 the excess of the public utilities over government bonds rose to .38%, demonstrating the sharp rise in the cost of money while the government bonds, artifically supported by the Federal Reserve's policy of sustaining the price level, remained relatively stable.

Of what value to the real estate appraiser are these unmistakable trends in the sharp rise in the rate of time preference? What conclusions may be drawn as to their influence on the capitalization rate in the valuation of real estate? Are these fundamentals too far removed from the actuality of appraising the value of a specific property to have any interest to the appraisal profession? A proper correlation of these facts to the realty situation will demonstrate their significance.

If one charted the upward trend in interest rates, he or she could prove that the volume of real estate transactions in Manhattan began to show an inverse trend at the same time. The results are interesting since they tend to show that the rise in the cost of money had so influenced investors that an increasing reluctance developed to commit funds to income-producing property, which was being offered for sale on the basis of the same general returns as in 1945 and 1946. Inevitably, the dollar volume of real estate transactions declined precipitously.

Figure 10.1 shows the volume of transactions in Manhattan real estate between January 1946 and February 1948. Commencing in December 1946, the monthly volume of sales showed a steady decline until a low of $18 million in volume was reached in November 1947.

Table 10.1 demonstrates that while the volume was dropping, the ratio of the sales prices to the assessed valuation remained relatively constant, indicat-

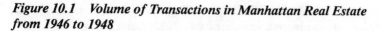

Figure 10.1   Volume of Transactions in Manhattan Real Estate from 1946 to 1948

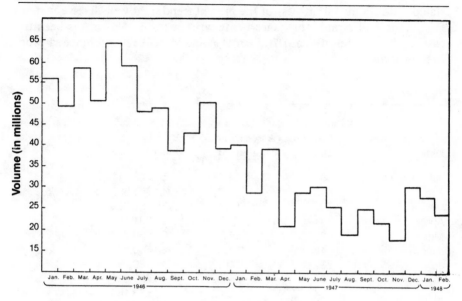

ing that conveyances occurred only when sellers realized the price they wanted. The vast majority of buyers, however, refrained from purchasing real estate at the current price level, preferring to invest their money elsewhere than to undergo the risks inherent in the ownership of real estate at the current low rate of return.

It is thus apparent that the revolutionary increase in the cost of money had some effect on real estate since the sales volume declined so sharply. It is safe to assume that if the trend in the cost of money continues upward, ultimately the rate of return on real estate will also rise, even though there has been no discernible increase at the present time. As pointed out earlier, the real estate cycle characteristically lags behind general business conditions. Appreciating this fact, however, the appraiser may draw certain conclusions that will help in selecting a rate with some degree of anticipation, and thus he or she will not be content with merely using the current rate.

The well-informed appraiser, keeping abreast of all developments in business and finance, may easily relate these events to the real estate market. As an example, in the *New York Times* of December 16, 1947, a prominent mortgage broker predicted that, as the result of the upward trend in the cost of prime commercial paper, the first change in 12 years, and because the yield on government bonds had risen to 2.34% (from 2.18% in 1946), real estate owners could not enjoy much longer the low interest rates on mortgages they had been able to obtain since the 1930s. It was pointed out that high-grade corporate bonds yield 2.70% and higher, in contrast to 2.40% in 1946. It was further stated, "It is doubtful, in view of the present trend, that we will see any more first grade real estate mortgages being written for 3.25% as has been the case. . . . Advances of ¼ of 1%, ½ of 1%, and ¾ of 1% in mortgage rates are to be expected."

Table 10.1

Date	Number of Sales	Ratio to Assessment in Percent	Dollar Volume
Jan. 1946	686	91.1	56,843,311
Feb.	613	86.3	44,895,523
Mar.	737	93.4	58,555,822
Apr.	781	91.1	52,391,168
May	836	98.7	64,939,772
June	742	102.0	60,560,572
July	737	100.01	48,180,288
Aug.	677	100.02	49,723,921
Sept.	494	100.02	38,536,188
Oct.	628	100.25	43,702,397
Nov.	571	94.8	51,167,484
Dec.	510	100.0	39,459,386
Jan. 1947	463	111.0	41,250,744
Feb.	369	112.0	28,981,705
Mar.	431	100.03	39,245,532
Apr.	342	97.5	21,265,278
May	405	99.0	30,471,431
June	346	100.02	31,299,528
July	339	99.3	26,797,484
Aug.	289	95.2	18,746,287
Sept.	328	93.6	26,847,671
Oct.	332	93.0	22,491,362
Nov.	341	95.4	18,055,784
Dec.	384	98.4	31,084,934
Jan. 1948	353	98.5	29,142,479
Feb.	289	103.8	24,397,746

What is the reason for these sharp upward trends in interest rates? The answer to this may lead to valuable conclusions as to the effect on real estate in general. It may be said that interest rates usually tend to rise in times of prosperity because business competes in seeking additional funds for expansion and working capital. Then, soaring material costs and wages, plus the shrinkage of equity capital due to the drain on profits occasioned by high federal income taxes, sharpens the demand for funds and a lender's market begins to evolve. Until the last few years, the Federal Reserve System has traditionally fostered high interest rates in times of prosperity as the conventional means of confining booms and mitigating the effects of excess credit and overfinancing.

Effect of Government Monetary Policy

In the last analysis, the recent inflationary spiral in the cost of living was created by the government itself. Depreciation in the worth of the dollar started its last downward spiral when, under the economic dislocation of a total war, the government borrowed money from the commercial banks and spent it in the war effort, then the money was promptly returned through business channels to the commercial banks and through individual incomes to the savings banks, and finally the money was immediately reinvested. The resultant high level of purchasing power and the demand for commodities unobtainable in quantity during the war, plus the agitation of labor for higher wages to meet higher prices and without regard for labor's productivity, led to a constantly increasing price level.

The means of correction, of course, does not lie in regulating the result—prices—but, rather, in the removal of the cause. Curtailment of government expenditures, continuance of a reasonably high tax level on private income, and reduction of the national debt are the primary factors that will stop the inflationary spiral.

The appraiser, however, is not a legislator and has no means of combating government fiscal policies. He or she is concerned only with the effects of this policy on the selection of the proper capitalization rates for real estate. It is customary and correct to appraise real estate in terms of today's dollars, not at a dollar pegged at what the appraiser may feel to be more indicative of value. It is hardly pertinent to select a past level of cost or dollar worth as indicative of future value; there may be no relation between the past level selected and that which may be anticipated.

New cost data must be accepted. Higher expenses of construction and maintenance, higher wages, and, most important, higher income must be recognized. An appraiser must not distort the meaning of conservatism by appraising in terms of what used to be. The appraiser's reaction should be anticipatory and prospective, not retrospective or current. The risk and uncertainty should be measured in terms of today's money and the capitalization rate selected accordingly.

The general inflationary problem created by government fiscal policy can be solved by the appraiser if he or she remembers the simple expedient of increasing the capitalization rate in a rising or a peak market. The traditional movement in the cost of money, such as is being experienced today, is no better proved than by a recital of the facts heretofore presented. Real estate, especially that not under federal rent control, is generally and substantially undercapitalized, in view of the depreciated worth of the currency. If the appraiser can grasp the incongruity of real estate returning the same yield today that it may have returned five years ago, despite the well recognized fact that today's dollar buys only half of what it did five years before, he or she will value property more realistically than if centering on past data. It seems only logical that some compensation must be forthcoming in the capitalization rate on real estate to combat the shrinkage of the dollar's worth as a medium of exchange. The appraiser should always keep abreast of the changing market and current events.

Government Regulatory Policy

A partial explanation for the confusion existing today concerning the proper capitalization rate for real estate may be found in the federal government's policy of enforcing ceilings on gross income of residential realty. Without discussing the social aspects of the problem, it may be said that such a policy has served to stultify the natural economic phenomenon of supply and demand. The consequent optimism of the investor in believing that ceilings on income would be removed soon after the termination of the war led to lower capitalization rates, particularly in the competition for desirable realty.

The appraiser is faced with an issue of paramount importance in the selection of a capitalization rate for realty under rent control. The market is demanding and anticipating higher rentals. How can this fact be rationalized in view of the general conclusion as to the undercapitalization of realty, and since the currency as a medium of exchange has been so depreciated? As a general rule, it is a more sound procedure to lower the capitalization rate than to predict successively higher rental levels for the future. This lowering of the rate, however, should contain a calculation involving the trend of money, which, in turn, has a vitiating effect on the demand for lower rates and tends to impede its downward path. Thus, we have had counteracting forces, one tending to lower the rate and the other tending to raise it. Belated recognition of this phenomenon in the real estate market was evident in 1947, when investors resisted current offerings because the return was not sufficient to justify the investment. A proper analysis of the influence of government regulatory and fiscal policy should have led the appraiser to the same conclusion at least a year earlier than the market recognition.

The Real Estate Market

The real estate market is the most important element in determining the proper capitalization rate for realty. The influence of the rate of return on other forms of wealth, such as stocks and bonds, has already been noted as well as the effect of general business conditions. The conclusion has been reached that the investor is generally influenced by stock and bond activity and by government fiscal and regulatory policy. These basic factors influence all types of real estate equally. Our next concern is with the factors peculiar to the real estate market itself, the proper interpretation of which will guide the appraiser to a proper selection of the capitalization rate. Since it has already been established that pure interest and financial management are basic components of interest and do not readily change, the variations in the capitalization rate in realty itself are almost wholly derived from a study of the risk factor.

Conditions of Supply and Demand

In a normal competitive market, an analysis must be made periodically concerning the conditions of real estate supply. The effects of cost must be carefully measured and the attitude of producers toward entering the market must be determined. This entails a study of rental rates according to the type of structure as a means of analyzing whether the costs of construction would be compensated by the net income obtained. Only when a well-documented conclusion can be reached justifying the investment in construction can the appraiser scientifically determine the anticipated availability of supply.

An analysis of demand, on the other hand, entails the determination of data on the specific nature of the demand, classified as to type of structure. Demand must be estimated against a background of data on population growth, constancy, decrease, or shifts from one section to another. Because of the localized nature of real estate as a commodity, some sections may experience a rapid gain. If population in the immediate area is constant, it may be naturally concluded that at least one other section in the general area has lost in population and, consequently, in value. District bursting, sliding, or shifting is a recurring real estate phenomenon and must be accorded proper weight in the selection of the capitalization rate.

There are other factors relating to supply and demand that must be carefully analyzed. The percentage of vacancies, or, as it is sometimes called, the occupancy ratio, the volume of new construction, and the ratio of sales prices to assessed valuations have a significance to which careful consideration must be given.

Earnings-Price Ratio

The most reliable market evidence of the proper capitalization rate is found in what H.B. Dorau, chairman of the Department of Real Estate and Urban

Land Economics of New York University, has called the earnings-price ratio. In short, the *earnings-price ratio* is the ratio of the net income, as if free and clear of mortgage indebtedness, to the selling price. In the case of private dwellings, it is the ratio of the gross annual rental value to the selling price. Gross income is used for private homes since the expenses are uniform and not subject to the same degree of variance as with income-producing property.

As an example, assume that an apartment house, after deductions for all expenses and contingencies, has a net income free of mortgage, of $10,000, and has sold for $125,000. The ratio of the net income to the selling price is 8%. This strongly indicates that the market deserves an 8% overall rate of return for that particular class and character of realty. In other words, the market demands a return of 8% before it would be attracted to the property for investment.

Next, assume that a private dwelling sold for $15,000 and had an annual rental value of $1,500. The ratio would be 10%, indicating that a return of that amount would be necessary to attract a prudent and well-informed purchaser.

A natural question that should arise is the manner in which the rate is to be found. This is a fairly simple procedure, yet it requires more exhaustive investigation and inquiry than the average appraisal demands. It is presumed that the appraiser has also made an analysis of sales of comparable properties in the neighborhood, and that the selections are comparable in size, anticipated utility, style, income layout, character of the tenancy, and neighborhood. It is then necessary, in income-producing property, to obtain the gross income and expenses, thus desiring a net income before the ratio can be established. If it is impossible to obtain the required income and expense figures, the appraiser may estimate them. Often they may be found in listings in the appraiser's office. If not, efforts should be made to obtain them from the owners of the property.

Suppose that five comparable sales of apartment houses similar to the one under appraisal were found. The method of determining the overall rate would proceed as shown in Table 10.2.

Note that four of the sales indicated overall rates of return varying from 7.37% to 8.18%. The fifth sale is obviously unrepresentative of market condi-

Table 10.2

Property	Plot	Rooms	Net Income	Sales Price	Ratio (in percent)
A	100 × 100	160	$14,000	$190,000	7.37
B	75 × 125	152	13,000	175,000	7.43
C	75 × 100	137	12,000	155,000	7.74
D	50 × 150	132	12,000	110,000	10.90
E	60 × 100	95	9,000	110,000	8.18

tions since it is at least 3% over the other percentages. These exceptions result from unwise or forced sales, or are often a result of an apartment house being maintained in extremely poor physical condition. In any event, sales such as that of Property D are so obviously out of line that they must be discarded or a gross error in the selective process might result.

The fundamental is the same in the case of private dwellings except, as previously noted, gross income rather than net income is used. Again, the comparable sales of five properties, as the method of determining the overall rate of return, is used in Table 10.3.

Table 10.3

Property	Size	Rooms	Gross Income	Sales Price	Ratio (in percent)
A	100 × 150	7-2	$2400	$24,000	10.0
B	75 × 125	6-2	2000	19,000	10.5
C	85 × 200	7-2½	2600	24,000	10.8
D	100 × 125	7-3	2600	28,000	9.3
E	100 × 100	6-2½	2100	19,000	11.0

In none of the instances observed in Table 10.3 does there appear any ratio significantly out of line and unrepresentative of market conditions. The rates found will inevitably vary, but the astute appraiser can select the applicable overall rate for the realty he or she is appraising (1) on the basis of its relative desirability in comparison with the other private homes, and (2) if income-producing property, on a basis of the risk involved in the property under appraisal in relation to the overall rates established in the comparable sales of other typical apartment houses.

The problem of then selecting the rate applicable to the property under appraisal requires mature judgment and analysis. It is not solved by obtaining an average of the ratios found in the market. Any such mechanical method has no validity in a process that is primarily an art and in which we can only hope to apply scientific methods rather than to obtain purely scientific results.

The Capitalization Rate

Heretofore, the study for the most part has been confined to a discussion of interest and interest rates and the overall rate of return as it is commonly known. What, then, is the capitalization rate? The capitalization rate is a rate of interest used for the specific purpose of converting a series of net income payments into capital value. In the process, the capitalization rate must demonstrate the degree of risk attached to the income, its anticipated duration, and its ability to recapture the capital investment as a means of providing for depreciation.

The earnings-price ratio, or overall rate of return, has been universally misinterpreted by the investing public and appraisers as a capitalization rate that would fit the above description. This is emphatically not so. To regard this ratio, as expressed in a percentage, as a capitalization rate negates every fundamental of sound appraisal procedure.

It contrives to ignore the depreciation factor in the depreciable portion of the property; it does not demonstrate the extent of the economic life of the improvement; it refuses recognition to the differential that may exist in rates between land and building; and it constitutes the treatment of land and building as a single entity, capitalizable as such. In short, its effect is only to measure the ratio of *current* rather than anticipated earnings to the price at which they may be purchased. Furthermore, it does not indicate whether land has been considered the residual product of the other factors of production or whether the building returns have been made residual. Those who have mainly relied on the earnings-price ratio in the valuation process may leave unanswered several questions that should be in the body of the appraisal report.

The earnings-price ratio, it should be made clear, is a simple mathematical ratio that expresses the market's conclusion as to the present total net income on a property in relation to the price at which it may be purchased. At the very best it measures the amount of money one could afford to pay for the privilege of receiving a certain net income for a period of, say, one or two years. The professional appraiser, however, should look beyond this limited horizon in anticipation of what the property may net for its remaining economic life, and determine from the earnings-price ratio what the real capitalization rate may be.

Before such an analysis is attempted, it is advisable to caution the appraiser against blind acceptance of earnings-price ratios. Many appraisers, when asked the basis on which the rate has been selected, reply somewhat vaguely that the rate "is in the market." That the rate is a market phenomenon cannot be controverted, but the appraiser must first learn how it is determined. It should be remembered that comparable sales (and hence the earnings-price ratio) are a past event. Value, however, depends on the future utility of the property and is anticipatory rather than retrospective. Therefore, it is conceivable that the ratio may have to be revised in view of certain significant and anticipated trends in demand, money cost, or other factors that may arise.

The second qualification in the use of earnings-price ratios may be found in the inflationary effects of secondary mortgage financing. It may be concluded that on the basis of terms existing in the market, such financing usually inflates the price at which a property is conveyed because of the premium paid for generous mortgage terms. Thus, the appraiser may be forced to make an adjustment of perhaps 3% to 8% in the total recorded price, according to the discount allowable if the second mortgage were offered for sale in the market. If care is exercised to see that the sale price is adjusted, where the property sold was with the assistance of a purchase money second mortgage, the possibility of a gross error in the selective process may be avoided, and the earnings-price ratio would then be reflective of the all-cash value of the realty or its reasonable equivalent.

From the overall rate thus determined, the capitalization rates for the fractional parts of the property—land and building—are selected, and land and building returns are capitalized separately.

Specifically, how can the earnings-price ratio help to determine the value of the property under appraisal? Assume the following facts:

I.	Total net income	$ 10,000
	Established earnings- price ratio—8%	
	Indicated capital value	125,000
II.	Total net income	$ 10,000
	Land value by comparison—$50,000	
	Return attributable to land—6%	− 3,000
	Residual return attributable to building	$ 7,000
	Capitalization of building return (7%—20 years—Factor 10.594)	$ 74,000
	Add land value	+ 50,000
		$124,000

Thus, the ratio of the total net income of $10,000 to the appraised value of $124,000 would still be 8%, even though the fractional parts of the property have been separately capitalized.

The reader may wonder why the capitalization rates ascribed to fractional parts of the property are substantially lower than the earnings-price ratio. That ratio, of course, is strongly influenced by the futurity of the income attributable to the building. The shorter the duration of the building's economic life, the lower will be the capital value, and the higher the ratio of the total net earnings to the appraised value. As an example, in the annuity system of capitalization, the capitalization rate remains the same but the applicable factor differs according to the duration of income.

It is felt that too little emphasis has been given to the study and determination of the proper capitalization rate for real estate. Many appraisers make no mention of the capitalization rate in appraisal reports. It is difficult to conceive how the appraiser expects to attain professional status if such faults persist. Statements such as, "The rate is selected on the basis of long experience in the real estate business," should be stopped, and the selection of the capitalization rate should be intelligently substantiated.

11
Beware the Abusers of IRR Methodology

There is nothing at all new about the use of the internal rate of return (IRR) methodology in valuation. It has had more widespread application in our inflation-ridden economy since the late 1970s because the older, traditional methods of capitalizing—converting stabilized net income into a present market value—seemed inadequate. Rents seem to rise almost inexorably during a sustained inflation, compelling a need to forecast, within a reasonable time frame, probable rent increases as leases expire. Computer programming has eased the task of dropping in new rents, dropping out old escalation provisions, and substituting a new base year for real estate taxes and operating expenses. In the hands of professionally trained appraisers, abuses in use seem improbable.

Our main concern is that owners and agents are now using revenue expense forecasting and discounting techniques as marketing tools. Any person with ulterior motives could easily inflate rent projections, understate expense increases, and use too low a discount rate, thus inflating prices to a frequently

This article was written with Robert A. Steele. Reprinted from *The Appraisal Journal* (April 1982): 204-11.

unsuspecting public and eventually discrediting an excellent analytical tool. Worse still, an unwarranted increase in prices accompanied by heavy secondary financing could lead to difficulties for owners paying debt service during a period of increasing vacancies and flat-to-declining rents. The problem for institutional buyers who paid high cash prices during the rising phase of a cycle would be confined to disappointment about the internal rate of return realized rather than any distress in paying debt service and operating expenses.

The Discounted Internal Rate of Return

The IRR may be defined as the present value rate at compound interest of a series of discounted annual cash flows added to the discounted gains or losses from a presumed resale at the end of the projection period. A self-amortizing mortgage loan provides an example of how this works. When a lender makes a loan, it is, in effect, making an investment. As the borrower repays the loan, the lender is receiving a return on and of its investment; this is usually labeled the debt service or constant factor. The interest rate becomes the IRR. An equity investor makes a down payment, receives a cash flow, positive or negative, over the investment period (usually a 10-year projection), finally obtains the benefits of resale, and from that an internal rate of return can be calculated. A simple example will illustrate:

IRR		Proof			
				PW of	
Time	**Cash Flow**	**Time**	**Cash Flow**	**$1 @ 10%**	**Present Value**
0	− $100,000				
1	10,000	1	$10,000	.909091	$ 9,090.91
2	10,000	2	10,000	.826446	8,264.46
3	10,000	3	10,000	.751315	7,513.15
4	10,000	4	10,000	.683013	6,830.13
5	110,000	5	10,000	.620921	68,301.35
					$100,000.00

(Calculation on an HP-38; IRR = 10%)

Note that the IRR study starts at time zero compared with year one for the discounted cash-flow study. The investment is made at time zero, but it is assumed the first cash flow does not occur until the end of the first year. The investment is shown as negative, because when all of the positive cash flows are discounted at the proper internal rate of return, the sum of present value will produce a zero answer, thereby proving that the present value of cash flows and the investment are perfectly balanced.

Solving for the IRR frequently involves trial and error. Usually, the trial discount rate produces a present value other than zero. By trying different trial rates and bracketing zero the proper rate will be achieved. Fortunately, financial calculators will do this automatically. In the special case of a level annuity, if the discount rate and capitalization rate are the same, that rate is the IRR. The reversionary value must be equal to the investment; however, interpolation becomes mandatory even on level annuities when the discount rate is different from the capitalization rate. The latter is the rate used as a divisor that converts the stabilized cash flow into a value at the end of the projection period. The resulting discounted total value theoretically reflects what the real estate is worth at that time at particular discount and capitalization rates.

Typical Uses and Projection Periods

The use of a projection period is particularly applicable to multiple tenancies where the lease-termination dates vary significantly, as in office buildings, shopping centers, and light industrial parks. Escalation terms in office buildings frequently vary considerably, not only because of refinements over time in these provisions but also because of market demands at a given moment. For example, in a saturated market, the tenant will demand and frequently obtain a ceiling on the extent of real estate tax and operating escalation for which he or she will accept responsibility. Where there is high demand, the owner will require and receive full tax and operating escalation reimbursement and sometimes even more. Where there are many tenants, lease variances almost mandate the use of computer analysis.

The difficulty of forecasting trends on percentage rents in shopping centers is formidable. Nevertheless, they must be estimated because there is no other effective way of valuing the property. It is frequently impossible to assemble sufficient comparable sales data to justify use of a capitalization rate alone because of differences in location, market competition, and income levels of the inhabitants in the trading area. IRR methodology must be relied on, supported by knowledge of mortgage interest rates and general money market rates.

A very basic question is the length of the projection period selected. At the end of the projection period, the following year's cash flow is assumed to be stabilized, and capitalization rate is then applied to derive a market value on the presumed resale. That lump sum or capital value is then discounted to the present day.

How long should the projection period be? A suitable period for valuation purposes is not necessarily suitable for internal study purposes. For valuation purposes, there is a consensus that generally no more than 10 years should be used. (An obvious exception would be prime property with 11 years remaining on an old, low, flat-rent lease for the entire building.)

For development properties, the usual 10-year projection period may be extended by the time required for development. New properties tend to be slow in achieving investment maturation; they frequently take 10 years after completion to achieve their occupancy and rental level potentials.

In our own investment analysis of properties, we project rents and expenses sometimes over a 20-year period or longer. The study period is often made concurrent to the self-liquidation of an existing first mortgage, or with an important, long-term lease. For long-range planning, it is crucial to have at least some concept of how the real estate will perform compared with other investments over a long time period, as long as it is clearly understood that no valuation implications may be drawn from an extended study period. Nor should there be any special objection to using an extended projection period in a sales brochure. The important point is not to base the *value* on a lengthy period involving significant income growth rates. The uninformed buyer could be misled.

Forecasting Techniques

Central to IRR analysis is the creation of a rent matrix for the property. A current rental value is placed on the premises, on an elevator zone, floor, or location basis or any combination thereof. The current rent levels are then projected, usually on a percentage basis of increase or decrease. In the case of the Pan Am Building, the tower rents were estimated in the spring of 1980 to average about $30 per square foot and to compound at 6% annually. These turned out to be extremely conservative figures. When agreement on price was reached with Metropolitan Life in the summer of 1980, average rent values had already risen to about $33 per square foot. Today, they are over $40 per square foot and are projected at $51 per square foot by 1983.

At the same time, real estate tax and energy costs proved to be underestimated, at least in the short run. We had forecast a tax increase of 15% per annum for three years and 6% per annum thereafter. The city of New York is now seeking to double the Pan Am real estate taxes as the result of its sale for $400 million, although the tax increase will probably be substantially less. We had estimated that the city would gradually increase all real estate taxes to reflect the surge in rents and to "catch up" to increased value. Of late, New York appears to be moving in this more moderate direction rather than extracting punitive increases from buildings just sold. It is clear, however, that the cash flow will be substantially higher than forecast just two years ago. To that extent, Metropolitan Life has already justified the purchase price and assured a basis for a substantially increased IRR over the original expectations.

Areas of Abuse in IRR Analysis

The first and most obvious potential abuse is the use of overly long projection periods with ambitious income growth rates, which inflate the value over that from a more acceptable projection period.

The problem of overestimating rental values over the projection period must be given serious consideration. One may well question the inexorability of compounded rent increases over 10 to 12 years. The 1974-1976 period amply demonstrated that rents could fall, vacancies increase, new construction cease, and foreclosures become common; and with increased volatility in financial markets, real estate cycles are likely to become shorter and more intense.

Those who forecast continuing rent increases maintain that interruptions in rent increases are invariably made up for by accelerated surges in rents during the recovery phase. Historically there is some substance to the argument. However, to ensure a reasonable valuation result, it is strongly recommended that discount rates be high enough to reflect the degree of risk involved in sustaining the rate of rent increases. A further conservative technique is to increase the capitalization rate to reflect the added risk of sustaining even stabilized income in the relatively remote future. There is a growing disposition of late to make the capitalization rate equal to the discount rate because it is used at such a remote time. Last, assumed compound increases in rent may be made at a lesser rate than one otherwise might think will occur.

In forecasting the probable level of land sales in a large-scale, master-planned community, for example, we have experimented with building-in recessions over an extended time frame. In the case of a very large project in Las Vegas, we assumed three recessionary episodes in which sales volume was adjusted sharply downward to reflect the decline in demand during recessionary periods. There is no particular market evidence to suggest that incorporating the effects on demand of recessionary periods is superior to assuming a conservative average annual compounding of sales prices or rents. The real adjustment should be in the discount and capitalization rates. The selected rates must synthesize at least the following factors:

inflation rate	shortage	equity availability
recessions	uncertainty	debt availability
oversupply	political-economic events	interest rates

The most conservative approach is to use a rate that would be at least 200 basis points over the expected average long-term capital rate. If, for example, the average mortgage interest rate is expected to be 12%, the IRR should be no less than 14%. In California, there is impressive market evidence that discounted IRRs have now reached 16%-18%. This seems to reflect market caution about future inflationary excesses in pricing.

Another obvious way to inflate prices is to underestimate the current level of operating expenses. This is especially grievous when the compound rate of operating-expense increase is also underestimated. Historically, but not recently, expenses and costs have compounded at a far lower rate than current high inflationary rates. Should one extrapolate at a significantly higher rate as a result of recent aggravated inflation, especially in real estate taxes and energy expenses? It is good practice to compound energy-cost increases at a higher rate than general operating expenses, since recent history clearly proves they have risen at a much faster rate. The recent increase in oil supplies and drop in prices may moderate the rate of increase but it is still expected to outstrip other costs.

Another potential abuse is to minimize unduly the possibility of future vacancies and contingencies. Prime properties today tend to be very close to 100% rented. Nevertheless, vacancy allowance should always be taken. Our recent practice in prime properties is to allow about 1.0%-1.5% for vacancies and contingencies, and then to also calculate the vacancy loss arising out of re-rental losses because a certain percentage of tenants vacate rather than renew their leases. This is a simple calculation when the computer is programmed to provide automatically for, say, a three-month rental loss for 30% of the existing tenant space on renewals.

The objective in using IRR methodology is to implement credible projections. However, who is to judge credibility? What does it really mean? We interpret credibility in this context to mean estimates that seem to be reasonably attainable, with the underlying assumptions fully stated on a line-item basis, and supported by historical trends. In the final analysis, the appraiser and the broker must seek market acceptance in the acceptance of clients or buyers. This is not to say that there may not be differences in some of the line items. The test is whether the figures on balance are accepted as thoughtful, documented, and objective.

To see the ease of manipulating the IRR, consider the following examples:

Assumptions:

	Case 1			Case 2	
Projection period		10 years	Projection period		15 years
Net income growth rate		8%/year	Net income growth rate		10%/year
Starting annual net income		$9,000	Starting annual net income		$9,000
Overall capitalization rates			Overall capitalization rates		
Going in		9%	Going in		9%
Going out		10%	Going out		9%
Resale commission		5%	Resale commission		-0-

IRR:

	Case 1			Case 2	
	Time	**Cash Flow**		**Time**	**Cash Flow**
	0	$100,000		0	$100,000
	1	9,000		1	9,000
	2	9,720		2	9,900
	3	10,498		3	10,890
	4	11,337		4	11,979
	5	12,244		5	13,177
	6	13,224		6	14,494
	7	14,282		7	15,944
	8	15,424		8	17,538
	9	16,658		9	19,292
	10	$202,576[†]		10	21,222
		IRR = 15.88%		11	23,344
				12	25,678
				13	28,246
				14	31,070
				15	$451,902[††]
					IRR = 19.00%

[†] $17,991 + ($19,430 ÷ .10 × .95) = $202,576
[††] $34,177 + ($37,595 ÷ .09) = $451,902

Even assuming the same value and overall rate of return, changing the specific assumptions slightly can result in a difference of over 300 basis points in the IRR. The novice investor, of course, would be attracted to the seemingly higher yield but the chances of realizing his or her expectations are greatly reduced.

If 15.88% were assumed to be an attractive market rate, the unscrupulous analyst could reprice the property by using the following analysis:

Time	Cash Flow	PW @ 15.88%
1	$ 9,000	$7,767
2	9,900	7,373
3	10,890	6,998
4	11,979	6,643
5	13,177	6,306
6	14,494	5,986
7	15,944	5,682
8	17,538	5,394
9	19,292	5,120
10	21,222	4,861
11	23,344	4,614
12	25,678	4,380
13	28,246	4,158
14	31,070	3,947
15	451,902	49,536
Total		$129,067

The analysis would seem to indicate that the property is worth $29,000 more than in Case 1 but really nothing changed except some plausible assumptions.

Conclusions

The professional appraiser and analyst are aware of all the pitfalls. In fact, some outstanding appraisers hold the view that IRR analysis is not truly a valuation method, but only a check against more conventional capitalization of immediate net income on a stabilized basis. This, however, is really a semantic difference. If market value is the present discounted worth of future income expectations, it is reasonable to say that this methodology represents a valuation technique. Surely it is adaptable to an inflation-ridden economy.

The potential abuse lies in the use of IRR methods as a sales tool by agents or owners anxious to obtain the highest possible price for a property. It is not difficult to engage technical help to prepare such estimates, or to engage a computer software company to perform calculations based on the projections. Persons or computer companies engaged as technical assistants are not subject to the ethical constraints of the practicing appraiser. In their enthusiasm for maximizing prices, they may attempt to inflate values over reasonable market levels by use of misleading estimates.

The purchasing public must be alert to this and engage professional appraisers and analysts to examine with caution the figures presented. Only in this way can the buyer be satisfied about the reasonableness or unreasonableness of the projections. Those companies serving as intermediaries must exercise caution. They will earn disrespect if they attempt to persuade the buying public with figures that appear to be deliberately inflated. On the other hand, those companies whose calculations stand the test of credibility will be recognized and respected.

12
Valuing Megastructures

Megastructures Defined

Webster's unabridged dictionary defines a megastructure "as a large body. . . of a major order. . . unduly enlarged." In the context of the real estate industry, a megastructure may be defined as a very large, major, single use structure, or as a very large multiple use structure or unified complex. A size of 1 million square feet is required to earn the megastructure title because *mega* also means "of a million," or 1 million times a unit of measure. Thus, we conclude that every building over this square foot size qualifies. Examples of predominately single use megastructures are the Pan Am and General Motors office buildings in New York City. Examples of multiple use megastructures include the John Hancock Building in Chicago, The World Trade Center in New York, and Renaissance Center in Detroit. The latter two qualify not only by total size but also because they are effectively joined not only at grade level but also at one level below grade by an integrated plaza, by concourses with retail shops, with easy access to all above-grade structures.

Mixed or multiple use "all-in-one" tower buildings are more difficult to design and more expensive to construct than single use buildings. In New York, Olympic Tower and Trump Tower are combinations of retail, office, and residential condominiums. The varied nature of the uses provokes design problems in framing structural steel, in window fenestration, in facade materials, and in elevatoring when all uses are concentrated in a single tower. Inevitably, premium development costs occur for mixed use tower structures. However, in single use megastructures, economies of scale may be realized and prove to be offsetting, especially when floors are of correspondingly large size. In New York, Olympia & York's 55 Water Street contains about 3.6 million square feet of rentable space and has floor areas of 53,000 square feet each. This allows more economical construction than slim towers and a higher proportion of usable to gross square feet. Both the investor and the tenant gain in this respect: the investor can build at a lower unit cost while the tenant has enhanced space flexibility and possibly lower rent.

Attractions of the Megastructure

The sheer sizes of megastructures give them unique visual identification, even in New York, where 1 million or more square foot structures are somewhat commonplace. Visual identity is an important factor in rental marketability. The outstanding vistas from upper floors create premium rents. The structure is generally well known to all in the sense it has a certain presence in the business community.

In some markets, a single or mixed use megastructure provides a basis for at least some degree of market dominance. Megastructures are pacesetters. To some extent, they may influence market rental levels, tenant installation allowances, and other terms and conditions. Their occupancy tends to be higher than smaller buildings, presumably because of their size and dominance. The mixed use megastructure, perhaps best exemplified by the highly successful Galleria in Houston, offers unparalleled convenience to the office user or hotel patron. One need never walk outdoors to satisfy almost every basic need in business, retailing, culture, recreation, entertainment, medicine, and shelter. The carefully planned and well-managed mixed use megastructure has a distinct advantage over single use buildings, where convenience to other needs may not be as good.

It is suspected that ego plays an important but nonquantifiable role in the development of megastructures. There is a certain fascination in size. Also, pride of accomplishment in completing a megastructure runs understandably high. As previously mentioned, economies of scale, at least to the point of diminishing returns, are very attractive to the developer.

Investment Characteristics of a Megastructure

Because they are so large and frequently disproportionately costly, megastructures are not easy to finance. Certainly in today's economic climate, development of a megastructure requires life insurance or pension fund participation as a joint venturer, in which the institution provides essentially all the development costs in the form of debt capital in return for which it receives a preferred return from 50% or more of the cash flow.

A contributor to higher total development costs is the more extended period of time required to build a multiple use megastructure and the longer absorption period to rent all the space. In the case of the 12.5 million square foot World Trade Center in New York, it was started in 1968 and was not fully completed and rented until 1981. The long development period results in continuing construction activity with resultant noise, debris, and dirt for new tenants to hear and see. For the developer, it means a period of time in which there is little or no income but a constant outgo of capital.

Appraisers must make special adjustments in their cost estimates for a higher proportion of so-called "soft costs" (i.e., mainly construction loan interest, real estate taxes, leasing commissions, and G & A) out of total development costs. They must also consider carefully the rate at which the space will be rented. By its very definition, a megastructure will offer so much competitive space compared with annual demand that it will frequently take years to achieve 95% occupancy. In the process, the added space may soften the rental market. It also results in a discounting of the low early year's negative or meager cash flow, which in turn impairs the value. When the Pan Am Building was completed in 1963, its intensive effort to rent 2.3 million square feet by completion caused an oversupplied market to develop, which undermined rents. Appraisers frequently underestimate this competitive effect. The developer of the multiple use, multiple building megastructure has an advantage in this respect over the single use tower megastructure developer. The former will perhaps extend himself to put in the entire infrastructure of retail, cultural, and recreational facilities, but he can at least attempt to pace the course of development of individual buildings tied to the infrastructure as demand dictates.

When Olympic Tower on Fifth Avenue in New York City was completed in 1974, it was an artistic triumph but financially unrewarding. At that point, the office market was oversupplied and the residential condominium market was less than robust. However, Arlen Realty and the Onassis interests, as joint venturers, had little recourse other than to build the entirety. There was no effective way of deferring the real estate construction until demand increased. If construction had been delayed because of market uncertainties, financing charges and ground rent would have contributed disproportionately to the total development cost. The decision to proceed was probably a wise one, despite the weak market.

Megastructures lend themselves, at least in part, to income tax syndication because of the high depreciation allowances and the usually high proportion of depreciable improvements to total cost. The Economic Recovery Tax Act of 1981 allows a 15-year straight line write-off, with an election to use 150% or 200% declining balance depreciation. This is a powerful incentive to wealthy individuals. The institution and the developer as joint venturers can arrange separate financing of buildings to achieve this. If the appraiser is engaged to value a multiple use megastructure after the financing and joint venture agreement are in place, he must make his value estimate subject to the financing arrangements. Essentially, the valuation becomes an equity appraisal, subject to the mortgages, ground rents, and preferred returns, if any.

The large sizes of megastructures enable the owners to engage directly renting and management personnel as employees of the owner, rather than granting a renting and managing agency. This is generally more economical and full time can be devoted by the staff to the recurrent tenant and operational problems of building management. Megastructures are characterized generally by superior day-to-day and supervisory management because their owners recognize their uniqueness and strive to provide high-quality, thoughtful services that are entirely on the premises.

Further, the multiple use megastructures frequently produce more stability because of the varied nature of their income. It is possible, for example, for hotel cash flow to be poor while office cash flow is excellent, or vice versa. Much like a diversified company, each element in the mixed use complex may bear a bigger burden at a particular moment than another, with overall results being better protected during market downturns.

Megastructure Valuation Methodology

Comparability remains the cornerstone of valuation methodology, quite without regard to type, size, use, or location. Comparable rents have particularly special meaning. Land comparisons are also always helpful. Comparable development costs and operating costs have less application because of the unique and special character of the operation. Comparability becomes too tenuous and strained to be totally credible. Surely it may be said that comparable market data are more readily available and have greater relevance in a single use tower megastructure than the mixed use type, whether the latter is a tower or a complex of structures tied together with a base infrastructure, as in the Houston Galleria or Detroit's Renaissance Center. In a multiple use megastructure, operating costs must be adjusted for increased public electricity because of 18-hour, or even 24-hour, public usage; for increased security; and for increased HVAC because of the higher proportion of public space to tenant space. Even in a single use megastructure such as the Pan Am Building, almost one entire floor is devoted to a public concourse, maintained by Metropolitan

Life, the owner, to enable pedestrian traffic flow through from Grand Central Station to the office district north of East 45th Street.

Megastructures are more complex because sheer size results inevitably in leases with varied lease terms and expiration dates. Owners attempt to standardize lease provisions but the bargaining power of tenants and the fluidity of market conditions invariably produce substantial differentials in the length of leases; in real estate tax and operating expense escalation; sublet and assignment provisions; and in interior maintenance requirements. In the case of The World Trade Center, there are close to 1,000 leases in existence which must be analyzed. The chief financial officer of Pan Am World Airways, prior to the Pan Am building sale, authorized the creation of a special software program so that a system of introducing new rent levels at compounding growth rates could be created as leases expired. At the same time, the system also dropped out the old tax and operating escalation, substituted the new base years and escalation provisions, and allowed for certain tenant installation costs and vacancies as an estimated proportion of tenants vacated.

By formulating a computer software program, we are able to project all line items of revenue and expenses over a projection period that varies from 10 to 12 years. In an inflationary economy, there is no valuation significance to initial cash-on-cash returns. Value becomes a function of estimating future rent increases in the most credible manner as leases expire. We not only reconstruct the expenses to estimate the net operating income but also compound these expenses over the projection period. After the projection period, we assume that income is stabilized. In other words, no valuation significance is given to the prospects for further rent increases beyond the selected time frame. The stabilized net income is then capitalized and discounted to the present time, along with the net operating income over the projection period. The discount rate is called the internal rate of return (IRR). IRR may be defined as the present value rate at compound interest of a series of discounted annual cash flows added to the discounted gains and losses from a presumed resale at the end of the projection period. Stated simply, it provides for an interest return on the investment and the presumed return of the investment at a given time.

In the 1981 Pan Am sale, the property sold for about $350 million over a $50 million first mortgage. The initial year's cash return was only $8.4 million, or 2.4%. It was not until 1985, as 51% of the leases expired, that the return rose to an estimated $32.3 million, or 9%, with steadily increasing income in ensuing years. As it happened, the actual rents that will be received through 1985 will be higher than the original Landauer projections, so Metropolitan Life, the buyer, will do better than the projections anticipated.

How is the discount rate established? Surely the best clues are in the analysis of properties which have been sold, such as the Pan Am sale. However, access to the essential revenue and expense data is difficult for the investor or appraiser to obtain. Another clue is the behavior of long-term money rates, principally long-term mortgages and bonds. Discount rates tend to be 100 to 200 basis points higher than mortgage and bond rates because the equity risk element must be consolidated within the debt rate. In the early stages of an inflation, when interest rates are still relatively low, discount rates are low as well. As interest rates rise, so do discount rates. As inflationary fires abate, interest and discount rates will gradually decline on a lagging basis. Thus, the marginal cost of capital is an all-important indicator and forms the basis for the appraiser's consideration of the appropriate IRR. In the process, he must be aware of the effect on IRR rates of location, design, use, strength of tenancy, degree of maintenance and repair, management, and market factors.

Summary

Megastructures have had a profound effect on the real estate market. They frequently become focal points for the community in a business, social, and cultural sense. They affect competitive market performance because of their sheer size by bringing on the market a significant proportion of the total existing inventory at one time. They attract the large financial institutions because of their market dominance and tendency to outperform smaller structures. They certainly require a special kind of computer analysis in order to reflect accurately what the future may be for the bottom line. They are bellwether properties because the IRR acts as a distinct guide for the space of smaller properties. Finally, they have made the general as well as the institutional public more aware of the role of real estate in the economy and its importance to our economic way of life.

Part II
Counseling

The practice of a professionally trained and certified appraiser is frequently molded to his or her personality and general business experience. Because I was fortunate to have had development, brokerage, and management experience in addition to MAI training and was very much a generalist at heart, I tended to have a broader interest in real estate. I welcomed assignments that did not necessarily call for a fixed valuation result and others that did call for advising clients on current events or on implementing appraisal recommendations. I was also enormously curious about the workings of the market and instinctively wanted to analyze the meaning of events.

Perhaps the best illustration of this curiosity is an article I wrote nearly 30 years ago, "Rent Control Crippling Urban Housing Market," which is as valid in economic principle now as then. Other illustrations of my preoccupation with the behavior of investors and developers are "How Real Estate Decisions Are Made" and "How to Plan and Build a Major Office Building." It is essential that appraisers know the mood of the market and how investors and developers typically think and feel. With this knowledge, more accurate appraisal results invariably follow.

Another concern that frequently surfaces in the articles is a disposition to analyze clinically why the market has not performed more effectively. In "An Economic Assessment of Large-Scale Projects," I comment both on the deficiencies in market planning and on innovative ways to finance a large-scale project. The articles do not necessarily demonstrate a direct relation to the market value of each subject property, but illustrate how the appraiser can become a market and investment analyst.

The crowning event of my career was working on the pricing and offering for sale of the Pan Am Building in New York. For this assignment, my experience in valuation, market analysis, and marketing strategy was invaluable. There is an old-fashioned concept that an appraiser or consultant can and should act only in an advisory or technical capacity. Not so! The best qualified person to implement a logical course of action is frequently the one who is technically trained. My MAI training and experience enabled me to carry the marketing program through to its ultimate result—a successful sale. In reading "A Marketing Revolution: The Sale of the Pan Am Building," you will see how the critically important MAI training, backed by actual field work and an excellent staff ensured the sale.

13
Rent Control Crippling Urban Housing Market

The Problem

The recent conflict over rent control in the New York State legislature, the somewhat inflammatory statements made in the press, and the positions of the protagonist and antagonist of this difficult problem point up the need for a detached and impersonal reappraisal of the economic aspects.

Far too much effort and thought have been devoted by the real estate trade associations to the legal aspects while the various tenant groups have concentrated their appeals for continuance of rent control on humanitarian and sociological grounds. The appropriate perspective of the problem has been lost in a maze of conflicting self-interest statements and has been ignored by many individual state legislators conscious of the need for supporting popular local issues which will give them greater assurance of self-perpetuation in public office. This view has been nurtured by that particularly fortunate group, the tenants who have been established in the same residential quarters since rent control. In an unguarded moment, they admit being in the "driver's

Reprinted from *The Commercial and Financial Chronicle,* Thursday, June 2, 1955.

seat." Their income has risen higher than other commodity prices while they still have a rental unit at a bargain price. This group is very anxious to have rent control retained and strengthened and the legislators pay this special interest group special heed.

On the other hand, the antagonists of rent control, the real estate owners and agents, have long since given up the prospect of winning a decontrol. They feel they are being "realistic" by agreeing to the continuance of controls while seeking means of obtaining minor increases by tortuous techniques of proving hardship, "voluntary" increases, installing new capital equipment, inequality, and other similar devices. During this period, they have failed the public and their own interests by forgetting the fundamental weaknesses implicit in long-term controls and through their inability to make the general public see the inequities, although admittedly, a sorely trying task. This is particularly tragic since over 50% of the families in New York State are homeowners.

In the interim, it becomes increasingly more difficult to terminate controls. Statesmanship is abandoned in favor of expediency. The community has fed so long on low rents that tenants honestly believe they cannot afford to pay more. New Yorkers have adjusted their scale of living to provide for a lesser allowance out of their income dollars for rent while, on the other hand, they state their desire for other commodities from the surplus money saved from uneconomic rents.

It is incredible that rent control has now been with us for 12 years and is assured of continuance for at least two more years beyond June 30 and probably thereafter. It is not so surprising, however, that it has become a virtual political impossibility to face the prospect of decontrol. The "shortage," we are told, is as acute as ever. Many well-intentioned people insist that controls continue until this "shortage" disappears, yet it is somewhat elementary economics to observe that a shortage will always exist where a commodity can be purchased or leased for less than its market value. The artificial restraint on rental prices provoked by rent controls thus tends to intensify and prolong rather than abate or eliminate a shortage as many have hoped.

The Historical Background

What are the facts, from an economic viewpoint, about rent control? Can we assess the economic ramifications of rent control from the vantage place of history? A brief review of market conditions and the circumstances under which rent control was imposed will serve as a necessary prelude to a full discussion of the topic.

The depression of the 1930s, intensified by a significant oversupply of housing and commercial reality, plunged real estate prices to inconceivable depths. Forced sales, high vacancies, cessation of construction, infrequent sales—all the indicators of a distressed market—were present. These conditions continued without significant improvement up to the start of the Second World War. Some slight relief was felt in local areas as defense needs in 1939 to 1941 increased employment and purchasing power, and as available space was gradually absorbed.

The advent of the war in 1941 resulted in economic and sociological dislocations which, in light of the lack of construction in the previous decade, gradually produced an increasing shortage. At the time controls were imposed, however, real estate had by no means made complete recovery from the depression. Although vacancies had decreased, rents were at abnormally low levels. Controls were imposed in most sections of the country before they were needed and in advance of full occupancy; under such circumstances, rents had no chance of rising.

That controls of some type were advisable during the war can scarcely be argued. Their continuance for 12 years and longer after the termination of hostilities leads inevitably to a different conclusion, when viewed from the perspective of history.

Long-Term Implications

Perhaps the most tragic result of continued rent ceilings has been the promotion by the federal, state, and local governments, consciously or otherwise, of the psychology that rent control is an essential and necessary peacetime function of our democratic system. This viewpoint has insidiously crept into the thinking of administrators and legislators alike to such an alarming extent that we can prophesy the residential real estate industry assuming all the characteristics of a public utility, with permanent rent controls, regulation of the rate of return, control of building operations and maintenance standards, and more important, loss of the advantages of a relatively free and competitive enterprise which has heretofore produced a standard of housing unparalleled in the world.

Present rent restrictions are so onerous that it is impossible to obtain an economic rent. Thus, since the public fully appreciates bargains where every dollar of rental value received only cost them $0.60 to $0.75, the shortage is intensified, rather than alleviated, by government edict. There never will be any appreciable diminution in the demand for a commodity which rents for less than its market value.

The stultifying nature of the prolongation of controls has also discouraged new production of conventionally financed (i.e., nongovernment underwritten or financed) residential apartments because of the widespread and uneconomic disparity between rents resulting from governmental restraints on used realty and those rents necessary to justify highly inflated postwar construction costs. There is no "floor" on new construction rentals—only a bottomless well between rent controlled and free market rentals. Had rents on used realty been permitted to seek their proper market level, the incentive to builders would have increased.

It is not surprising to realize that through 1952, over 80% of our postwar multifamily construction has been under indirect government sponsorship (FHA 608, 207, 213, etc.). The government found it essential to provide mortgage insurance for loans which theoretically were 90% of the value of the housing project in order to prod builders into relieving the acute shortage. Without the assistance which certain sections of the FHA legislation provided, builders were unwilling to risk large amounts of risk capital under conventional financing plans for the purpose of competing with rent controlled realty. Thus, we witnessed the spectacle of solving a political dilemma by a government "give-away" program.

The result of this rather illogical government solution of the housing problem will inevitably be bad. It may be contemplated that the federal government eventually will be in the real estate business under the impetus of a wave of foreclosures of government-insured mortgages held by institutional lenders whenever we approach a period of oversupply of rental housing or witness a significant constriction in the present level of economic prosperity. The FHA legislation, partially because of the pressure of rent control, has permitted an unsound policy of unnecessary overfinancing and shoddy housing standards. The mushrooming frame, ill-kept garden apartments dotting the countryside constitute a memorial to this specious legislation.

Another result of the continuance of controls has been the withdrawal from the market of untold thousands of rental units because of the complete inadequacy of the interest return. Space designed for residential use has steadily been converted to business and commercial use (where local zoning codes permitted) as a means of ensuring the owner a fair return on his investment. In many instances, rented homes were sold for owner-occupancy because the investor could not realize an equitable return. Thus, controls again tended to intensify the shortage by reducing the supply of housing units available for rent.

Certainly the continuance of rent control has accelerated the physical depreciation of existing realty. If an investor feels he cannot obtain sufficiently high market rentals because of the control imposed on his gross income, he nevertheless will make an effort to obtain the net income to which he feels he is entitled by simply failing to maintain the property. A portion of the income which under the stimulus of competitive rental conditions would have been committed to prudent maintenance and operation is instead allocated to the investor's yawning pockets. Since rents below economic levels will ensure full occupancy, the investor does not have to maintain his real estate by any standards except his own. The benefits and advantages of competitive spurs are lost, and both tenant and owner suffer. The inevitable consequence is physically delapidated housing with a high degree of depreciation and heavy evidences of deferred maintenance.

Although the owner can escape certain expense burdens under rent control, there are expenses that recur and cannot be avoided. Taxes, fuel, wages, insurance, electricity and gas, supplies, water, and major repairs will at least remain constant and, under the impact of inflation, rise to discouraging heights. Whatever benefits have accrued to owners through 100% occupancy have in general been more than vitiated by the sharp increase in operating expenses.

Rent control has also resulted in a somewhat artificial increase in the rate of family formation. Rents are so far below economic levels that many families can afford to maintain the luxury of two apartments when at economic rents they could afford only one. Other families of one or two persons are living in large units which they could not otherwise afford if it were not for the benign protection of government controls. This seemingly paternalistic and humanitarian attitude on the part of government is actually decreasing the supply and unfairly depriving many deserving families of residential space which would have become available to them under a more logical approach to the problem.

One other factor of paramount importance pervades the whole problem of rent control. The long-term real estate investor is being steadily liquidated by the insidious evil of inflation. The federal and state governments, through the habitual practice of deficit financing or discriminatory control, have created a situation where the prices of all other commodities have far outstripped the puny and meaningless increase in rents and prices of rent controlled real estate. Since it is obvious that the real estate investor's dollar is worth no more or less than that of anyone else (tenants included), he is forced to pay double for most commodities with about the same amount of dollars which he had before the war-borne inflation. This alone would be justification for an increase in rents. The long-term real estate investor thus joins the other investors who are being liquidated by inflation—the bondholders, insurance policy holders, pensioners, and all others living on long-term fixed incomes.

French Housing Standards

The abject condition of our residential real estate market today recalls the classic illustration of housing conditions in Paris, France. Rent ceilings originally imposed in World War I still remain in effect today. It would be political suicide in Paris to remove controls because the public has tasted the fruits of subsidized rents and acquired an unbreakable habit for them. Since a spiraling inflation has increased the prices of all other commodities many times more than rents, the average Parisian wage earner only pays about 2% of his income dollar for rent and luxurious apartments rent for $10 a month.

New construction in Paris is also subject to rent controls and there has been virtually no building. Of the improvements 99% are 15 years or older, the vast majority without central heating or sanitary facilities. Apartments are available by public requisition or bribe, and Paris, long regarded as the cultural seat of the world, is now known to have the most degenerate and obsolete residential housing in Western Europe. The French investor has been reduced to the status of a porter for the French government. It is not inconceivable to foresee that dreary market in this state also, unless we are willing to confront the problem of rent control.

Proposed Solution

Does a housing shortage actually exist? The answer, after reflection, seems to be in the negative. What really exists is fewer housing units than is demanded at existing prices. It is relatively simple to create a shortage of any commodity by the device of lowering the price to less than it would be established by the working of supply-demand phenomena in the market place. If we now increased rental ceilings another 30%, or a total of about 50% over 1943 levels, it is strongly suspected that the "shortage" would disappear. Within a year, apartments at every conceivable price level would be readily available. And the tenant, what would happen to him? Recent statistical studies indicate that urban residential dwellers are paying less than 10% of their income dollar for rents. Thus, if we supposed a 50% rather than a 30% increase in rent, it would increase the tenants' allocation for rent from their income dollar to only 15%, an amount which any sociologist would readily admit can easily be paid for housing shelter. Thus, the "shortage" is an illusion created by artificially low prices.

What is the solution? As it is recognized that an immediate complete decontrol would provoke some limited hardship, a possible compromise exists in the adoption of a long-range, orderly program of decontrol extending over a two-year period. During this interval, statutory rents should automatically rise 5% at six month intervals. Concurrently, the so-called "luxury" controlled rentals, that is, those above $50 per room monthly, could be decontrolled. At succeeding six-month intervals, increasingly lower rental levels should also be decontrolled until only the lowest rentals would remain to be freed from controls at the end of the two-year period.

What would be the market reaction to a program of this type? Salutary indeed? Those tenants who for years postponed a decision to buy private dwellings or move to more expensive apartments because of low controlled rents would have ample opportunity to make a decision. Other tenants would decide to remain in their present quarters at the higher rentals. Still others would find smaller or more modest apartments within their financial reach if free market rentals proved onerous for them.

Free Market Conditions

What a boon for housing if this course was resolutely followed! For the first time in many years, the builder could effectively assay demand and adjust his construction accordingly. The spurs of competition would force better maintenance, and the landlord would exert every effort to attract tenants. The builder would produce better dwelling units. The tenant would be settled in housing he could afford and not necessarily that which he desires. The tragic waste of space under rent control, as previously reported, would be eliminated completely. There would be, for example, no logic in living in six rooms beyond one's rental reach when a fair choice of three rooms within one's income requirements was available.

Advocates of rent control contend that free market rentals would initiate an inflationary spiral and spark rising costs and wages. The absurdity of this contention is apparent when it is recognized that a rise in the price of an individual commodity (i.e., rental housing) means only that the wage earner has less money to spend on other commodities; a lessening in demand for automobiles, food, recreation, or appliances will in turn create lower prices for these commodities and the net inflationary gain is negligible. In the mature, non-emergent economy as is presently our own, it is the government's fiscal and credit policy which creates inflation, not the control of individual prices.

The return to free market conditions might also serve notice to our various government bodies that the "shortage" was actually a product of rent control and that the need for public housing for the few (at the expense of those not qualified to enjoy its subsidized benefits) is not quite so acute as supposed. Free market rentals might also tend to expose the fiction that every family deserves a new housing unit. With current estimates of the duration of the profitable, useful life of multiple housing at 50 years, it is patently fraudulent to sell the concept that all families should have or, yes, even deserve, new housing. This is an obvious impossibility. Our innate sense of individual dignity and self-reliance should help us conclude that, with minor exceptions, we should enjoy only that housing which we can reasonably afford.

There is no escape, however, from the fact that rents will rise should controls terminate but this is properly so. The discriminatory subjugation of the property owner's investment to the will of the tenant, far beyond emergent market conditions, seems a callous political effort to gain political votes. In the interim residential housing has assumed all the characteristics of a public utility yet without the property owner's consent. Such confiscatory concepts of government threaten the foundations of our economic independence and the cherished institution of private property ownership. This blatant political irresponsibility must terminate.

14

Economic Assessment of Large-Scale Projects

Failings in market research account for many problems encountered in assessing large-scale projects, and this inadequacy is manifest in two major analytical areas. One concerns forecasting the quantity and quality of the total market's allocations to the project, and the other concerns the potentially greater accuracy of microanalysis over macroanalysis. This discussion concentrates on these two areas, as well as on the critical importance of adequate equity and mortgage capital and their effect on profitability.

What is meant by *large-scale project?* There is no agreed definition of size in this instance, and generally speaking, *large-scale* implies quantity and uses of a magnitude that compels a study of a metropolitan market. A smaller project can be analyzed and forecasts can be made within the political area or even a section of a city, whereas a large-scale project demands study of a wide market, transcending political boundaries and limited only by accessibility to places of work and the time required to commute.

Another dimension of *large-scale* is the need for real estate uses other than housing. These various commercial, institutional, industrial, recre-

Reprinted from *The Appraisal Journal* (July 1969): 360-71.

ational, service, and government uses are required as a consequence of the quantity of planned housing. Smaller housing projects, on the other hand, rely on other entrepreneurs to provide essential retail and business uses to serve the project.

Inadequate Market Analysis

Sales volume projections frequently have not been realized, and market research has experienced difficulty in three critical areas. With the advantage of retrospection, they can be identified as follows:

1. Projections of the annual market demand for housing, which might be allocated to the project, have tended to be over-optimistic. Subsequent market capture was disappointing and adversely affected cash flow and profitability.
2. Feasibility studies have recommended housing and lot prices that were too high to capture the optimum share of the market, thus reducing sales volume and profitability.
3. Consumer demand for style and function was poorly interpreted, and styles too often reflected the tastes of developers or architects rather than those of the public. This reflects the failure to apply microanalytic marketing techniques.

Not all the difficulty can be attributed to market analysts, as their recommendations often have been ignored or modified by architects or developers. Experience now is enabling analysts to forecast more accurately the mass market and its distribution by size, cost, and style. Excessive allocations of the total market to the project also have been tempered by experience, and a more conservative trend is evident.

Housing Projections

Optimism can be damaging when injected into market forecasts. The first optimistic conclusion generally occurs in defining the total market area. Frequently this is done by plotting automotive travel time on a map from an assumed focal point, and sometimes the total market area is considered synonomous with a political entity because statistical data is easier to obtain on this basis. A third technique is to base the market area on population concentrations in relation to travel time to the project area. It is quite customary to consider all three means.

The mistakes lie in miscalculating geographic and consumer attitude factors that can easily alter one's definition of a market area. Few physical barriers remain in the 200 largest U.S. metropolitan areas. Roads cut through mountains and divides; great bridges span bodies of water; grade separations at rail and auto intersections are commonplace; rail service is adequate if not good. Psychological barriers do remain, however. How often the analyst hears that one side of the river will always be better than the other; that no one wants to live on the other side of the divide; that one side of the railroad tracks is in public disfavor.

Public prejudices and preconceptions may be illogical, but they exist; the analyst must respect these attitudes because the public and not the analyst make the market. He must know these conditions and weigh their effect in defining the area from which the large-scale project will logically draw its customers.

The original error of dependence on an unjustifiably large effective market area may then be compounded by over-optimism on the proportion of housing or commercial unit volume that can be reasonably ascribed to the project. There is no mathematically precise technique for estimating this allocation. One obvious method is to subdivide the actual housing volume performance in a series of concentric rings away from the large-scale project. Thereafter, one can estimate varying proportions of capture from each ring and evolve a composite annual capture rate.

This task will be simplified as we are able to study clinically the actual performance record of large-scale projects within their market framework, and it may become possible to correlate more precisely the influence of architectural style, access, environment, population, income, and other factors. As these studies emerge, we are slowly beginning to frame viewpoints that will be refined constantly.

It is considered foolhardy to believe that over 10% of the total market area can be attracted to a large-scale project that provides little or no industrial employment base within its boundaries. We think it more prudent if a project appears profitable with a 5% capture of the market. The capture rate can be revised upward to the extent that the master plan provides for actual industrial construction and firm commitments have been made. When the plan provides for some industrial use but no companies have agreed to relocate there at the time of the analysis, the analyst is ill advised to increase his or her market allocation rate over that of the nonindustrial large-scale project. Industrial portions of master planned communities generally have grown very slowly and have not greatly influenced the residential sales volume.

Advanced Procedures in Market Analysis

Increasing use of survey techniques in market analysis is evidence of a growing trend to microanalysis. In past years macroanalysis was almost uniformly employed. But, largely because developers did not wish to commit extensive funds to market research, the analyst was forced to adopt techniques that were confined essentially to sampling and statistical analysis in a broad but not necessarily deep manner.

It was considered prohibitively costly to minutely examine the existing real estate inventory and the characteristics and attitudes of its inhabitants as a clue to demand potential. Thus, the analyst frequently was removed from the heart of the market and truly was viewing it from a remote location without the advantage of refined scientific tools. The results in housing style and functional utility in commercial structures were too often unsatisfying and unappealing to the public.

To illustrate the frequent inadequacy of macroanalytical techniques, many master planned projects have been greeted indifferently by families who have resisted the order and precision of the master plan concept. The busy bits of outdoor sculpture and small scale of the First Village at Reston, Virginia, reminiscent of a Hollywood motion picture set, create vague but troubled reactions in many families accustomed to a less structured environment. Thus, the aesthetic security and physical discipline of the planned environment do not wholly overcome the feeling of over-planning, over-cultural, and over-civic activity attached to large-scale projects. These factors and attitudes should have been identified and dealt with in the planning stage.

Thus, the analyst, however grudgingly, attempts to master the role of socioeconomist and behavioral science specialist in assessing the public's moods and impressions. These can be understood best by the widespread use of consumer preference and attitude surveys. The most effective technique is personal interview because mail questionnaires evoke a low response and frequently are completed casually. Nevertheless, they are better than nothing.

Project planners are realizing they must achieve a deeper penetration into the characteristics of the existing inventory and people's preferences. Developers now appear willing to expend more money on microanalysis, and frequently they employ full time market researchers and economists to investigate and plan comprehensively. Cost is now considered insignificant in relation to the greater profitability resulting from microanalytic techniques.

Cash Flow Techniques

More attention is being directed to preparing cash flow analyses to reflect profit prospects over at least a 10-year period. We now recognize that market forecasting in itself is an insufficient service for the profit-motivated developer. More advanced analytical techniques are being devised constantly to translate the results of market and land use studies into a comprehensive cash flow chart.

The term *cash flow* has a radically different meaning for investment analysts than for appraisers or perhaps even accountants. Simply stated, it means "cash in" and "cash out"—it dispenses with the traditional separation of capital and income. Equity capital, mortgage proceeds, and sale and rental income are viewed as contributions to the total income stream. Traditional development costs for roads, utilities, buildings, and all overhead are recognized as expenses. In addition, interest on debt, mortgage amortization, and federal income taxes are considered part of the expenses. Cash flow analysis is prepared both to estimate cash needs and measure profitability in place of the conventional profit and loss statement.

In conventional appraisal thinking, real estate represents investment in a fixed asset; the investment is expected to earn income; income is a combination of interest and capital returns; amortization is not an expense but a saving because it reduces a liability; depreciation is an expense because it recognizes the terminable existence of the asset and is intended to return one's capital as its value diminishes; the effect of income taxes cannot be calculated in the analysis because the owner's tax status or the type of ownership differs so greatly.

The sophisticated developer is impatient with these traditions and tends to cast them aside. He or she expects the market analyst to proceed first on the basis of detailed assumptions regarding the owner's tax status. The developer expects major policy decisions to be made on the basis of his or her particular tax situation. The developer regards depreciation not so much as an expense but as a valuable ally in reducing taxable income and increasing cash flow. The developer realizes the importance of high ratio mortgage financing and knows that he or she can increase cash flow and maximize profits by obtaining the highest possible mortgage. The developer regards amortization as an expense burden that must be paid from income, not as a saving.

Table 14.1   Discounted Present Worth of Future Cash Flow

	Cash Inflow			
1	**2**	**3**	**4**	**5**
	Cash Income		**Draw against**	
	from Sale of	**Proceeds of**	**Working**	**Gross Cash**
Year	**Serviced Lots**	**Land Loan**	**Capital**	**Inflow**
1—1970	$ 560,960	$2,000,000	$ 0	$ 2,560,960
2—1971	1,274,905	0	178,059	1,452,964
3—1972	1,995,271	0	0	1,995,271
4—1973	2,301,594	0	0	2,301,594
5—1974	2,715,565	0	0	2,715,565
6—1975	2,761,224	0	0	2,761,224
7—1976	2,601,941	0	174,930	2,776,871
8—1977	2,154,025	0	0	2,154,025
9—1978	2,090,000	0	0	2,090,000
10—1979	2,002,000	0	0	2,002,000
11—1980	1,322,000	0	0	1,322,000
12—1981	620,000	0	0	620,000
Total	$22,399,485	$2,000,000	$352,989	$24,752,474

The cash flow statement in Table 14.1 sets forth revenue and expenses over an assumed 12-year development period on a 1,600-acre section of a 6,000-acre tract. The tract fronts on a 1,500-acre reservoir on the fringe of a large southern city. Most of the numbered column calculations are supported by tables (not included) showing the source of the figures and the manner in which they are derived.

In this instance, the developer planned to install all major roads, utilities, and recreational facilities at his own expense. He would then sell lots, in bulk, to builders or individuals, and did not contemplate constructing homes or other types of buildings. He also assumed that commercial land would be sold to other developers. Essentially, this is a process of subdividing and wholesaling land in accordance with a master plan.

A land developer may do the building him or herself. In some cases the developer does so to create interest and activity. He or she may construct stores and offices to ensure necessary local shopping and service conveniences for initial home buyers. Subsequently, the developer may do additional commercial construction, thinking that it is the best investment among all alternatives.

Except for the smaller resort communities, master plan developers rarely attempt all building construction. The land developer encourages wholesale sales to other developers; not only does this reduce his or her own investment

	6	Cash Outflow 7	8	9	10
Year	Payment of Development & Carrying Costs	Deposit Cash in Working Capital Account	Payment of Income Taxes at 50% Rate	Repayment of Land Loan	Gross Cash Outflow
1—1970	$2,207,971	$352,989	$ 0	$ 0	$ 2,560,960
2—1971	1,325,728	0	84,824	21,206	1,431,758
3—1972	806,157	0	580,211	304,452	1,690,820
4—1973	834,359	0	655,547	405,844	1,895,750
5—1974	774,723	0	845,703	547,570	2,167,996
6—1975	689,789	0	776,735	647,350	2,113,874
7—1976	988,542	0	872,712	73,578	1,934,832
8—1977	735,475	0	682,281	0	1,417,756
9—1978	376,023	0	647,100	0	1,023,123
10—1979	31,400	0	712,000	0	743,400
11—1980	0	0	661,000	0	661,000
12—1981	0	0	310,000	0	310,000
Total	$8,770,167	$352,989	$6,828,113	$2,000,000	$17,951,269

but it also introduces attractive and different building designs, thus avoiding the stylized homogeneity that can otherwise result. Sometimes the large-scale developer will also sell a section of subdivided lots on an individual lot basis. Thus, the developer may be a wholesaler and retailer simultaneously.

In this instance, the 6,000-acre tract was a former timberland holding which had benefited from a newly created reservoir on which the tract owner held waterfront ownership rights. This was made possible by granting an easement of use to the local government rather than land ownership for reservoir purposes, thus enabling the owner to retain the valuable upland area. Rights for boating and swimming were obtained as well.

The land's book value was truly negligible. It had been acquired in the depression of the 1930s for as little as $50 an acre. In connection with the study the first section of 1,600 acres was appraised at $2,000 an acre, based on liberal terms, or 40 times its acquisition cost. The tract was 12 miles from the center of the city on a modern four-lane divided highway and immediately adjacent to a planned circumferential highway. The standing pine and oak trees were to be retained where possible.

Referring to the cash flow table, it is interesting to note in Columns 2 and 3 that more than 90% of the project, excluding land equity, was to be financed from land sales. It was estimated that only a $2 million bank loan was required to create enough improvements to finance the balance from sales. This assumption places a great responsibility on the market analyst to be reasonably accurate in his sales predictions. Not only must the prices be correct, but the sales volume must be attainable. Otherwise, additional borrowings must be obtained in the face of lower profitability under difficult circumstances. It must be pointed out that the cash flow analysis looked more promising than normal because the land was owned free of mortgage debt and was held at a very low value.

Cash Flow

Year	11 After-Tax Cash Flow	12 Discount 10% Factor	13 Discounted Present Worth of Future Cash Flow
1—1970	$ 0	.8264	$ N/A
2—1971	21,206	.7513	15,932
3—1972	304,451	.6830	207,940
4—1973	405,844	.6209	251,989
5—1974	547,569	.5645	309,103
6—1975	647,350	.5132	332,496
7—1976	842,039	.4665	392,811
8—1977	736,269	.4241	312,252
9—1978	1,066,877	.3855	411,281
10—1979	1,258,600	.3505	441,139
11—1980	661,000	.3186	210,595
12—1981	310,000	.2897	89,807
Total	$6,801,205	.4377	$2,975,345

Column 6 illustrates the heavy burden of development and carrying charges in the early years of a master planned community. Some $3.5 million is planned to be expended in the first two years against subsequent annual costs averaging no more than $800,000, or half the annual rate for the first two years. This places a special strain on profitability in the early years.

These heavy costs are caused not only by the heavy expenses of road installation and utility systems. In order to attract buyers in volume to a planned area, it is almost mandatory to create varied recreational facilities at the outset. Rising personal income, the declining work week, the increasing emphasis on leisure time, and the growing trend to family sports compel construction of golf courses and country clubs, lakes, community swimming pools, tennis courts, and riding trails. Community facilities also must be offered in the form of public meeting halls for civic and social functions, teen-age canteens, and various cultural activities.

Somewhat more than $1,250,000 of the first two years' expenditures, or over one-third, was budgeted for these recreational and cultural needs. These facilities obviously cannot be profitable immediately, and income from this source will tend to lag far behind the capital expenditure. Also note in Column 2 that sales income for the first two years is relatively low and does not really intensify to a desired volume until the fourth year. This is a consequence of land sales on an installment plan, both to lot buyers and bulk builders, normally over a five-year period. Thus, the master planned community faces a slowly gathering sales volume in its early years, matched against extraordinary starting costs and capital expenses.

Column 8 estimates the income taxes payable by a U.S. corporation at an assumed 50%. It is important to remember that reportable income for tax purposes differs significantly from cash income. The Internal Revenue Service will permit a disproportionate allocation of the land cost if a supportable rationale can be made for it. In this case, because of the reservoir and main highway influence, some 50% of the value of the 1,600 acres is concentrated in the first 25% of the land. On the same basis, general development expenses benefiting the entire project may be allocated for tax purposes. Other development costs that benefit specific sites alone cannot be estimated until the time of sale.

What constitutes our cash flow? Column 11 is simply the net income remaining after inflows from borrowings and sales, and after outflows for actual development costs, financing charges (including amortization), general overhead, and federal income taxes. We then discount the after tax cash flow to estimate the present worth of this expected future income, and this is compared to the land value established on a comparable basis to estimate profitability over the period.

Discounting techniques applied to cash flow can be used to solve a variety of problems. When the land is owned free and clear, the discounted cash flow produces a residual land value. When an option with specific cash flow requirements exists, the discounted cash flow measures ability to meet the terms and produce a present value above the purchase price. It can also be used to develop the terms which can be offered in view of the project's present worth.

Cash flow analysis really is meaningless when extended past 10 or 12 years. It is impossible to predict accurately what will occur so far in advance, and the income is so discountable that it loses valuation significance. In this instance, of the 6,000 acres, the absorption rate would permit full use of only 1,600 acres over the 12-year period. Hence, we also must think about the remaining land's value in 12 years. A present discounted value for the remaining land had to be estimated to see the entire profit picture in an appropriate perspective. The figures persuaded us that the project was logical and supportable by the market.

It is important to stress that cash flow alone is not a sufficient measure of productivity. Historically remaining land appreciates much faster than general land. Thus the analyst must estimate what the capital value of the remaining land will be after the 12-year period. If the value increase is expected to be significant, it can justify a less profitable initial development during the first decade. Thus, combining income and capital gain is the most reliable and accurate way to estimate profitability. The well located and well planned large-scale project will, with patience and forebearance, prove an excellent investment.

Investment Problems

The crushing combination of initial land investment and initial costs of road, utility, and recreational installations normally eliminates any positive cash flow for the first several operating years. When taxable income does materialize, the development corporation must pay a 50% income tax on earning. At this time cash flow is affected adversely by the required repayment of principle on land mortgages.

More than one new town developer has wryly commented that only the original land seller makes money from a large-scale project. More optimistically, however, as we reduce our errors by experience the large-scale project can be a profitable venture indeed for the well-capitalized company.

Lenders have been wary about the safety of loans in large-scale projects and heretofore have advanced relatively conservative sums. Robert Simon, developer of the well-publicized new town of Reston, Virginia, has stated publicly that the difficulty of achieving investment objectives has been caused in part by appraisers and mortgagees who failed to recognize the remaining land inventory's appreciation following initial construction. Equity investors have been equally cautious about profit prospects. Many projects therefore have been hampered by chronic undercapitalization. To my knowledge, no developer is strong enough to carry these large-scale projects with conventional financing.

Two recent financing developments might improve the capitalization picture. First, federal legislation has been enacted to ensure private loans made by lending institutions on land and subdivision costs. Loan terms are extremely liberal. Second, insurance companies are underwriting large-scale projects in a variety of ways, including purchase and leasebacks, land loans with equity participation, and other devices. Each of these will be discussed in turn.

Title X Financing

Title X of the Federal Housing Administration's regulations provides for federal insurance of land mortgages advanced by lending institutions. The maximum loan is $25 million. The loan may be advanced in one of two ways: 50% of FHA's market land value estimate plus 90% of the value of improvements, including roads, utilities, and recreational facilities; or 75% of FHA's value estimate after development costs are complete. The loan's term is seven years and may be extended. No amortization is required in the initial years when development costs are highest. The mortgage insurance premium is 1% of the loan balance and reduces to .75% when amortization commences. The maximum interest rate is 6%.

Few of these loans have been made because of the unrealistically low interest rate, and there is every indication that Congress will eliminate interest ceilings. In the interim, the loan can be obtained only by the developer paying points, that is, accepting a discounted amount that must be repaid in full. The current point spread is from 8% to 10%, raising the effective interest rate from 8½% to 9% or more.

Title X loans are important financing devices that ease the problem of creating requisite capital improvements before lot and acreage sales begin to achieve a substantial volume. The loan proportion FHA is willing to ensure is extremely liberal and assures the developer of sufficient funds to cover the cost of critical initial development expenses and overhead, thus eliminating chronic undercapitalization. When sales volume falls short of expectations, lack of funds is particularly dangerous because it defeats the prospect of financing the major portion of development costs through land sales. Title X offers a basis on which costs can be met effectively even when sales volume does not reach expectations, and it will enable developers to avoid bankruptcy or dilution of their equity position when sales are miscalculated.

New Communities Act

A major new financing method, the New Communities Act of 1968, has been proposed to Congress by the president to provide a federally guaranteed cash flow debenture to protect the investments of private backers of new communities at competitive rates of return. Moreover, the developer would not need to make large principal debt payments until he or she received cash returns from sales of subdivided land. The proposed legislation offers an incentive for joint government (local and state) financing of utility systems and public facilities through federal grants.

It is not clear whether the legislation will pass, but the fact that it was proposed indicates the federal government's desire to ensure the success of master planned communities.

Sale and Leaseback Financing

One finance technique is for an insurance company to purchase the entire tract at market value and lease it back to the developer at an agreed rental rate equal to 6% to 8% of the price. In effect, the developer thus obtains financing for 100% of the land value. The developer then agrees to repurchase the tract at intervals and at prices that total the purchase price over a 25-year period.

Provisions normally are inserted to enable the insurance company to share in the land appreciation. For example, if the developer repurchases the land for immediate resale to a third party, the price serves as a formula for participating in land profits.

Another typical provision is a right of first refusal on all long-term mortgage financing for individual building projects. An additional provision enables the insurance company to purchase improved property at 85% of its market value and lease it back to the developer at an agreed rate.

Equity Participation

Large-scale project lenders are no longer content with interest alone on mortgage loans. Many lenders now want to share in either the equity or the income from projects they have financed.

In a recent negotiation for a $20 million loan, the lender required 7½% interest plus 25% participation in the cash flow of all income-producing properties erected during the 15-year loan period. In this instance they also demanded a capital sum of 12 times their share of the cash flow after 15 years. This is true equity participation because the lender also realizes the capitalized value of his or her share. An alternative provision is cash flow participation by the lender during the loan period, but without equity participation.

In large-scale industrial parks it is common for the lender to share in the sale proceeds of subdivided land over an agreed schedule of prices. The extent of participation is always negotiable, but it is not uncommon for it to reach 50%. Of course, the interest rate and minimum lot resale price levels influence the extent of participation.

The insistence of lenders to become equity or income participants reduces the developer's profit potential, although this disadvantage is more than compensated by the assurance of enough available funds for a well-planned community. The liberal terms buffer the developer against unforeseen market conditions and provide an ample contingency against disappointing sales.

No amount of financing can create profits for a large-scale project that is ill conceived or has inadequate market support. Nevertheless, the availability of funds in large amounts can and will pull many sound projects through the critical first five years to a point where profits start increasing significantly. For less successful projects it will enable ultimate success, though at a somewhat reduced profit.

Conclusions

The pace of master planned community developments will resume after this period of doubt and disillusionment. It is quite evident that no large-scale project can be successful without the commitment of institutional funds on a basis heretofore considered imprudent. The major life insurance companies and a few New York commercial banks currently are the sole financing sources, but industrial corporations ultimately will enter the community development field. Tentative steps have been taken by a few companies. To the extent that sponsorship passes to well-staffed, financially strong corporations, it will be possible to achieve much more rapid strides in optimum planning and execution.

Industrial corporations can bring two essential strengths to large-scale projects. First, we sorely need to apply industrial technology and management practices, and second, the financial staying power of large companies is essential to the long-term success of large-scale projects.

It is evident that investors are expressing renewed interest in fixed assets because of pressure on the U.S. dollar and monetary problems affecting the sterling bloc. Land perhaps is the best investment refuge in this economic climate. This is a compelling reason for equity participation in land development by financially stronger companies.

Market analysis techniques are improving steadily and fewer forecasting mistakes can be anticipated. Surely, the gross errors of the past will be avoided. The need for more comprehensive market research is also recognized.

Finally, there seems no disposition whatsoever in this country for the government to directly sponsor master-planned communities. Government at all levels is limiting its real estate involvement to public and publicly aided housing for low- and moderate-income families on an individual project basis. Its participation in master-planned communities is confined thus far to insuring loans, making grants to local government to finance utility systems, and guaranteeing cash flow, as proposed by the President.

The initiative, basic financing and planning for large-scale projects is still the prerogative of private investment, with government backing and support.

15
Attitude of Investment Trusts toward Office Buildings

A considerable unanimity exists among real estate equity trusts concerning the current office property market.

To understand why requires a look at two recent periods in which the office market first experienced a period of stability and tranquillity, and then entered an era that was inflationary, expansionist, and probably unlike any prior market for office property. It is important to contrast these markets to see where we stand today.

Stability, Then Inflation

Starting at the end of a mild recession in 1961, and continuing through 1965, the market was characterized by minor but creeping inflation of less than 2% a year. Office rents in New York City rose by no more than 2% a year, and other

Reprinted from *The Appraisal Journal* (April 1971): 194-99.

prices were moving upward at a similar slow and leisurely pace. Conditions were sound and we were making real dollars.

Then the wild market of 1966 to 1969 occurred as the nation heated up the economy through faulty and late financing of the conflict in Indo-China. Office rents in New York began to rise at an annual rate of about 10%, or five times as rapidly as during the 1961-1965 period. This expansionary binge in the office property market was fueled by the high level of the general economy, which required a very sharp increase in the white collar force and a consequent need for additional office space, and by the demand from corporations to upgrade their office accommodations as a reflection of the high profits they were making.

The Peak in 1969

New York reached peak land prices in late 1969 with typical sales of about $600 per square foot. Some sales were higher in the course of assemblage, but overall the $600 figure was about the peak price in land. The peak rent as an average on a *full-floor* basis (notice the qualification—not for small bits of space, but as an average for a full floor) reached a peak of $12 per square foot in prime locations in New York. These rents have already dropped to $11 per square foot and probably will fall further.

In Boston, 10 million square feet of office space were constructed. At the peak of the market there, land prices rose to $150 per square foot and rents to $10 per square foot. Nothing like it has been seen since.

A Drastic Change in the Office Market

The year 1970 marked the beginning of a different phenomenon, with significantly different conditions in the office market. Demand has abated considerably and the reasons may be set forth as follows:

First of all, a squeeze on corporate profits has required a widespread reordering of priorities by corporate users of office space in favor of capital spending programs that will produce immediate profits. You don't get immediate profits by upgrading your office space, though you realize benefits in the long term in the improvement of environmental conditions that affect worker attitudes. Therefore, industrial corporations preoccupied with the need for getting corporate profits moving upward again and showing immediate returns reduced their demand for better office space.

A further complication was the development of a natural caution by corporation managers because of the recessionary episode through which we are now moving. This caution works as a moderating force on office demand even for those companies whose profits were not unduly squeezed.

So the market has experienced a natural settlement and abatement of those hot inflationary fires that were experienced for those four previous years.

Diversion of Demand

One more complicating situation especially visible in New York City, but also in some other cities, is the diversion of demand to the suburbs or smaller metropolitan areas, away from the inner areas of major cities. Continental Oil has just moved its executive headquarters out of Rockefeller Center to Stamford, Connecticut, some 40 miles from New York City. American Can has already moved out of the heart of New York at 100 Park Avenue to Greenwich, Connecticut, and, in a real shocker, the Borden Company, occupying 240,000 square feet on Madison Avenue in New York, has moved its executive offices to Columbus, Ohio. Shell has left New York in favor of Houston, Texas, and other examples could be cited.

One should not be too lugubrious about the situation that exists in New York but the fact is that a spreading sense of disillusionment has developed regarding New York's seeming inability to cope with its problems—social, physical, environmental, and transit.

All these factors have caused a settlement in office demand, and even the naturally buoyant and optimistic observer of this market is inclined to view this market with some pessimism.

Consider, for example, the case of the Borden Company Building. Consultants to the Borden Company recommended that the building be sold by sealed bid at the middle of that heated economy early in 1969. The building was owner-occupied, and the consultant felt that it might appeal to another owner-occupant because it is reasonably modernized, though an older building. The necessary information was provided to brokers and to a selected list of possible buyers. The high bid was $24 million for an office building that was constructed in 1930, containing 240,000 square feet of space. That $100 per square foot of building area was really the peak of the market.

Supply

The supply side of the picture represents almost a mini-repeat of 1929, when demand evaporated while so many buildings were irrevocably committed. Three, four, sometimes five years pass between the time land can be assembled and title established and the necessary architectural and planning and feasibility studies can be completed, and financing can be obtained and the building is erected and rented. What happened in 1929 was that the demand vanished long before such office construction as the Chrysler Building, the Empire State Building, and even Rockefeller Center could be completed.

We are not going to have that situation now. This point should not be taken out of context to suggest that we are. But the classical situation is occurring in which much office space is committed—impossible to pull back—in the face of diminishing demand. The handwriting, at least temporarily, is on the wall. In many metropolitan areas (which have to be evaluated on an individual basis because of the highly localized nature of real estate as a commodity)—reduced rents and increased vacancies are a likely result over the next two and possibly three years.

A Weak Market

Consider what this does to an already weak real estate market. (Here the term *weak* is used in a relative sense to say that a supply-demand imbalance is present.) The current pullback in demand will adversely affect the weak areas that have been oversupplied with office space. Atlanta, New Orleans, some areas of southern California, and other cities are especially affected, and even strong markets such as New York, Boston, and Washington, D.C., can be included. Indeed, Washington, D.C., is now very quiescent with the General Services Administration pulling out of the office market and not making as many leases on behalf of the federal government. The major source of demand in Washington has simply vanished temporarily.

Patience is needed in the face of such conditions, but in the meantime the problem is there and producing some trying circumstances. During a period like this, the absorption rate declines, particularly for the new developer who has financed the construction rate of a building with interim financing at 12% to 14% interest rates and compensating balances.

The indirect costs are particularly destructive in this kind of market. Classically, the balance sheet has provided for field cost plus 20% for indirects. Later we said field costs plus 25% for indirects. Right now the indirect costs are 35%, and sometimes as high as 40%. The major reasons have been interim financing costs and the stretch-out in the period of time to obtain normal occupancy.

The older building is undergoing severe competitive pressure because market conditions have resulted in some deterioration in the previous high occupancy rate in which existing tenants re-rented and modernized their space.

Effect on Equity Trusts

In assessing the effect of these conditions on equity trusts, it is important to understand that the trusts have never been development-minded. Most, as a matter of policy and not of law or regulation, have refrained from a building program in which they would forego *immediate* income. The trusts have opted for existing properties, office buildings with a proven record of success, because they wanted the immediate earnings and did not want the risk involved in a developmental program. Thus the holdings of office buildings by the equity trusts have not been as adversely affected (at least not immediately) as the projects of individual developers caught in this tough market of declining demand and declining rent.

The negative factors described are occurring in the face of high fixed costs, extraordinary contract costs for construction, peak prices for land, and record-breaking indirect costs. It is thus very difficult to make the properties show a return. The trusts are thus being even more selective on office investments: first, by checking much more carefully the competitive status of the market, especially as it relates to impending new construction, which would affect potential investment; and second, as to financing. Certainly preference is given to older mortgages at lower interest rates, provided that the amortization is not too high. However, in the trust field, special problems arise. The principal payments cannot get too high in relationship to depreciation because then the trusts can get into an untenable position in which the shareholders would have a taxable income greater than their cash income. Low-interest mortgages are highly desirable, but on the other hand, trusts can't afford to pay too much amortization, so they walk a chalk line all the time.

The 1969 Tax Reform Act

The 1969 Tax Reform Act has had only a temporary effect on the purchase of office buildings. Because unsatisfactory financing potential currently exists, the second user, although entitled to a straight-line depreciation, may have difficulty in avoiding high interest rates. Straight-line depreciation does not contain enough tax shelter and higher rates of return therefore are required as compensation. In this sense the Tax Reform Act has hurt the resale market of older office buildings.

However, as financing problems ease, the adverse effect of the Tax Reform Act can be eliminated through refinancing. This would involve selling the land to a pension fund or insurance company, leasing it back, and then establishing a leasehold mortgage at low amortization on the lease-hold, thereby eliminating the possibility of too much amortization.

Most likely, straight-line depreciation will not significantly deter the marketability of older office buildings. If properly financed, such buildings provide considerable depreciation on a straight-line basis.

Rates of Return

A trend toward higher equity rates of return in both the real estate and stock market currently is reflected in lower multiples, falling prices, and reduced profits.

Moreover, due to heightened competition, more risk, and the imbalance in supply and demand in the office market, the equity investor is demanding a higher rate of return as a provision against the high debt service anticipated on refinancing. For example, those equity investors satisfied with 10% free and clear two years ago would seek 12% today. In refunding the existing first mortgage the debt constant will be at least 11%, thereby necessitating a higher rate of return to obtain a margin.

Rates of return are dependent on how expenses are computed and analyzed. Fifteen months ago a large number of properties in Houston, Texas, were purchased at an 8% rate of return, whereas a month ago a comparable group of properties in Houston were purchased at approximately a 10% to 11% rate of return.

During 1966 through 1969 overall rates of return did not increase as rapidly as debt service, particularly in 1967, 1968, and 1969. As a result equity returns dropped to as low as 5%, and frequently did not exceed 8%. These very low rates will *not* continue, at least for the next several years.

The Appraiser's Role

How do appraisers or counselors serve the investment trust, particularly the equity trust? Today, appraisers have an obligation to become more market oriented and less stylized. In the past appraisers have been preoccupied with technique, including computer applications, failing to recognize the importance of basic input data and unconsciously minimizing the more important influence of hard market facts over technique.

The appraiser must assume responsibility for

1. Reconstructing the income statement, taking into consideration the escalation provisions within office leases
2. Anticipating supply and demand conditions, to estimate within reasonable bounds a property's rent and vacancy potential for the immediate future when discounting doesn't take such a toll
3. Recognizing the importance of financing and its effect on the investment
4. Effectively measuring the effects of depreciation, realizing that property is not purchased on a cash basis but on the basis of both tax and investment implications
5. Becoming thoroughly acquainted with sales and rents

Regarding trusts, counselors will be responsible for

1. Screening property for purchase
2. Giving advice regarding a property's sales potential
3. Determining whether to refinance or modernize a property
4. Anticipating profitable new forms of investment in the ever-changing world of real estate

16
Have Central City Land Values Fallen?

There is growing evidence, both inferential and direct, that central city commercial land values are undergoing a significant deflation from the peak prerecession level of 1969. However, it is less clear whether the deflation is transitory or whether a long-term devaluation in land prices has in effect occurred. As the largest commercial center and trend leader, New York City provides interesting clues to this question. The prospect of decline in central city land values is not, however, peculiar to New York City. It is expected that the same trend in varying degree will follow in the major metropolitan areas such as Los Angeles, Chicago, Houston, and Boston. Land values had risen in New York to unsupportable speculative peaks during the 1966-1969 boom and a wholesome and natural downward adjustment is taking place. This adjustment should not, on the other hand, be construed as threatening the preeminence of New York City as the world's leading commercial center.

Boom in Land Values

Which economic forces led the central city area to this significant halt in land

Reprinted from *The Appraisal Journal* (July 1972): 351-55.

appreciation? In the wildly inflationary "guns and butter" economy, from 1966 through 1969, Manhattan land prices doubled. Inflation psychology was pervasive and found ample expression in real estate. Premium Park Avenue sites that would have commanded $300 per square foot in 1965 would readily have brought $600 per square foot or more at the peak of this frenzied era. Indeed, a prominent Manhattan office builder was heard to comment publicly in 1969, "I would pay $1,000 a square foot for the Racquet and Tennis Club land at Park Avenue and East 52nd Street if it could be delivered."

The boom in land values was felt throughout Manhattan in both commercial and residential areas. For example, in 1969 the Cathedral High School site on Lexington Avenue and East 51st Street was sold to Sam Rudin and Sons for approximately $400 per square foot. In 1969 IBM was reported to have paid up to $500 per square foot for small parcels in enlarging the plot area surrounding its main office building at Madison Avenue and East 57th Street. One assemblage on the west side of Third Avenue and East 49th Street in 1969 produced startling prices, ranging from $417 to $500 per square foot in a peripheral location. None of these sites would command such prices today.

During this frantic four-year period, rents for absolutely prime office space rose a minimum of 50%, from $8 per rentable square foot to $12 per square foot. Smaller units were rented at $14 to $16 per square foot. In prestige buildings, such as the Union Carbide Building on Park Avenue, small units reached a high of $20 per square foot. These sharply escalating rents encouraged office developers to feel they could afford to pay virtually any price for a land assemblage because the added capital cost could easily be recouped in higher rent. Speculative fever gripped the market. Land assemblages were taking place in secondary locations on Third and Second Avenues, Broadway, and 7th Avenue because of the lack of sites on prime thoroughfares.

Recession

The first signs of the imminence of deflation appeared in 1969 and 1970. A spreading sense of impatience and disillusionment with the city's problems, however unjustified, caused a significant number of industrial corporations to move or plan to move from Manhattan to outlying or other metropolitan areas, thus diverting an important source of demand. The list was impressive: Stauffer Chemical, Continental Oil, General Telephone, Shell, Borden, Cheseborough-Pond, and many others. In the context of the size of the Manhattan inventory, the relocations were undoubtedly overemphasized but the psychological impact was devastating.

The 1969-1971 recession also reduced demand as the financial community and industrial corporations deferred office expansion plans in favor of operating policies that would have an immediate and positive effect on their after-tax profits. Large scale relocations and expansions within the City were assigned a low priority.

This sharp contraction in demand after almost five years of intense activity was further aggravated by an impressive and growing oversupply that stemmed from the 1966-1969 boom psychology. In midtown Manhattan, some 27 million square feet of office space have been or will be completed in the 1971-1973 period. Close to 15 million square feet of this is vacant. The magnitude of the problem is evident when one considers that in 1971 only 3 million square feet of Manhattan office space was rented for future occupancy. This figure has been as high as 10 million square feet during the boom era and had varied from 2 to 6 million square feet annually in the pre-1965 period. Although an increasing intensity of demand is anticipated, it could be 1976, possibly later, until a restoration of a reasonable supply-demand balance is achieved.

Under the dual blows of recession and oversupply, office rents in the past two years have declined precipitously while vacancies in most buildings have increased. The $12.00 per square foot rental of 1969-1970 is now at $9.50 and may drop still lower. Meanwhile, construction costs, realty taxes, and operating expenses continue to climb, though at a moderating rate. Land values have to be a casualty of this combination of market circumstances and must wilt under the continuing pressure.

The $12.00 per square foot office rental implies a capacity to pay as much as $700 per square foot for land. A rental value of $9.50 per square foot, on the other hand, implies a capacity to pay only $200 per square foot. Thus, it is conceivable that a 20% drop in rent revenues theoretically could produce a 70% drop in land value! Of course, these relationships do not always move in precise ways since the other variable can change as well. Nevertheless, Table 16.1 dramatically portrays the relationship of land value and rental income.

Table 16.1   Required Rent at Varying Land Values

Land values per sq. ft. of land area	$200	$300	$400	$500	$600	$700
Capital costs per sq. ft. of building area						
Building	$ 45	$ 45	$ 45	$ 45	$ 45	$ 45
Land[a]	+ 11	+ 17	+ 22	+ 28	+ 33	+ 39
	$ 56	$ 62	$ 67	$ 73	$ 78	$ 84
Net return on capital cost at 9%	$5.04	$5.58	$6.03	$6.57	$7.02	$7.56
Add r.e. taxes, oper. exp. and vacancies	+ 4.50	+ 4.50	+ 4.50	+ 4.50	+ 4.50	+ 4.50
Required gross rent per sq. ft.	$9.54	$10.08	$10.53	$11.07	$11.52	$12.06

[a]Land value expressed in square feet of permissible building area, assuming a floor area ratio of 18 times the lot size.

It is astounding to realize that under a given set of circumstances a developer can pay $100 per square foot more for land if he or she increases the gross rents only $.50 per square foot. It is not difficult to see what occurred during the boom period. Rents were escalating so sharply that almost any land price seemed reasonable, even though the other variables of construction costs, taxes, and operating expenses were also increasing. Speculative excesses were inevitable.

Evidence of Decline

On the downside, the negative leverage works against the land and causes disproportionate declines in land value that may be triple the decline in the rent. At the moment, extensive evidence of a decline in land values is lacking because there is little market activity for land in Manhattan. Thus, the question is somewhat hypothetical. There is no assemblage activity of any significance. Virtually all plots held by developers are for sale but there are no bidders. Who would risk a purchase in the face of the oversupply?

Past market experience indicates that real estate land prices do not decline in the face of a mild recession or mild oversupply. Owners tend to hold firm during a transitory supply-demand imbalance in anticipation of an upturn in the market. Opinions are being offered that this is not the case now.

Two Sample Cases

Two recently proposed sales transactions, neither of which has yet been completed, suggest quite strongly that the first widespread declines in land values have begun. The Penn Central Railroad Company, now in bankruptcy, offered for sale 21 fee interests comprising its land and other real estate holdings in the Grand Central and Park Avenue sections of Manhattan. Only six acceptable offers to purchase were received for what is regarded as the best commercial section in the world. The majority of the offers were based on the anticipation that land values on renewal of the ground leases would not exceed $300 to $400 per square foot. Equally significant is the manifest disinterest in the properties and in the central city as demonstrated by the unacceptable character of bids on 15 of the 21 properties. These bids can only be interpreted as a sharp discounting of the future of the central city.

The second example involves a tentative valuation of $150 per square foot for the 10-acre commercial portion of Battery Park City, the landfill operation on the Hudson River, as the basis for establishing land rent, as reported in the offering prospectus for the $200 million bond issue required to finance the public and land improvements. A similar development plan known as Manhattan Landing exists in a more formative state for the East River. In 1968 the commercial land value at the proposed New York Stock Exchange site of this

East River landfill and platform development scheme was established by a City-appointed Committee of Appraisers at $200 per square foot. This value was based on the institutional character of the Stock Exchange building and not on the best commercial use of the site. The committee stated that the value of the landfill site in its highest use was $275 per square foot. On the other hand, the Battery Park City plan clearly represents the best use of its site. In spite of the intervening boom, the quite comparable Hudson River site has been valued at 45% less than the East River site.

The Prospect of Deflation

The present depression in rents and the extensive oversupply shrouding the market seems serious enough to provoke a troubled question: Are we witnessing the beginning of a long term, fundamental deflation in Manhattan land values? It is not beyond reason to foresee that the combination of (1) the recession's sobering effects, (2) New York City's social, educational, fiscal, and transit problems, (3) the diversion of office demand to outlying or other metropolitan areas, and (4) the debilitating effects of the office space oversupply have unintentionally conspired to create a long-term downward adjustment in land values that may extend well beyond the expected restoration of a reasonable supply-demand balance in 1976. It took Manhattan almost 40 years, from 1930 to 1970, to regain the peak land levels of the pre-1929 depression. This historic rhythm surely does not have to be repeated nor are market conditions in any sense precisely comparable. Real estate nevertheless does tend to have a sluggish and attenuated secular cycle, which suggests that a recovery in central city land values is not in the immediate offing.

Another national trend affecting central city land values and confirmed by the 1970 Census is the growing size of metropolitan areas. We are quite literally spreading out—using land more extensively and less intensively in the central city. Commercial and residential density of people will tend to decline in the core areas. The decentralization of commerce and industry will continue. This will act to inhibit any sharp recovery in central city land values.

Conclusions

The probabilities are that a significant downward adjustment in land values has taken place. Manhattan land prices have risen to unsupportable speculative levels and a natural corrective devaluation is not only inevitable but desirable. This adjustment in the real estate market's land pricing mechanism should not be interpreted as implying the decline of New York City. Instead, it should be regarded as a needed correction of the excesses of the pre-recession boom. Indeed, in lowering the unit cost of commercial space, New York will find itself better able in the future to retain and attract the major users of office and retail space.

Finally, if an equilibrium in commercial supply and demand is attained by 1976, to what level will prime land values then recover? It is expected that prime commercial rents will recover to an average of $10.50 to $11.00 per square foot at that time. This would suggest maximum land values in the $400-to-$500-per-square-foot price range, probably more towards the lower end. While this is far short of the $600 per square foot of 1969, it is a more realistic pricing of central city land.

17

How Real Estate Decisions Are Made

Investment decisions in real estate are made on the basis of a sometimes in-
stinctive and at other times a mathematically disciplined series of *comparative
analyses*. Investors and developers tend to a less formal and less documented
decision-making process; appraisers use more complex methods. But in both
cases, ultimate judgments are reached primarily on the basis of comparative
analysis. The income capitalization method in common use in this country is a
form of such analysis since all the sequential estimates are made on the basis of
a knowledge of similar investments and their costs, revenues, expenses,
financing, net incomes, and rates of return. Thus, both developers and investors rely primarily on market comparisons when evaluating real estate investments.

Less appreciated is the fact that real estate as an investment competes with
all other forms of investment available at a given moment. It competes against
fixed-income investments and the vast array of securities from which different

Reprinted with permission from *The Real Estate Review* 5(3), Fall 1975 pp. 42-46.
Copyright ©1975 Warren, Gorham & Lamont, Inc., 210 South Street, Boston, Mass.
All rights reserved.

proportions of income and capital growth may be anticipated. It also competes against speculative mineral exploration ventures with high tax shelter features, against direct investments in existing service or manufacturing business, and against investments in other tangible assets such as art, antiques, and jewelry.

The relative attractiveness of real estate tends to ebb and flow, dependent on international monetary conditions, the state of the economy, and real estate market conditions. Whenever monetary affairs are uncertain or unstable, as they were in the period preceding the 1971-1973 worldwide currency realignments that culminated in devaluation of the U.S. dollar, real estate has had a special attraction as the best of the tangible assets.

Real Estate as an Inflation Hedge

Continued investor interest in real estate throughout 1974 was based on its capacity to act as an inflation hedge. The specter of annual inflation rates of 10% sustained this high level of investment interest despite low rates of return. The sharp increase in operating expenses, especially energy costs, together with the natural lag in gross revenue increases reduced net revenue to the point where many properties have been, at best, at break-even levels.

Another factor in the continuing popularity of real estate investments has been the performance of the stock markets. The more popular stock indexes have shown no demonstrable growth since 1968. Over the past six years, stock prices have risen and fallen in an unusually broad range, but the net current gain is negligible. Investor disenchantment with stock performance has caused a moderate-scale switch to real estate investing in a continuing search for long-term growth as well as income.

Tax Shelter Attracts Investment in Real Estate

The federal income tax law gives real estate a competitive advantage over many other investments. On new residential developments, 200% declining-balance depreciation allowances may be taken. On a 40-year life, this means starting depreciation at 5% annually. In contrast, nondeductible mortgage amortization is rarely more than 1% in the first year, although it increases slowly in the subsequent years as part of a constant debt service amount. The excess of noncash depreciation over amortization payments is used to shelter from income taxation the cash flow from the real estate (and often, outside income as well).

Another provision of the Internal Revenue Code allows the expensing, for federal income tax purpose, of certain items generally considered part of the "soft" capital development costs (e.g., real estate taxes, mortgage loan interest, and insurance during construction). Thus, the investor's net capital outlay is reduced by the extent of his income tax saving. Similar tax advantages are obtainable in mineral exploration ventures, but the risks are commonly considered far greater than in real estate ownership.

The tax-shelter benefits of real estate ownership have probably had the most direct and significant effect on the equity rate of return in forcing its downward movement.

How Real Estate Returns are Defined

Real estate investment rates of return have historically been quoted on a pretax "cash-on-cash" basis. Cash income consists of all revenue less real estate taxes, operating expenses, and debt service. Thus, cash income is reduced by mortgage amortization but does not consider depreciation. Cash flow is commonly defined as the return after all the foregoing expenses and federal income taxes, if any. The term *net operating income* has frequently been substituted for the term *cash flow* by the real estate industry in an effort to persuade analysts that a real estate venture was thriving despite the relative absence of after-tax income. Since net operating income as used by the real estate industry is usually determined by computing taxable income, adding back depreciation, and subtracting mortgage amortization and taxes, it is merely another way to characterize cash flow.

In recent years, acceptance has been given to the theory that well-located, well-designed real estate does not depreciate but in fact can be expected to appreciate. If this premise has merit, it is proper to include amortization in the investment return since in reducing the mortgage liability, the investor is effectively saving on a deferred basis. Americans call this *equity buildup,* while Europeans think of it as a deferred return on investment.

In a sense this is a most dangerous theory. It is presumptuous to the extreme to anticipate an inexorable increase in real estate values. Even under idyllic market circumstances, some degree of depreciation is taking palce. Advances in design, equipment, and materials are inevitable, and some of these place existing properties at a competitive disadvantage. Thus, it is fair to say that only the excess of mortgage amortization over market depreciation may be added on a deferred basis to the return on equity. Astute real estate analysts have developed mathematical relationships for the components of yield, or return, by breaking out the relative influence that cash flow, recapture of amortization, tax shelter, capital gain, and sales expense play in overall returns over a presumed or actual time span.

How Mortgage Financing Creates
Positive or Negative Leverage

Investors finance real estate purchases with mortgage loans for three basic reasons:

- The size of the average investment is so great that the investor usually lacks sufficient equity capital to make the purchase without incurring substantial mortgage debt.
- Mortgage interest is tax deductible.
- The investor seeks to take advantage of "positive leveraging"—the borrowing of mortgage money at a rate such that the mortgage constant (interest and amortization) is less than the overall rate of investment return free of mortgage debt.

Assume, for example, that 75% of the investment can be borrowed at 9% interest, that the equity capital will constitute the remaining 25%, and that the overall rate of return on the project is 11%. The return to the equity investor may be thought of as (1) a return on the portion of the project purchased by equity (11%), and (2) a return on the portion purchased with mortgage money (11% minus 9%). The latter portion of the return is on an investment three times the size of equity. Thus:

$$Return = .11 + (.11 - .09)\frac{.75}{.25}$$
$$= .11 + (.02)3$$
$$= .11 + .06$$
$$= .17 (17\%)$$

To the extent that the loan-to-value ratio increases, the equity rate of return becomes disproportionately higher. If the investor considered amortization only as cash outgo rather than as a form of saving resulting from the reduction of his mortgage loan liability, he must add the cost of amortization into this formula. Assume a debt service constant factor of 10% for both interest and amortization:

$$Return = .11 + (.11 - .10)\frac{.75}{.25}$$
$$= .11 + (.01)3$$
$$= .11 + .03$$
$$= .14 (14\%)$$

In recent years, real estate investment decisions have been rendered more difficult by the occurrence of "negative leveraging." Negative leveraging occurs when the mortgage interest or the mortgage constant exceeds the overall rate of return, adversely affecting the equity return. Assuming an interest rate of 8.5% and an overall rate of return of 8%, the following occurs:

$$Return = .08 + (.08 - .085)\frac{.75}{.25}$$
$$= .08 + (-.005)3$$
$$= .08 - .015$$
$$= .065 (6.5\%)$$

The problem is compounded when the debt service constant (assumed to be 9.5%) is substituted for the mortgage interest figure:

$$Return = .08 + (.08 - .095)\tfrac{.75}{.25}$$
$$= .08 + (-.015)3$$
$$= .08 - .045$$
$$= .035\,(3.5\%)$$

Mortgage interest and debt service constant factors have fluctuated violently since the credit shortage of 1966, but their long-range trend has been upward. On the other hand, overall rates of return have moved within a narrow range and have not demonstrated cyclical extremes. Equity returns have consequently been reduced because increases in overall rates have not matched increases in interest or debt service constants.

The 12%-15% equity returns of a decade ago are only a memory today. Indeed, transactions are occurring in which equity rates of return are in a range of 5%-8%. Why, then, do investors continue to purchase at higher equity prices and lower equity rates of return?

We have summarized the following reasons:

- Refuge from inflation and monetary instability
- Investor disenchantment with the stock markets
- The availability of accelerated depreciation, even as this benefit was reduced by the 1969 Tax Reform Act

In addition, the recent and growing international interest in United States real estate has contributed additional equity demand and driven prices up while further lowering equity returns.

The Overriding Influence of Mortgage Cost and Availability

Undoubtedly, the amount and cost of financing is the single most important element in real estate investment decision making. In the case of existing income-producing real estate, the terms of the existing mortgage contract significantly affect the equity price.[1] Ideally, the investor prefers a mortgage with a high loan-to-value ratio, low interest rate, low amortization requirements, and unlimited prepay-ability. Properties carrying such ideal mortgages command higher equity prices than properties on which the existing mortgage is deficient in one or more of these attributes.

[1]For an excellent example of the effect of mortgage terms on sales price, see Zell, "Pension Fund Perils in Real Estate," *Real Estate Review* 65 (Spring 1975).

Heavy annual amortization requirements are unattractive to an investor because they do not provide basis for sheltering income through the substitution of depreciation for amortization. If annual amortization is $10,000 and the depreciation allowance is $8,000, the investor's reportable income for tax purposes is higher than his cash income. When amortization becomes equal to depreciation, a crossover point is reached that dictates that the property be either refinanced to reduce amortization or sold to avoid an untenable income tax position.

The mortgage amount and terms have an even more profound effect on new real estate development. The availability of mortgage money is obviously a major factor affecting real estate supply. Financing terms also affect supply. In a sense, the volume of new construction is controlled by mortgage terms. Since overall rates of return move within a relatively narrow range, the debt service amount becomes critical to the decision to commence development. If, for example, overall returns for new office buildings are 9.5% and the debt service constant is 9%, a good climate for development exists. On the other hand, if the debt service constant is 11% and negative leveraging exists, the developer becomes disinclined to proceed.

The Effect of Tax Shelter on Return

Next to mortgage financing, the amount of tax shelter most influences equity yields. The greater the noncash losses that can be shown, the lower the cash equity return the investor will accept. Currently, equity cash yields on properties with high and continuing tax shelter (say, for 10 years or more) are in the 3%-7% range. On rare occasions, investors will purchase on a break-even basis, that is, with zero equity yield. The after-tax yield to an investor in the 50% tax bracket may range from 12%-18% on such properties.

Until recently, certain types of FHA housing projects with 90% loan-to-value, interest-subsidized mortgages and controlled rents were sold to tax-conscious investors with cash yields ranging from zero to 5%. The experience of such investors generally has not been up to expectations. Many of the projects suffered cash losses because of high vacancy rates or high operating expenses. There is a growing realization that these investments are not as attractive as they once appeared.

A principal deficiency is the absence of capital gain potential. Since rents are controlled, increases in the equity value are unlikely. The result has been greater interest in nonsubsidized investments where rents may be raised as market conditions permit.

Influence of Foreign Investment Capital

The influence of foreign capital has had a profound psychological effect on investment decision making in the United States. Heretofore, Americans have been almost slavishly devoted to income capitalization as a method for deciding what to pay for a real estate investment. True, the income capitalizations were based on a comparative analysis of properties, but the alpha and omega of investment decision-making was the income stream.

Foreign investors appear to place a greater emphasis on "inherent asset value"—that value which reflects the relationship between the purchase price of the real estate and its replacement cost, provided the real property under consideration is well located and of quality design and construction. This school of thought holds that all existing real estate must be analyzed in terms of its competitive parity. How does the proposed real estate investment relate to a new and similar but not necessarily identical building, either existing or hypothetical? The approach obviously has less relevance for real estate that suffers significantly from a poor location, deficient design, or inferior construction. As a general proposition, the more marginal the investment, the less application the "inherent asset value" concept may have.

The concept is an interesting one because it recognizes the economic fundamental that in the long run, under conditions of equilibrium between supply and demand, replacement cost is the governing factor in pricing real estate. While this approach does not disregard income, it does permit purchases for the inherent asset value rather than for current return, particularly if leases are of short duration and opportunity exists for increases in rent. It assumes that in the long run, rents will be sensitive to and responsive to replacement costs.

Inflation and Real Estate Prices

Inflation causes development and building cost increases that tend to ensure the profitability of any existing real estate development meeting the basic criteria of modernity, location, and quality. Inflation does not, however, preserve real estate values during cyclical downturns when the market is oversupplied. Nor is it effective in preserving values in real estate that has pronounced obsolescence or an inferior location.

During the first four years of this decade, investor confidence in the effectiveness of real estate as an inflation hedge tended to raise the prices of prime real estate by putting an additional premium on prices of relatively superior property. It did not, however, influence to any great extent the prices on non-prime real estate. For these properties, income stream still was and is the ruling consideration.

To Sum Up

The use of comparable data (as evidenced by rents, real estate taxes, operating expenses, mortgage terms, equity rates of return, and capital costs) is the cornerstone of investment decision making. The comparative process is not limited to real estate; at least in part, the rate of return an investor demands is determined by indicated returns on competitive investments of similar risk characteristics. In recent years, real estate has had a special attraction for the investor as refuge from inflation.

Income tax laws provide special tax benefits that enhance real estate as an investment. For new construction, varying amounts of accelerated depreciation allowances are permitted that are far in excess of market depreciation and thus tend to reduce the taxable income while providing the basis for adequate replacement of the investment. The income tax laws also allow the expensing for tax purposes of certain items commonly regarded as part of the capital development cost. This has the effect of reducing the capital investment to the extent of the tax savings.

The availability and terms of mortgage money is a major factor in investment decision making. Investors leverage the purchase by attempting to borrow money secured by a mortgage at a lesser rate of interest and amortization than the overall rate of return. Of late, sharp competition for real estate has driven prices up and returns down, thus causing negative leveraging (overall rates of return that are lower than debt service constant factors).

In recent years, foreign investment in U.S. real estate has influenced a shift away from an almost complete reliance on income capitalization and rates of return to a collateral consideration of inherent asset value. Inherent asset value recognizes the relationship between the competitive price of the real estate and its replacement cost. This school of thought will on occasion minimize the importance of the immediate return on the equity investment in favor of what may be expected as a return under conditions of market equilibrium and constantly advancing prices.

18
How Foreign Money Buys U.S. Real Estate

An understanding of the magnitude of the capital markets in the United States is essential to grasping the long-term implications of foreign investment in real estate in this country.

The total size of our capital markets is about $3,500 billion. The commercial banking system contributes some $800 billion. The life insurance companies, excluding insured pension plans they are administering, are a $235 billion industry, while the pension funds themselves total $405 billion.

By contrast, foreign investment in the United States is only $30 billion—less than 1% of the total domestic market, and about 5% of the pension fund and life insurance markets.

Foreign Investors and the Domestic Market

Foreign investment is growing rapidly in this country, however. Although the

Reprinted from *Basis Point* magazine, Summer 1978, published by Investment Affairs, The Equitable Life Assurance Society of the United States.

entry of the Arab nations in force could have a profound effect on the market and the ratio of foreign to domestic real estate investment, this has not yet occurred.

Both individual and institutional foreign investors are contributing to higher prices and lower yields by competing with the life insurance companies and with the huge amount of domestic personal wealth for desirable investment properties. New York State insurance law allows life companies to invest the equivalent of 10% of their general account assets in equities. The percentages may vary by state, but the point is that only a limited percent of their total assets may be invested in real estate equities. Many big life companies in time will get close to their legal maximum investment in equities as based on their general accounts. Once they reach it, they will be able to invest further only as their general account assets grow (there is no legal limit on the amount of separate account funds that can be invested in equities).

What does all of this have to do with foreign investment? There is a definite shortage of real estate product because there is so much equity money vying for the available offerings. The foreign investor has to compete in this vast domestic market.

Although foreign investors are undoubtedly contributing to higher prices, there is simply not enough foreign capital in the market to say that they are *establishing* those prices. The market is being made by all the competing elements—the life insurance companies acting for themselves, lending institutions, pension funds, and the enormous amount of available personal wealth. An educated guess is that the foreign pension fund monies now being invested annually are in the range of $1 billion. By contrast, the life companies and the domestic pension funds together well may invest as much as $4 billion to $5 billion a year in equities.

Some of the latter figure is a *potential* market because the pension funds have been relatively slow about investing in real estate to date. It is probable, however, that they will step up their activity in the future. That sector of the market is potentially many times larger than the foreign sector. The foreign institutional market is mainly, but not exclusively, pension fund money. The German banks, in particular, have made some fine purchases in the United States.

The West Germans, the Dutch, and the Swiss are among the most active foreign investors because they can export capital with relative ease and without penalty. They can invest directly by creating American corporations; or they can, if they choose, invest through a Netherlands Antilles company. In many cases, they prefer to invest directly.

Why Buy in the U.S.?

Most of these investors tend to create American subsidiary corporations, which are subject to federal income tax. They like to leverage for many reasons. The tax deductibility of the interest on the mortgage, plus the generous depreciation allowances permitted under United States tax laws, enable them to minimize the income tax they pay.

The English have a very special problem involving the sterling premium that must be paid to take capital out of England. To circumvent this tax, the English engage in back-to-back financing. The Bank of England is reportedly considering eliminating the pound sterling premium. If that happens, we will see considerably more English investment in American real estate.

Meanwhile, Canadians are quietly buying up much American real estate. They are a much more important source than generally is recognized and will continue to be because they have a basic familiarity with the American market. So far, Arabs have not been as active as they had been expected to be.

What motivates foreign investors to buy real estate here? Obviously, there is a lack of buying opportunities in their own countries; they have a product shortage, too. Foreign pension funds have grown so large that a sensitivity has developed about owning too much of their own land. The choices are surprisingly limited abroad when the stringencies of investment criteria are recognized. Many are seeking a haven from socialism and economic and political instability.

There is a general feeling among foreign investors that, expressed in international terms, United States real estate is underpriced, despite the high prices currently being paid. Why? American developers have had such an enormous production capacity that many markets, despite their prodigious growth, have been plagued periodically by oversupply. A continuing chronic overhang of too much real estate in the market depresses rents and relative values. An imbalance between replacement cost and net income results. Rents in the United States, in general, have lagged behind international rents.

In the last decade, the public has developed an increasing awareness of the importance of ecological considerations. Regulatory actions in terms of real estate development have been increasing: zoning, planning, ecology, environmental impact statements, and the like. "Permit time" has increased significantly. Not only has the time involved in planning new construction tended to stretch out, but the cost has increased because indirect costs of development rise with the time the land must be carried during this longer development process.

What does all this mean? Foreigners do not believe that we are going to experience the same extent of oversupply that characterized the American market in the pre-1977 era. If a better equilibrium between supply and demand is achieved in the years ahead, we will witness some truly significant appreciation in the value of American real estate.

The Selectivity of Foreign Investors

Investors from other countries generally use certain criteria in considering the purchase of American real estate. Their respect for and sensitivity to inflation is much greater than our own. Most Americans, it seems, have adjusted to the anticipation of higher inflation rates, including an additional overlay of inflation arising from more expensive imports. We are prepared to live with it.

Foreign investors, on the other hand, not only feel that inflation will continue at an accelerated rate, but they also buy real estate in the anticipation that true runaway inflation may occur some day. As a result, foreign investors look with disfavor on any long-term leased property. They do not like flat rent for any extended periods of time, unless percentage increase potential is built in as in a shopping center, or without some application of indexing such as a consumer price index. They feel that real estate will be more sensitive and responsive to inflationary conditions.

Foreign investors tend to be more selective than American investors. They want the best locations. They want buildings of superior quality, free of the built-in obsolescence that can result from faulty design. They willingly pay substantial prices for prime property that meets these criteria. They believe in mortgage financing up to 75% or 80% of the purchase price. The debt service constant on a first mortgage is, in their view, the best protection in the world against inflation. They are attracted to the calculation of interest on a progressively declining balance with the difference credited to amortization. They recognize amortization on a discounted basis as part of their rate of return.

Computer analyses comparing the owning of property free and clear to mortgaging property have shown that, over a 10-year period, returns are 100 to 150 basis points higher by mortgaging, and foreign investors are aware of this. They generally do not compete in this respect with the American pension funds, which, as a matter of policy rather than as a matter of tax laws, tend to buy on a nonmortgaged basis. On the other hand, the foreign funds occasionally will buy for cash when the investment is negatively leveraged, as long as substantial increases in the income are forecast.

Let's presume a purchase price of $10 million for a piece of property on an all-cash basis. Let's also presume that the initial cash return on that $10 million is $850,000, or 8½%. Let's say that there are two competitors for this property —one an American pension fund, the other a foreign investor.

The foreign investor will get a $7.5 million mortgage at 10% constant, including 9¼% interest. Subtracting the 10% debt service factor on $7.5 million, or $750,000, from our $850,000 free and clear net income leaves an equity return of only $100,000. Thus, the foreign investor is making only 4% on equity. The reason? He or she is negatively leveraged. The debt service constant factor on the mortgage is higher than the free and clear rate of return on the property. Naturally, the American domestic pension fund, because it is tax-exempt, has the advantage of buying on an all-cash basis at higher yields.

To compete, a foreign investor must decide whether he or she wants to buy for cash or traditionally finance the purchase of the property. At least for the first several years, the investor must accept an extraordinarily low equity rate of return. This interesting competitive situation puts the foreign investors at a disadvantage.

Foreign investors also are attracted to our practice of nonrecourse mortgage financing. They prefer to buy existing income-producing property, tending to avoid development or new construction. They bypass properties requiring extensive renovation or rehabilitation, preferring what is called *track record* property without inherent flaws in terms of building or location.

Foreign investors are not unduly influenced by the initial cash-on-cash return on an equity investment. They analyze real estate on a minimum 10-year projection of revenue and expenses. Taking as their cue the expiration dates on existing leases, they recalculate the revenue on a year-to-year basis; account for inflationary rises in operating expenses; and presume that after 10 years the real estate is sold. They then compute both a pre-tax and after-tax discounted internal rate of return. Value appreciation is the extent to which subsequent years will show substantial improvements in the net income as increases are obtained from expired leases.

Equity cash-on-cash returns range widely. The only nonreturn transactions are those in which the properties are suitable for conversion to condominiums. There are few if any equity initial cash-on-cash returns of less than 4%. With remote chances of near-term increases, the returns can run as high as 10%.

The investor's reaction to the rent schedule, the market, and other considerations determines the initial return. Concerning the discounted pre-tax and after-tax internal rates of return, property should not show a less than 12% pre-tax discounted rate of return. On an after-tax basis, the objective is 10%—although it is not always possible to achieve this goal.

Today's Real Estate Market

In which type of market are foreign and U.S. real estate investors operating today? Prices have risen strongly over the past two to three years. Free and clear rates of return—i.e., before any financing—have declined about 150 basis points. The 10% all-cash return of three years ago is now 8½%. Returns on equity have declined even more because of negative leveraging—from 200 to 250 basis points over the past three years.

If the common stock market were to experience a sustained upturn, it would tend to take the pressure off real estate prices in the marketplace. Much more domestic pension fund money might be allocated to the securities market instead of seeking a haven in real estate. If this were to happen, we could see an ultimate swing to higher rates of return. However, if the Dow Jones Index continues to go nowhere—as it has for 10 years—strong upward price pressures will characterize the real estate market.

Foreign investment in U.S. real estate should continue indefinitely, although the volume of investment will vary depending on market conditions, availability of product, and competitive investment opportunities.

Despite the concern over Arab wealth, the proportion of foreign to domestic investment will remain relatively small. Foreign investors have taught their American counterparts to respect inflation, to stress location, to look beyond the near term, and never to compromise quality. They have been a wholesome influence on the market.

19

How to Plan and Build a Major Office Building

The process of development planning and of carrying out a construction scheme is an involved, multiphased, detailed activity. The most difficult problem is that of project coordination, that is, arranging that all the professional disciplines and construction processes interact in the most efficient and cost-saving manner. The efficient use of land, labor, and capital in their most economical proportions is what provides the entrepreneurial profit that motivates the developer.

Critical to a successful effort is the strong coordinating leadership of an executive who can control the sequential activities of development without waste, faulty planning, or poor judgment. This article is an overview of the planning and building of a major office building in an urban area like New York City. The principles of control, nevertheless, apply to any office development, large or small, in any urban or suburban location.

Reprinted with permission from *The Real Estate Review* 10(1), Spring 1980. Copyright ©1980, Warren, Gorham & Lamont, Inc., 210 South Street, Boston, Mass. All rights reserved.

Site Selection and Assemblage

The identification of the best available site and the steps taken to assure its purchase are the most difficult stages of the development planning process. Vacant land is a rarity in cities like New York, Boston, and Chicago. The developer frequently finds it necessary to buy underutilized land, usually in many different ownerships, in order to assemble an economically sized plot. Since the land is in short supply, land prices per square foot of permissible building area are very high. Currently in New York, they range from $10 to $40 per square foot.

Obtaining possession of the appropriate property interests is the developer's most difficult task. Commercial tenants may have long leases that do not include sale or demolition clauses. They must be bought out at high prices. It is almost impossible in, for example, New York City to relocate a residential tenant by the permissible government process. It is, therefore, usually a major expense to persuade an apartment tenant to move. The office developer must occasionally conceal his identity or buy through others if he is to avoid paying "hold-out" prices. Once the developer's assemblage effort becomes known, leasehold tenants' demands for payment accelerate rapidly. At the height of the building boom that occurred in New York in the late 1960s, it was not uncommon for a developer to pay tenants up to $10 per square foot of permissible *new* building area in order to obtain possession of obsolete space to be demolished.

A special analysis of Manhattan (New York) land values for 1960-1972 found that the price per unit (per square foot of land area or for permissible building size) declined in plots over 30,000 square feet. It discovered that land values in the premium locations were frequently two to three times higher than they were in conveniently located good sites, sometimes only a few blocks away. In 1970, the highest prices for land assemblages, inclusive of the cost of possession, were close to $600 per square foot. (Sales of individual parcels within an assemblage were made at prices as high as $1,000 per square foot.)

During that bygone boom, the seller would, in many cases, give the buyer a purchase-money mortgage for 50% or more of the price. These loans customarily required the developer to pay off the loan out of the first advance he received on any construction loan. These assemblage loans were rarely, if ever, subordinated to a construction loan. Given the high interest rates prevailing in the late 1970s, substantial developers today are obtaining commercial bank financing and paying all cash for the land they acquire.

Planning and Zoning

At one time, zoning codes prohibited residential uses in office districts. The statutes usually provided only that office, retail, service, and a small proportion of light manufacturing be permitted in commercial zones. There is a current trend to mixed-use zoning, in which offices, retail uses, and residential apartments or hotels are all included in a single zone. Proponents of such zoning see many benefits for urban revival in the concept. One of the most modest of the results is that in mixed-use areas, unlike office areas, the city does not empty out at night. There is always activity in the streets. Another important change in zoning attitudes creates codes that tend to discourage parking in the central business district in order to prevent cars from entering already totally congested areas.

Another modern control technique may be illustrated by New York City zoning regulations. In that city, the developer may erect a building whose floor area is 15 times the size of the lot area. The height is dictated by a *sky exposure plane* concept that forces smaller floors as a means of ensuring greater light and air. If the developer installs a high-ceilinged gallery or otherwise makes provision for open public space, it may receive a floor area bonus up to three times the lot area.

Rezoning is a difficult, often tortuous proceeding. There is widespread popular feeling against increasing use density in the central business district. Government attitudes tend to vary somewhat with the state of the local economy. If, for example, a developer requested a zoning ordinance in New York during the horrible market conditions of 1974-1975, he was sympathetically received. Now that New York's recovery is assured, it has become more difficult to obtain a zoning change or even a variance. Perhaps the most significant impediment encountered by developers seeking variances or changes is time delay. In many major U.S. cities, up to two years may be lost in the rezoning process. There is, of course, less need for zoning changes in the central business district than in outlying areas. However, in the central business district, the zoning pattern becomes so well established that change is more difficult.

While many new ideas in zoning have been introduced in the last decade, their efficacy is yet to be established. One such idea is the transfer of development rights from one site to another. The object of the development right concept is to enable a specific developer to erect a larger building without increasing the total density within a given district. The overbuilding developer is required to purchase development rights from other property owners in the district, thus assuring that these other properties will remain underbuilt and the district's average density will not be exceeded. The theory is ingenious, but in practice, it may create problems. Dense shadow patterns and spot overpopulation and crowding can result. One circumstance in which such transfer of development rights appears warranted is that in which a building that underuses the site has been declared an historic landmark. The owner should have a right to sell his unused development rights anywhere in the district.

Marketability and Feasibility Studies

Marketability and feasibility studies are mandatory first steps in most developers' building programs. Developers tend to conduct these studies themselves. A small proportion of developers employs outside consultants who specialize in feasibility analysis and who bring to the studies the advantages of objectivity and detachment.

The analyst who seeks to determine a building's marketability is trying to establish its rentability or salability at given rent levels or sales prices and to determine the time period that will be required to achieve normal occupancy or a complete sale.

The feasibility analysis is an extension of the marketability study. Not only is it concerned with the size and timing of income flows, it also estimates the relationship between projected net income and development cost. This entails calculations not only of revenue but also of financing costs, real estate taxes, operating costs, and total development costs.

Methodology is changing somewhat. Analysts now place less reliance on the so-called land residual capitalization method in deciding feasibility. They are beginning to prefer the discounted, internal, after-tax rate-of-return technique because it establishes the long-term return on the estimated investment cost rather than relying on the difference between cost and value as the major measure of success. New computer software programs have been devised that, at minimal costs, allow analysts to make numerous forecasts each based on small changes in estimated variables and projections. Sensitivity analysis techniques can be used that greatly enhance the valuation and investment analysis results. For example, numerous analyses may be made, each assuming different data for rent levels over the absorption period, or each assuming absorption periods of different length.

Establishing the physical characteristics of the structure that yields the highest site utilization remains a key element in planning a new building. In the central business districts of the major cities, the zoning maximum is commonly regarded as the best use. Even if this is the case, there are countless other design features that must be carefully studied. The size of the floors, the location of the core area (elevators, stairs, mechanical equipment, and lavatories), the mechanical equipment itself, facade and lobby materials, interior finishes, etc., all have an important bearing on achieving the highest profitability. Energy considerations have intensified the study of more advanced heating, cooling, and ventilation systems, and of fenestration changes as a means of combating soaring energy costs.

The least scientific aspect of the planning process and the one most subject to error is the estimation of rent levels and absorption periods. Market analysts and appraisers have tended to be overoptimistic about the share of the total market a particular project will command. Since the allocation is largely judgmental, and since no proven methodology exists for the purpose, it is important that developers arrive at their judgments with the assistance of outside consultants who are both professional and detached. Developers' problems are compounded by their natural disposition to be overoptimistic about the rents and absorption period for their own projects. Developers' enthusiasm can frequently be moderated by a respected professional opinion.

Architectural and Engineering Selection

It is of the utmost importance that the developer select an architect who understands and accepts the investor/developer's objectives and criteria in the construction of the office building. The architect who is capable of designing only costly monuments is not the person to engage to design an investment-grade office building in which little or no preleasing is anticipated. The architect must accept the challenge of keeping costs to a minimum consistent with the risk involved. In major cities, the selected architect usually chooses his engineering subcontractors with the developer's consent. Some architectural firms have complete in-house engineering staffs, but most subcontract the mechanical and structural engineering to engineering specialists.

The developer has a critical interest in the actual design and supervision experience of both the architect and his subcontractor specialists. The developer should not only interview architects, he should have them submit a list of their designs, together with locations, descriptive data, and graphics of their work. He must then visit a sufficient number of completed buildings to gain insights into a preferred architect's design ability. The depth of an architect's staff is another significant consideration. Particular attention must be paid to the architect's capacity to offer working drawings that are errorless and complete, leaving little to the general contractor's imagination.

Once the architect is chosen, he must start the process of evolving a design that not only reflects the client's needs but also follows the market and investment recommendations of the marketability and feasibility consultants. For example, if the marketability and feasibility analyses resulted in recommendations for a lower-height building with larger floor areas as most marketable, the architect cannot attempt to persuade the developer to erect a tall tower with small floors. Similarly, the interior finishes and mechanical systems must be commensurate with the client's needs and desires as well as the dictates of the feasibility study.

From the teamwork of various professionals, there evolves a design concept that satisfies the developer, architect, engineer, and real estate consultant. Every possible factor must be thought of and considered for its influence on the final design. The schematics that the architect finally creates must be sufficiently detailed to enable the costing process to begin.

It is also desirable to have chosen the general contractor at this early stage so that his consideration of the cost implications of the design may also be received.

Selection of a General Contractor

Until recently, general contractors, in addition to dealing with the various subcontractors, have performed one or more of the trades themselves. The general contracting organization might itself have undertaken excavation, foundation, and concrete work, or carpentry, plastering, painting, and plumbing, or any combination of these. This type of general contractor has been largely superseded by a *broker* type (also called a construction manager) that performs no trade work itself. Instead, it estimates costs by inviting all the trades to submit bids for their respective specialties. It maintains a staff of cost estimators, purchasing agents, and construction superintendents, in addition to necessary support personnel. This relative handful of personnel exerts profound influence on the efficiency of the construction process.

Traditionally, it has been the practice of developers to invite competitive bids from at least three, sometimes more, general contractors, based on a complete set of working drawings. This is still the practice of government bodies and many large industrial corporations. Competitive bidding can also work well on smaller projects. However, in major U.S. cities, especially New York, Chicago, and Los Angeles, the bidding system has yielded to a new procedure. Now the developer/investor selects a construction manager carefully and requests that it prepare cost estimates based on design development drawings. Developer and contractor negotiate a contract based on the contractor's estimates. These negotiated contracts are especially effective in labor-short or high-salary markets where the premium is placed on obtaining the most skilled labor. The proficient general contractor knows all the trades and can bargain effectively with subcontractors. When choosing the general contractor, the developer relies heavily on the contracting firm's record of performance, and he may reward a past record of excellence even if he must pay a higher price.

The general contractor company, working on a negotiated bid base, usually (but not always) receives a monetary award for completing the improvements below budget. Conversely, if the project costs exceed the agreed budget, the contractor company may be liable for the cost overrun. This is a serious liability and raises the question about the credibility of such a contractor's budget estimate. Why would a general contractor accept such risk if his budget was even remotely competitive? General contractor fees rarely exceed 5% of project cost, and on big contracts they may be only 2% of total field construction costs. Nevertheless, the special skills of the general contractor usually enable him to avoid the crushing burden of cost overruns.

The negotiated contract makes good sense for large commercial development in the major cities. Under this arrangement, the general contractor is a member of the development team. He is an ally rather than an adversary. He will work hard to bring in prices from all the trades that are as low as feasible.

Another important reason for the popularity of the negotiated contract is that it permits the involvement of the general contractor in the architectural and engineering planning. That organization's input on materials, design, equipment, and even layout can be invaluable. The experienced general contractor is conversant with the latest innovations in energy conservation in improved heating and air-conditioning design and equipment, in better lavatory equipment, and in a host of other areas. The general contractor can help to restrain the architect's tendency to overdesign and overspecify. His expertise in material selection is especially useful. Last, his ability to purchase by negotiations with the subcontractors such critical items as steel, elevators, and HVAC plays a pivotal role in keeping costs at the lowest possible levels.

Selecting the Marketing Agent

The exclusive renting agent or consultant is an important member of the development team. His leasing skills and knowledge of tenant prospects are critical to the project's success. Most developers select an agency or consulting firm to be responsible for rentals, although some developers believe in direct employment of renting personnel. Developers considering agencies or consulting companies find it easy to identify those with a proven record of success. It is also easy to discover which agencies have the depth of staff that is essential to success. All too frequently, the powerful personality of the agency head is not sufficiently backed up by a proficient staff. Thus, the wise developer interviews all those who will be involved in the rental effort. Another factor that the developer must consider when rating candidates for rental agent is the number of competitive buildings that an agency may be simultaneously renting. Problems of overextension of staff and conflicts of interest must be avoided. It is sometimes rewarding to select a younger or lesser known agency that will exert an extra effort and that has no conflicts. However, such an agency is likely to have fewer high-level tenant contacts than an experienced agency. The choice is never an easy one.

An exclusive rental agency can specify that commissions will be paid on one of two bases:

- The rental agent may merely be authorized to split commissions with an outside broker who concludes a lease transaction.
- If an outside broker negotiates the lease, that broker receives a full commission on the transaction, while the rental agent receives an override com-

mission (usually one-half of the full commission). This arrangement is much to be preferred in a competitive market. It gives extra motivation to brokers and enhances the project's rental prospects.

Since commission rates are not regulated, they must be negotiated between developer and agent. Obviously, the relative size, experience, and market positions of the parties affect their negotiating clout. It is good procedure to engage the rental agent before schematic design starts. The agent can then join the general contractor, the developer, the engineer, and the architect in working on the best possible design for the office floors. The agent can also aid the developer in establishing the rent schedule. It is also the agent's responsibility to plan the total marketing campaign. This includes the preparation of a brochure, compilation and dissemination of mailing lists, devising of an advertising budget, and planning of a promotional and publicity campaign. The agent and the developer must also agree on the solicitation and other sales tactics to be employed in the leasing effort. The agent also assists the developer and his attorney in formulating the *work letter,* that is, the document setting forth the standard finishes to be provided for the tenant's space. He is instrumental in recommending the business provisions of the lease.

The Permit Process

Increasing government regulation of the approval process places almost intolerable handicaps on development in major cities. Traditionally, localities have regulated the integrity of the construction frame, the quality of separating partitions, the access of interior spaces to light and air, the fire egress, and the quality of heating and ventilating. Since the first applications of zoning in 1916, public policy has recognized the need for orderly planning of land use. There are few major cities without zoning or building and fire codes.

Of late, new agencies have multiplied. The environmental protection statutes have become thorns in developers' sides. True, these affect factory or shopping center locations more than office locations. They nevertheless threaten the development process in many ways. The same is true of clean air legislation. No one denies the importance of such restraints. However, the manner of regulation is a concern to developers and users of new buildings. The multiplicity of permits required to build in today's market extends the development planning and tends to increase development costs significantly.

Financing the Office Building

Developers generally will not consider beginning construction unless they have obtained in writing a first mortgage commitment from an institutional lender, the funds from which are to be disbursed on completion of the project. A first mortgage loan in prime locations amounts to 75% of the estimated market value of the project as established by an accredited appraiser. Most such mortgage loans require a debt service constant that liquidates the loan in 25 to 35 years. Prepayment is usually permitted after seven to ten years at 5% penalty, declining subsequently by 0.5% per year to 1%. Mortgage financing is usually nonrecourse in the sense that no personal guarantees (nor parent company guarantees, in the case of corporate borrowers with substantial net worth corporate parents) are required. A shell company whose sale assets are the real estate to be built is permitted to sign the bond or note.

Once the developer has obtained a commitment letter from a permanent lender, he can apply to a commercial bank for a construction loan. These banks usually will not lend for construction unless the developer has arranged a *take-out* (i.e., a long-term mortgage loan), the proceeds of which will be used to pay off the construction loan. The construction loan is made in an amount close to or equal to the long-term loan. If there is a gap or short-fall between the two amounts, the developer may have to obtain a temporary loan elsewhere.

The construction lender typically pays out monthly installments as the development work progresses. An engineer or architect must certify that the work has reached a point where the payment is warranted. Interest costs of construction loans usually float 1% to 3% above the prime rate. In addition, the borrower may have to pay one or two points at the outset, plus all legal and closing expenses. Construction financing is particularly expensive and contributes significantly to high development costs.

We indicated earlier that when the developer acquired the land, he may have obtained a purchase-money mortgage or third-party mortgage financing, usually from a commercial bank. These early lenders rarely, if ever, subordinate their interests to construction financing. Thus, the developer must be prepared to pay off the land financing out of the first advance that he receives from the construction lender. He must also have sufficient cash reserves to pay his contractors' bills.

Even though the permanent loan is based on value rather than on development cost, it is difficult for a developer to *borrow out,* that is, to arrange for 100% financing of his development cost.

All developers seek to create positive leveraging in their long-term mortgage financing. Positive leveraging means borrowing money at a lesser rate of interest and amortization than the overall rate of return. Recently, many projects have been started although they will exhibit negative leveraging at the outset, but leverage is expected to turn positive in the foreseeable future.

The cash equity for a project comes from many different possible sources. The developer himself contributes cash or is given equity credit for development, financing, and renting fees. He frequently has active or passive individuals or institutional partners as shareholders. The institution frequently seeks a more conservative preferred return but also participates in the appreciation potential. The developer's awards are a combination of fees, income tax shelter, and his share of the excess of market value over development cost.

Conclusion

The development of urban office buildings has, in recent years, been an activity that has rewarded its participants generously. Many wish to enter the field and to share in its rewards despite the difficulties of obtaining appropriate financing and despite the increasing risks that escalating government regulation impose on development efforts.

To the newcomer, it may appear that the rewards are there for the asking. What is needed is to spot the opportunity, the underbuilt plot, the unrecognized market. Apparently, one need only take the entrepreneurial plunge to reap the rewards of vision and daring.

But the experienced developer knows that development is a complex discipline. Development rewards those who capitalize on opportunity with professionalism. Complex developments require the selection and coordination of multitalented teams, intricate planning, and efficient coordination.

20
Commercial Condominiums

The growing recognition and acceptance of the inevitability of an entrenched, relatively high-level inflation has many implications for the real estate industry. The tenant has particularly felt the effects through the significant surge in rents which has occurred from early 1977 to date.

Although commercial rent and escalation reimbursements are deductible for tax purposes, the escalating cost of rental occupancy has become a major concern to both small and large businesses.

Another irritant that has contributed to higher rents is the relative shortage of office space. For example, in the northeast, Middle Atlantic region, over 96% of all reporting office space was occupied. Similar low vacancies are reported throughout the nation.

This puts added pressure on rent increases. The Federal Reserve's tight money, high-interest policies to reduce inflation have a counterproductive, short-term effect of increasing rents.

This happens because as developers defer new construction, lessened

Reprinted from *Building Operating Management,* June 1980.

competition causes even further rent increases. The market outlook for continued tenancy is indeed a poor one.

The well-capitalized, major industrial concerns can thwart the high cost of rent by undertaking a program of construction of general-purpose office buildings. Indeed, many Fortune 500 corporations have recently made major policy decisions to emulate IBM in building major office buildings throughout the country for their own occupancy.

Probably the single most important factor in this decision was the conviction that ownership in the long run was less expensive than tenancy.

Other considerations included the better image of ownership; support of the central city's economic base; and the ability to consolidate scattered locations.

But what about the smaller companies who cannot build on a scale where both development and operating economies can be realized? A very small building is usually uneconomic in high land value locations, especially in the central city areas. Remote, outlying locations where land is inexpensive may not be a proper choice in an energy-conscious environment.

A smaller space user also generally cannot afford the support services of a restaurant or cafeteria, or other service and retail uses.

Commercial Condominiums

The solution lies in the creation of economically sized office buildings in which many companies can realize the benefits of ownership at an attractive cost basis and in the most convenient, energy-saving location.

The commercial condominium gives the smaller space user all the income tax advantages and capital gain potential of individual property ownership. Instead of the endless process of paying rent, it is possible to build a substantial equity.

Not only does the condominium owner increase the value of his holding from amortization payments on a mortgage, but he also stands to experience a real gain in the value of his investment.

Many persons have counted as a negative the unrealized nature of the gain during the period of occupancy. This is not so. The gain can in fact be realized in as little as five years, and surely within ten years.

Most important, the investor does not have to give up occupancy to achieve the gain.

The first way to take cash out of the condominium is to obtain a larger mortgage than the original mortgage. This can occur in any situation in which rents and values are rising. The extra mortgage proceeds are tax free to the condominium.

Another way of realizing the gain without losing occupancy to achieve it, is to sell and net lease back the space to an investor. True, you lose the owner-ship, but you may realize a significant after-tax capital gain.

In the meantime, you can deduct the net rent as a business expense and invest the gain in one's own business . . . or, purchase another condominium unit.

Other Financial Options

It will be even possible in time to trade condominium units as a means of defer-ring or minimizing the capital gains tax. In other words, you may seek a larger or smaller unit of space, or, you may want to change your location.

You may be able to find another owner willing to trade a unit for yours. Of course, a goodly number of units of all sizes and types must be evaluated before this can be achieved.

Commercial condominiums have been criticized by some on the grounds that the space user lacks flexibility for growth. This is simply not the case.

The condominium buyer can purchase more space than his move-in re-quirements, just as the tenant may lease more space under similar circum-stances. The extra space may be leased for a three-to-five-year period, until needed.

True, the owner would have outfitting costs, but chances are he can sal-vage most of the partitioning, carpeting, etc., when he occupies the space.

Also, added space elsewhere in the building may be purchased as it inevi-tably will become available.

What is the best size for a commercial condominium? We would recom-mend a minimum 100,000-square-foot building. This size provides economies of scale and also can accommodate small as well as relatively large space users.

However, we see substantially bigger buildings in the heart of the major cities. I foresee commercial condominiums in the 500,000-square-foot range.

New Construction vs. Remodeling

Commercial condominiums work best in new construction rather than conver-sions. Conversions can be successful if the building is substantially vacant. This enables the investor to offer large blocks of modernized space.

In a building that is well tenanted and has varying lease expirations, the problem of getting sufficient space becomes troublesome. It can work if exist-ing rental tenants would uniformly be interested in purchasing their space.

Unfortunately, it doesn't happen this way to any great extent.

How is the condominium financed? The procedure is very similar to a res-idential condominium development.

The first step is to obtain so-called "end loan" commitments from thrift institutions or life insurance companies on an agreed basis per square foot of space, subject to approval of the credit standing of the purchaser.

With this commitment in hand, a construction loan can then be obtained from a commercial bank equal to 75% of the development cost. The equity sponsor could be a company who wished to retain a unit for its own occupancy. The sponsor could also be a local investor or developer.

The most frequently asked question is, "How do I go about this as a businessman without real estate experience?"

The first step is to pre-qualify the best investment broker or, alternately, the best local developer in your area. Working through either or both, the inexperienced company can avoid the pitfalls of real estate development, best exemplified by an inadequate location, cost overruns, or poor design.

Until now, most condominiums have been very small. On the West Coast, there has been a proliferation of commercial condominiums in Orange County, south of Los Angeles . . . but also in many other areas as well.

In the case of a typical one in Santa Ana, the condominium consisted of 21 small one- and two-story buildings totaling 150,000 square feet of space, with office sizes ranging from 5,300 to 13,000 square feet.

The site was close to 12 acres and density was very low. Sales prices ranged from $80 to $100 per square foot. Prices for similar units reached a maximum of $125 per square foot.

The concept of individual buildings is fine in low density, outlying areas, but will not work in close-in urban areas. We foresee a major building erected in a central city location in which the space is subdivided and sold in individual units as the next logical development.

There should be a wider range of commercial condominium types available. We are confident this will happen.

21

A Marketing Revolution:
The Sale of the Pan Am Building

One day in 1972, I read in the *New York Times* that James H. Maloon had been made senior vice president–finance at Pan American World Airways. Because James D. Landauer, founder and chairman of Landauer Associates, Inc., had taken a leave of absence from the company from 1962 to 1968 to become president of the corporation that owned the Pan Am Building, Grand Central Building Inc. (GCB), I wrote and told Mr. Maloon of our involvement in the real estate. Three years later, in 1975, Jim Maloon asked us to do the first in a series of investment analyses of the real estate. Although at that time we did not delve deeply into a study of the myriad of leases and operating cost data for the building, we did learn something about the building and how it functioned.

The Pan Am Building had been completed in 1963. The developer, who also owned 45% of the stock in GCB, was the highly regarded Erwin Wolfson. Tragically, he became terminally ill during construction but persuaded Jim Landauer to finish the development and to arrange mortgage financing that would cover the hard and soft development leasehold costs. Mr. Wolfson had given 5% of the stock to his attorney, William Zimmerman. Another 45% of the initial capitalization was owned by companies of Jack Cotton, a British developer and investor. In September 1963 Pan Am, the principal tenant, exercised an option it had acquired during its lease negotiations to purchase for $3 million the remaining 10% of the stock. GCB's investment was in the leasehold, the building. The 150,000-square-foot land parcel underlying 200 Park Avenue was owned in fee by companies wholly owned by the Penn Central Transportation Company and on which a percentage lease rent was paid annually under the provisions of a long-term land lease.

Earlier Ownership Changes

In the 10 years following the building's completion, many changes occurred in the building's ownership, which profoundly affected the building's destiny. First, in January 1969, after the death of Jack Cotton, Pan Am purchased from the estate his 45% interest for only $17 million cash over a leasehold mortgage held by New York Life Insurance Company, originally $75 million, at 5⅝% interest, but somewhat reduced by amortization thereafter. This gave Pan Am a 55% leasehold interest for an aggregate $20 million in cash. Second, to the surprise of some, Penn Central went into Chapter 11 bankruptcy. This did not immediately affect the operation of the building because ground rent continued to be paid. However, although Pan Am now owned 55% of the stock, it had only 50% of the voting rights because of provisions in the stock agreement.

In early 1977, I mentioned to Jim Maloon my concern over the building's continued, fragmented ownership in which it was difficult to obtain unanimity of opinion by the shareholders over even the most basic operating issues. Although Jim Maloon agreed with us concerning the advantages of consolidation, he was under the capital constraints of a cash-short company, to say nothing of the operating differences among the shareholders. A management study requested by Mr. Maloon, and subsequently made by Landauer Associates in early 1979, only confirmed my earlier views and those of Mr. Maloon that complete consolidation of ownership in one company was critical to the future investment performance of the real estate. A "laundry list" of necessary improvements in accounting, operations, physical maintenance, and required capital expenditures set forth in the management study was a nagging reminder of the need to upgrade before the 1983-1984 leases came up for renewal.

Consolidating the Ownership in Pan Am

To return to the sequence of events that preceded the sale, in early 1978 we learned from Mr. Maloon that the estate of Erwin Wolfson, acting through William Zimmerman, seemed intent on disposing of their combined 45% interest. From time to time, informal inquiries of Pan Am's interest in purchasing the shares had been made by Mr. Zimmerman; but with the circulation of an offering sheet to the market, it became obvious they were serious. Knowing that Harry Helmsley had been approached and was considering the purchase, Mr. Maloon realized that Pan Am should move with alacrity to make an all-cash offer. After discussing this with my client, I reasoned that Mr. Helmsley would offer only part cash and ask the estate to take back financing for the balance. Thus, cash would have a special appeal to the estate. Thanks to Jim Maloon, we were authorized to initiate negotiations. Within a few weeks, we bought for Pan Am the 45% of shares for slightly under $10 million cash. Even at that time it was an incredible price. True, it was a minority leasehold interest, but in relation to the leaseholder's original cost of about $90 million, or of its replacement cost of $450 million, it was indeed breathtaking. Now Pan Am controlled 100% of the leasehold for a total cash outlay of $30 million and a gross price, inclusive of the then $60 million leasehold mortgage, of $90 million.

Emboldened by the success of the Wolfson stock purchase, Pan Am then authorized our company to purchase the land (fee) interest. Before any purchase could be made, we needed to obtain the approval of the Bankruptcy Court in Philadelphia. We were wary of proceeding because of the furor occasioned by the unsuccessful but unsettling efforts to "piggy back" on the New York Realty Hotels proposed purchase when offered for sale as a group by Penn Central. In that instance, a group of Saudi investors associated with former U.S. Treasury Secretary William Simon sought to interpose a bid. The court granted their request, but the original bidder, the Tisch interests, prevailed in a courtroom competitive bidding drama. It was nevertheless a tense moment for the Tisch interests. I was determined to avoid this circumstance. In other words, a carefully researched and prepared offer might go for naught if a last minute interloper, relying on Landauer's experience or seeing the opportunity to play "hold out" in frustrating Pan Am's objectives, interposed a last-minute higher offer before the court. It was decided to forego this strategy in favor of making our purchase immediately following Penn Central's release from bankruptcy, thus avoiding competition from a last-minute speculative trader.

Patience worked. The moment Penn Central emerged from the Chapter 11 bankruptcy, in October 1978, we made an offer of $25 million for the land, or about $167 per square foot, subject to the lease. Penn Central accepted, and in December 1978 Pan Am owned 100% of both the land and improvements, completing the consolidation we had so earnestly recommended. It was a very low land price, compared with the $1,000 per square foot unencumbered land value then prevailing. In all fairness, the land price was low because the ground rent was low. But Pan Am held the ace card because the purchase could eliminate the obvious encumbrance of the lease. Their total investment then was only $55 million over an approximate $60 million amortized balance of the mortgage, or $115 million. Before the property was sold, another $10 million was paid in amortization. This brought Pan Am's investment down to about $105 million at the sale. (I have quoted only approximate gross purchase costs, inclusive of the mortgage. These figures bear no direct relationship to the book cost of the real estate, which of course was reduced by depreciation allowances.)

Lawsuits

One principal reason for consolidation of the various interests was the number of lawsuits that were outstanding not only among the shareholders, but between the shareholders and Penn Central. In the most serious case among the shareholders, the Wolfson estate and Mr. Zimmerman had sued GCB and Pan Am, alleging that Pan Am used its 50% voting right to block dividends that should have been paid. Pan Am's defense was that any cash flow would have to be retained for anticipated capital expenses arising principally under the fire safety provisions of Local Law 5. In fact, there was little or no net income. In an equally serious suit, Penn Central alleged that Pan Am was calculating the 8% percentage rent provision on base rents alone, when in fact the lease provided that percentage rent be based on 8% of all gross revenues, not simply rent. Penn Central's case had merit. It was quite apparent, in my judgment, that a decision would go against Pan Am. Legal counsel for Pan Am agreed. All lawsuits, however, were terminated as a condition of purchase of the leasehold and fee interests and the parties waived all claims to any future monies in this respect.

Building Description

The Pan Am Building was designed by architects Pietro Belluschi and Emery Roth & Sons. It is a 59-story octagonal building, with a structural steel framework. The first 10 stories consist of a base that contains a public concourse running from Grand Central Terminal to East 45th Street, eight office floors of from 60,000 to 100,000 rentable square feet, and an elevator parking garage for 350 cars. The 49 tower floors contain 32,000-36,000 square feet. The building is amply served by 60 passenger, 5 service, and 4 automobile elevators. According to 1969 Real Estate Board of New York measurements, the gross building area is 2.5 million square feet and 2.25 million of rentable square feet. The building has since been remeasured. According to 1983 REBNY guidelines, the building has more than 2.5 million rentable square feet.

The facade is pre-cast concrete panels, with a coarse aggregate finish that attracts soot and pollution stains. The roof is masonry covered, with five-ply membrane, tile on setbacks, and copper flashings. Windows are pivot-mounted for interior cleaning. The finish of the elevators, public halls, lavatories, hardware, and doors are of a lower quality than one would generally consider for such a major building. This concern ultimately led us to recommend in our management study that any buyer must spend a minimum of $5 million for specific improvements to the lobby, elevators, public halls, and lavatories as a condition of purpose. (Metropolitan Life ultimately decided to spend $15 million, which also included steam cleaning and the elimination of leakage from all windows.)

The building's interior finish consists of a two-story lobby with terrazzo flooring, tempered glass, stainless steel and marble veneer walls and column finishing, and tile and plaster ceilings with decorated lighting throughout. The lobby finish and general function will be substantially modified in 1983 or 1984.

The building's heating source is a Consolidated Edison high-pressure steam system; air-conditioning is provided by a high-pressure, high-velocity system zoned for each major exposure. Electrical service is provided from vault locations. Energy conservation is effected through a computerized Honeywell energy management system.

The location and convenience of the building are noteworthy features. One can gain access to the building by escalators from Grand Central Terminal and entrances on Vanderbilt Avenue at 44th Street, the 45th Street entrance on the north side of the building, and on the ramp at lobby level on Park Avenue.

Selling on Futures

In January 1980 Jim Maloon asked us again to study the feasibility of selling the shares in GCB, and in the process to update the figures to reflect the rapidly escalating rents and lowered discount rates. As pointed out earlier, we had made previous, somewhat ineffectual analyses without adequate computer modeling of the course of future income. With Jim Maloon's encouragement and consent, our services included conceiving or modifying software programs that would provide better insights into the building's future. As a result, some 60 days later we could submit with confidence a report of the revenue and expenses that automatically accounted for changes in rents as leases expired. Assuming a 6% annual growth rate, the report also provided for the insertion of new rents based on a rent matrix by elevator-floor zone, the change in expenses as they increased annually, the temporary vacancies created by presumed changes in tenancy as a percent of total renewals, the effect of real estate tax and operating cost escalation, the assumption that Pan Am would take back a lease for 350,000 square feet at the market level, and the effect of periodic major capital improvements and leasing commissions.

It would have been impossible to calculate accurately all these changes using calculating machines. The rent schedule was exceptionally complicated because there was little or no conformity in the standard lease provisions. In addition, a substantial number of leases were capped, that is, had ceilings on the tenants' responsibility for proportionate increases in operating expenses. The number of changes to be made in the forecasting was almost infinite. The computer made the essential difference. It also enabled us to dramatize that inclusive of Pan Am's 16%, some 67% of the leases (expressed in square footage) would expire by 1984, only four years away. Most of these leases had been initially made in the very soft rental market of 1962-1964 and were as low as $5.75 per square foot in the building base and $8.00 per square foot in the tower.

The Valuation Process

The discounting of the cash flow in the 12%-to-14% range for a 16-year projection period and the capitalization of the stabilized cash flow thereafter at 10% brought significant surprises to the study team. The initial studies indicated that the real estate could be sold for as much as $325 million. No one at Pan Am or Landauer previously had thought such a price was obtainable. Frankly, we had been thinking in the $250-$300-million range. Thanks to the computer, it became clear that the inherent value of the property was higher than anyone had anticipated. The average rent was as low as $10 per square foot, plus some tax and operating escalation. The assumed increases to $35 per square foot made a profound upward difference in the valuation, even when discounted to the present time. The assumptions were then constantly reviewed and adjusted so that we eventually decided $350 million was obtainable. Pan Am agreed.

The detailed cash flow projection (Table 21.1) over a 16-year period provided 6 line items of revenue and 14 line items of expenses, including interest and amortization on the mortgage. There were two reasons for the 16-year projection period. First, it was the date of the self-liquidation of the original mortgage. Second, some 95% of the original rentals would have expired by that time. This does not necessarily mean that the pricing was based on that period. Generally, we are reluctant to go beyond 10 years in any valuation analysis. However, the longer period is helpful to buyers in their own analysis. We did not attempt to estimate over that period the total capital improvements the building might require. Instead, we planned to alert buyers to the need for certain basic cosmetic upgrading and suggested this cost be subtracted from whatever they decided to bid for the property. We did provide a very modest replacement reserve for small items but never attempted to suggest what the building's mechanical replacement needs might be over its lifetime; instead, we left this consideration to the buyers. The projection was backed up by eight pages of explanatory assumptions about the rationale for the estimates. Base rents were currently estimated at the market level and assumed to grow at a 6% compound rate during the projection period. Expense escalation was based on the so-called "porters' wage formula," which called for the tenant to pay one cent more per square foot in rent for each one cent increase in the porters' wage rate, then about $10 an hour. The utilities, however, were separately assumed to grow at a 12% rate because of excessive costs in New York, over which Con Edison had little or no control.

Pan Am's willingness to cancel its own lease and take back a replacement lease at rents close to the market greatly influenced the price that was paid. Our rent matrix (Table 21.2) formed the basis for the revenue projections of base rent at a 6% compound rate. It is somewhat interesting to note that the 1980 projection for 1984 rent in the middle of the building (see Floors 30-39) was $36.61 per square foot. Today, the same space has a rental value of about $42-$45 per square foot. Thus, our projections were, if anything, conservative.

The existing mortgage had been reduced to about $50 million as the amortization payments became successively larger under a constant payment schedule of 30 years at 5⅝% interest. Even though the nonrecourse mortgage was valuable to retain, it was too low on a loan:value ratio basis to influence any buyers or the pricing. The ultimate price of $400 million represented $350 million cash over. The first year's cash flow of $8.4 million was only a 2.4% return on equity. However, by 1985, when the full effect of the 1983-1984 renewals took effect, the cash flow was forecast to increase to $32.3 million, or 9%. However, based on current rent values, the most likely cash flow by 1985 would be about $40 million, or an 11.4% return on the original cash investment. The internal rate of return, that is, the discount rate used to discount each year's cash flow over the 16-year period as well as the discounted residual value in 16 years, was at a relatively low 12%. That low rate has, of course, been improved as the result of Met Life's success in obtaining higher rentals. Surely this price was a high watermark in the sale of real estate. Yet in making a pre-emptive bid, Met Life assured itself worldwide publicity that would bring new vibrancy to an insurance company with a reputation for conservatism. I think it was a sage move for them.

Marketing Strategy

Ordinarily, analyses such as the Landauer investment analysis would exist for the private knowledge and use of the seller and for the purpose of enlightening the seller to the probable range of selling prices. It was certainly not customary to reveal this information to a buyer. However, we decided to use the rental

Table 21.1 *Cash Flow Projection (in dollars)*

	1981	1982	1983	1984	1985	1986	1987	1988	1989	1990	1991	1992	1993	1994	1995	1996
Revenue																
Base Rents	28,157	28,384	32,621	47,743	58,279	58,432	58,547	66,164	73,232	74,067	74,378	75,796	83,684	105,231	121,119	121,394
Escalation Income	6,749	8,398	9,423	8,497	9,587	13,436	17,722	18,386	20,512	26,203	32,707	39,597	42,132	33,138	31,703	43,057
Cost of Living	173	200	145	84	95	106	119	48	0	0	0	0	0	0	0	0
Percentage Rent	607	655	504	429	446	482	520	562	607	655	708	764	730	669	723	781
Tenant Sales	1,659	1,791	1,935	2,089	2,257	2,437	2,632	2,843	3,070	3,316	3,581	3,867	4,177	4,511	4,872	5,261
Credit Loss	−187	−197	−223	−294	−353	−374	−398	−440	−487	−521	−557	−600	−654	−718	−792	−852
Total Revenue	37,158	39,232	44,405	58,549	70,311	74,518	79,143	87,562	96,934	103,719	110,817	119,425	130,070	142,832	157,625	169,641
Expenses																
Payroll	3,561	3,881	4,231	4,612	5,027	5,479	5,972	6,510	7,096	7,734	8,430	9,189	10,016	10,917	11,900	12,971
Related Labor	784	855	931	1,015	1,107	1,206	1,315	1,433	1,562	1,703	1,856	2,023	2,205	2,404	2,620	2,856
Electric	5,824	6,523	7,306	8,182	9,164	10,264	11,496	12,875	14,420	16,150	18,088	20,259	22,690	25,413	28,463	31,878
Steam	2,365	2,602	2,862	3,148	3,463	3,809	4,190	4,609	5,070	5,577	6,134	6,748	7,422	8,165	8,981	9,879
Elevator Maintenance	514	555	600	647	699	755	816	881	951	1,027	1,110	1,198	1,294	1,398	1,510	1,630

Other Operating	1,006	1,086	1,173	1,267	1,369	1,478	1,596	1,724	1,862	2,011	2,172	2,346	2,533	2,736	2,955	3,191
Water & Sewer	82	89	96	103	112	120	130	141	152	164	177	191	206	223	241	260
Management	474	484	510	574	604	614	626	647	670	687	705	727	753	785	822	852
Insurance	320	345	373	403	435	470	507	548	592	639	690	745	805	869	939	1,014
Real Estate Taxes	8,404	8,908	9,442	10,009	10,609	11,246	11,921	12,636	13,394	14,198	15,050	15,953	16,910	17,924	19,000	20,140
Reserve for Replacements	100	105	110	116	122	128	134	141	148	155	163	171	180	189	198	208
Total Expenses	23,433	25,433	27,634	30,077	32,709	35,570	38,702	42,144	45,917	50,046	54,575	59,550	65,015	71,023	77,628	84,880
Net Operating Income	13,725	13,799	16,771	28,472	37,601	38,948	40,441	45,419	51,017	53,674	56,242	59,875	65,055	71,809	79,997	84,761
Interest	2,790	2,650	2,502	2,346	2,181	2,006	1,822	1,627	1,420	1,202	971	727	469	196	5	0
Amortization	2,430	2,570	2,718	2,874	3,039	3,214	3,398	3,593	3,800	4,018	4,249	4,493	4,751	5,024	321	0
Debt Service	5,220	5,220	5,220	5,220	5,220	5,220	5,220	5,220	5,220	5,220	5,220	5,220	5,220	5,220	326	0
Cash Flow	8,505	8,579	11,551	23,252	32,381	33,728	35,221	40,199	45,797	48,454	51,022	54,655	59,835	66,589	79,671	84,761
Total Leasing Commissions	75	17	1,918	3,282	39	65	24	3,110	478	53	154	264	5,626	7,934	109	130
Adjusted Cash Flow	8,430	8,561	9,633	19,970	32,343	33,663	35,197	37,089	45,319	48,400	50,867	54,391	54,209	58,656	79,562	84,631

and expense projections, descriptive material, and market data—in fact, everything except the discount process itself, which we considered to be confidential, in the offering.

Table 21.2   Schedule of Projected Office Space Base Rents per Square Foot (electric not included)

Year	Floors 3-9	Floors 10-19	Floors 20-29	Floors 30-39	Floors 40-49	Floors 50-56
1980	$16.00	$25.00	$27.00	$29.00	$30.00	$35.00
1981	16.96	26.50	28.62	30.74	31.80	37.10
1982	17.98	28.09	30.34	32.58	33.71	39.33
1983	19.06	29.78	32.16	34.54	35.73	41.69
1984	20.20	31.56	34.09	36.61	37.87	44.19
1985	21.41	33.46	36.13	38.81	40.15	46.84
1986	22.70	35.46	38.30	41.14	42.56	49.65
1987	24.06	37.59	40.60	43.61	45.11	52.63
1988	25.50	39.85	43.03	46.22	47.82	55.78
1989	27.03	42.24	45.62	48.99	50.68	59.13
1990	28.65	44.77	48.35	51.93	53.73	62.68
1991	30.37	47.46	51.25	55.05	56.95	66.44
1992	32.20	50.30	54.33	58.35	60.37	70.43
1993	34.13	53.32	57.59	61.85	63.99	74.65
1994	36.17	56.52	61.04	65.57	67.83	79.13
1995	38.34	59.91	64.71	69.50	71.90	83.88
1996	40.65	63.51	68.59	73.67	76.21	88.91

At this point it became necessary to create a brochure and to devise marketing strategy. It was first decided to write a comprehensive brochure that would contain all the information a large institutional buyer required for a searching analysis. In this respect, my valuation training served me well. Years of experience in arraying figures and writing reports made the task far easier. The 65-page brochure was then keyed to a documentation book, which would be given only to serious buyers who had made or intended to make offers for the property. The documentation book that accompanied the brochure contained the survey, the mortgage documents, the ground lease, the itemized rent schedule, service contracts, and a draft form of the proposed Pan Am lease.

One complicating factor was the onset of the consumer-induced recession of the first six months of 1980. First-quarter GNP declined sharply. The prime interest rate went from 12% in February to 20% in mid-April. Despite these adverse factors, the real estate market blithely carried on with its surge in rents and prices. It was also widely felt that the inflation rate would hold firm at about 10% or even increase. The brochure pointed out that as a result of inflation, market value could only be estimated on the basis of the discounted present value of the projected future cash flow. No one really argued the point during the marketing campaign. Thinking was somewhat universal about the inevitability of continued inflation. (It is interesting to note that scarcely two years later, buyers were criticizing the projecting of cash flow and the discounting of future cash flow on the grounds that it was unrealistic and beyond forecast.)

What price does one ask for a property during a rent surge period? Our client was determined to avoid an "asking price" because it implied a ceiling of value. In the past few years, however, more than one large transaction had been concluded at more than the so-called asking price. Most noticeably, it happened when Prudential Life Insurance Company paid in excess of the asking price for a group of shopping centers. We did not want to miss the same opportunity. I finally hit on an old definition of market value originated by the late Professor Richard Ratcliff of the University of Wisconsin: the most probable selling price. This definition was strategically used as Landauer's best estimate of the all-cash price at which the real estate would sell. I reasoned that we would tell the buyer the most probable selling price was $350 million and would invite the buyer to pay more if it were so inclined. Pan Am approved this strategy.

However, the price was not stated in the Landauer offering brochure. It was left exclusively for verbal transmission to the prospect. During the three-month marketing period from mid-April to mid-July of 1980, constant further evaluation of the rental values and discount rates was being made by Landauer professionals. It was decided not to revise upward the rents stated in the rent matrix, but it was felt the price might increase to $375-$400 million, or about a 12% internal rate of return at the higher price. Pan Am was well served by Joseph A. Weinberger, Esq., its outside counsel, and Edwin F. Malloy, chairman of the Fred F. French Investing Company, who acted as additional special adviser to Pan Am.

In incomplete form, the previous offering of the Wolfson estate's 40% interest revealed that many of the biggest leases had ceilings on the amount by which the tenants would proportionally reimburse the owner for interim increases in taxes and operating expenses. As a result, it became even more widely known about the "caps." The building inevitably suffered an image as being without a "bottom line" because of the lack of full escalation coverage. We were determined to correct this image in the minds of buyers with a superior offering brochure that featured the future income stream and by creating an aura of exclusivity. This exclusivity was achieved as well by asking the Landauer pre-selected and Pan Am-approved buyers (about 40) to sign confidentiality agreements before the submission. Essentially, the agreement provided that the prospect would accept any brokerage liability and that Pan Am had no obligation for fees except to its advisers and counsel. It further provided that the prospect would keep the information confidential and would not distribute such information without the written approval of the seller or its consultant, Landauer Associates. Only one major prospect, a large insurance company, refused to sign the agreement. Everyone else willingly agreed, although a few requested, and were granted, some modifications.

An audio-slide presentation was prepared in case history form. Our company had seen some multislide, fast-paced, kaleidoscopic presentations that varied from incomprehensible to merely slick. We were determined to present all essential facts in an informative, low-keyed manner, without fanfare. The slide presentation would be particularly helpful to foreign buyers. Surprisingly, even the most experienced institutional domestic buyers appeared to be impressed with the presentation and found that it was not only useful, but could sometimes be substituted for an inspection due to its thoroughness. All presentations were made in person. Nothing was mailed. The telephone was used only to establish the prospective interest and to make appointments. Follow-ups also were conducted in person. If buyers wanted to use brokers for advisory purposes, they were welcomed, provided they signed the brokers' confidentiality agreement, in which it was understood they would be paid by the buyer.

The criteria to qualify for the presentation included knowledge of the prospective buyers' net worth and experience. It included the need to find leaders who would be willing to form a consortium to consider purchase of the real estate. The prospective buyers who had expressed confidence in New York's future were favored. Because of the magnitude of the transaction, it was assumed that only institutional or large, publicly traded companies would qualify. The leading investors were not thought to be potential buyers because commercial bank financing would have been prohibitively costly at the time and there was a limit to their ability to raise the cash. Thus, life insurance companies and pension funds were favored as buyers, plus some large public investment companies and a few foreign buyers. Foreign institutions were not particularly good prospects because of the deal size and foreign disinclination to form syndicates. Nevertheless, we sent a disposition team to Europe to offer the property to a select few. Unfortunately, on the eve of our initial sales effort, James H. Maloon resigned as executive vice president of Pan Am to accept the chairmanship of Itel Corporation. It was Mr. Maloon's foresight and organizational ability that was so critical to the eventual sale of the property. It was the best example I'd ever seen of complete cooperation between a disposition consultant and an owner's representative. Jim Maloon also provided a smooth transition in arranging for Mr. William T. Seawell, chairman of Pan Am, to take over the sales responsibilities for Pan Am.

The Sales Effort

The actual mode of closing the sale was not fully decided by Pan Am and Landauer until midway through the sales presentations. Above all, we wanted to deal privately with each buyer while protecting the confidentiality of all offers. We also wanted to communicate the features of the property more effectively than our competitors. How could this best be achieved? The clue came with the realization that any price close to $400 million would mean that the Pan Am real estate was worth more than the market (not book) value of the parent company's shares! It became critical to ensure adequate market coverage and a bidding procedure that would be fair to all parties. It was important to avoid any shareholder legal action that questioned the extent of the marketing effort, the bidding procedures, or the price. I then telegraphed about 10 serious prospects to make an initial offer in writing by July 9, 1980, with a Landauer response by July 16. Landauer would then encourage a second, final bid by July 23, with the winning bidder to be announced by Pan Am on July 28.

Why the need for the two-phased procedure? It protected the Pan Am shareholders and management to the fullest possible extent. It created a reasonable timetable. It insulated Pan Am against an initial pre-emptive bid that might not have resulted in the best price. It enabled us to talk privately with each prospect between the bid dates without divulging the terms or price of any competitive offer. We at Landauer have been offended by loose criticism that we traded on the offers with others. Nothing could be more inaccurate or untruthful. On the contrary, we talked in confidence with each prospect only about the issues and conditions set forth in the offering brochure, including the Pan Am leaseback and the stock purchase agreement. We wanted to compare bids on an equitable basis. This was our sole motivation. For example, we were intent on a 20-year flat rental leaseback for Pan Am with sublet privileges. Since this had been misunderstood by some in the first bidding round, we were sure to specify this condition. The various bid prices were never divulged to any of the bidders.

We informed five of the ten first-round bidders that for all purposes they were substantially out of the competition because their offers were so low. All withdrew on our advice. Four of the remaining five bidders re-bid. On July 23, before noon, officials of the four finalists delivered their final offers to me. Two of the offers, those of Met Life and Olympia & York, were clearly superior. However, Met Life's bid was by far the better of the two. On July 25, Met was notified that its bid had been accepted by Pan Am in principle, subject to the signing of the documents and to a January 1981 closing. Met Life was properly elated. It was an exhilarating moment in Met's efforts to enter the equity real estate market more decisively. Many have asked the purpose of the stock sale rather than the asset alone. The reason simply was to avoid a New York transfer tax that applied only to real estate assets and not to leaseholds nor to corporate stock transfers. Subsequent legislation was passed by the New York State Legislature to include leaseholds and real estate stock sales. Aside from some small cash and a few receivables, the sole asset of the corporation was the real estate so the sale was very close to an asset sale.

Some Concluding Observations

The sale brought a new era to the methods used in the marketing of real estate. No longer was the process a secretive exercise on the seller's part. Full disclosure of detailed, pertinent information became the rule. In fact, we urged buyers to use our computer facilities and suggested they run any sensitivity analyses involving changing any of the line items of revenue and expense. The sale surely demonstrated the effectiveness in an inflationary market of projecting revenue and expenses over an extended time in accordance with lease expirations and probable inflation rates. The technique is especially useful when there are a substantial number of old leases at low rents where the rent increases are very substantial. Improved computer software programs, which were the joint product of our real estate investment analysts and consulting software experts, enabled both buyer and seller to make an infinite variety of assumptions about future cash flows. Both pre- and after-tax analysis was a simple matter.

We also realized firsthand the importance of a comprehensive, accurate, and graphic presentation in an offering brochure. Above all, selling real estate at the highest level demands effective communication with potential buyers. If the presentation is well prepared, the real estate will sell iteself. The institutional buyer was especially grateful for the time saved when facts and figures were carefully arranged and presented.

This sale particularly dramatized to financial officers of major corporations that owned their headquarters buildings the existence of another means of financing to strengthen a balance sheet that, for example, may have been laden with excessive short-term debt. The sale and part leaseback, at the market rate, of a portion of the space (as in the Pan Am case) or the sale and leaseback of the entire building as a financing device had real meaning to financial people. The cash raised and after-tax capital gain realized are strong inducements to many companies. The leaseback rental also could be structured to avoid the need for showing a long-term lease liability under FSAB Rule 13.

The most important result for me was the increase in confidence felt by institutions to our kind of sales effort. Our full-disclosure policy and spirit of candor were particularly appreciated and tended to draw us more closely to the buyers than otherwise would have been possible. Moreover, our projections were credible. As it turned out, in the two-and-one-half years of Met Life ownership, they are obtaining about $7-$8 per square foot more in rent than our matrix projected.

As I was quoted in the Summer 1982 issue of *Real Estate Review,* "We've really come full circle. We were advisors to Mr. Wolfson before the Pan Am Building was even built. Jim Landauer. . . was involved in completion . . . of the building. Now, we achieved a record price. Pan Am made a $300 million pre-tax profit, but at the same time the future is bright for Met Life. I really feel happy."

Part III
Forecasting

Recently, I heard a commentator remark that baseball was the only game in which one could be deemed an excellent hitter with a .300 batting average! Believe me, the same can apply to a real estate forecaster. At any given moment, it is difficult to comprehend all the internal, i.e., industry, occurrences that will affect a forecast, let alone the multiplicity of external factors that can prove especially upsetting. Nevertheless, despite the obvious frailties of predicting the future, the effort must be made. The basic premise is our conviction that market value is the present discounted worth of future expectations.

While not all are specifically forecasts, the following group of articles and comments were written or stated with an eye to the future. The real estate analyst must constantly be monitoring current and near-term market conditions and deciding what they may portend now and for the future. A case in point is "Changes in the Equity Real Estate Market," in which I comment on the meaning in the mid-1960s of the entrance and the probable effect of life insurance companies and large-scale syndications into the investment market.

My writings also tend to stress the importance of adequate marketability and feasibility studies of large-scale projects. Many of my business associates tend to think of me primarily as a market and investment analyst rather than an appraiser. "Improving the Quality of Feasibility Studies" illustrates this perception. Published in October 1976, as our deep recession was ending, the article attempted to analyze what went wrong with the industry's forecasting capabilities, which were so dramatically exposed with the oil crisis of late 1973 and the ensuing recession. Overplanning, oversupplying, and overfinancing were common. Some of the deficiencies were obviously procedural, but much of the problem occurred because developers and lenders were unable to predict accurately the timing or occurrence of the double blows of oil shortage and recession. In "How Manhattan's Fiscal Problems Have Affected the Office Market," external causes, this time of a positive nature, are explored. The beginnings of a solution to New York City's severe fiscal crisis were the generator that sparked the 1977-1981 office boom after six abject years of demand retrenchment and development inactivity.

As we grow in market knowledge and maturity, increasing industry attention is now devoted to analyzing the external and internal causes that prompted or influenced a phase of the real estate cycle. It is gratifying to see the diminishing influence of a provincial mentality in real estate circles that has judged events purely in terms of a local economy, without recognizing the national and international events that affect all local real estate performance. Much of "Real Estate Market Forecast for 1983," for example, is an exposition of general economic conditions, including inflation, interest rates, the extent of the general recovery, income, and employment, as essential background to an understanding of how real estate would perform that year. "American Real Estate Remains an Attractive Investment" was published in October 1981, a particularly sensitive time. As events turned out, the five-year market peak was reached in the third quarter of 1981. Questions were nevertheless raised about the extent of inflation, higher interest, the course of discount rates, and the rate of development activity. One must of necessity look beyond current events for market answers. At the same time, my view of the market tended to forecast the oversupply that was subsequently experienced as likely to occur mainly in 1984-1985. In fact, the oversupply occurred in mid-1982 and will persist through 1984, possibly 1985. That the recession of 1981-1982 was deeper than expected no doubt hastened the acceleration of the soft market, but my estimate nevertheless was poorly timed.

An interesting contrast exists between short- and long-range forecasting. In "Real Estate Market Forecast for 1983," a much higher degree of success, or a significantly higher batting average, is readily apparent. Yet, when one attempts to prophesize the decade of the 1980s, as I have done in various articles not included in this volume, the batting average slips. On balance, I feel fortunate with the general way the real estate markets have gone as compared to my predictions. Yes, a .300 batting average is not so bad after all!

Finally, the development of a sense of perspective over time is extremely helpful in one's business career. My clients have forced me to become more contemplative about the true meaning of real estate history for its effect on both the present and future market conditions. In "Trends in American Real Estate," I have attempted to trace the major general economic and real estate events since 1965 and to characterize the evolving nature of the real estate industry. The changes over time have indeed been profound. External factors such as highly increased financial volatility, secular increases in inflation and interest rates, and employment and income trends seem to be more important to real estate than our own industry indicators. There has been a deep lesson for me in gaining an historical perspective. It somehow eases the constant problem of understanding current events and forecasting the course of future events.

22
Changes in the Equity
Real Estate Market

Some sweeping changes have transpired in the equity sector of the real estate market. In the early postwar era, traditional forms of equity capital were operating. These consisted of wealthy, long-term investing families; the real estate operator and dealer; the private syndicate composed of several well-to-do people; the small investor influenced by brick and mortar; and the builder, operating on mortgage credit and subcontractor's credit.

In the ensuing years, the market became too large for this group. Private syndicates became successively larger. Institutions such as life insurance companies became more active in equity investment.

Public syndication started in 1954 when Lawrence Wien & Associates successfully syndicated the Equitable Building at 120 Broadway, New York. The proliferation in public syndication thereafter was incredible. Growth was so rapid and success so easy that careless practices inevitably resulted. For one, price was seemingly no major concern since the public would in any event pay more. Representations on rents and operating expenses were poorly presented, underestimated, or omitted. By 1960, many syndicators were moving into the

Reprinted from *The Appraisal Journal* (October 1964): 576-78.

public real estate field through an exchange of syndicate units for stock. The motivations were expansion through a smaller unit represented by the stock share; liquidity that was lacking in syndication; and a chance for promotional profits through warrants, tax options, and different classes of stock.

In 1961, the Investment Trust Act was passed, which permits real estate trusts meeting certain rigid requirements to be free of income tax and instead passes as a conduit to the individual shareholders any tax based on their personal income.

The stock market decline of May 1962 exposed many of the public real estate corporations (especially those of syndicate origin) as far weaker than their representations. The trusts, on the other hand, escaped relatively unscathed since the public had greater confidence in the investment policies of trust managers and in the more restrictive regulations growing out of the legislation. The small investor's confidence in the real estate market was badly shaken in 1962-1963. This lack of confidence was not followed by any discernible price declines.

Today's Market

Despite the drying up of public dollars as a source for equity financing (there have been no flotations of any significance of real estate issues since May 1962), the prices of desirable, well-located properties continue at the same general level. Substantial declines in property values have occurred in small properties (walk-up apartments and neighborhood stores), but these were not the type the syndicates and corporations have been buying. Many real estate trusts have found to their dismay that the syndicate's and corporation's revelations and scandals have not brought any downward pressure on prices.

Two recent developments have brought money into the equity market to counterbalance the withdrawal of funds and the inability to raise equity money publicly. First, there is a significant amount of institutional sponsorship of construction of office buildings, principally by commercial banks and insurance companies. Second, many prominent corporations, such as Reynolds Metal, Alcoa, and General Electric, are investing in large-scale urban renewal and other projects to demonstrate their products and to diversify their activities. This has had a stabilizing effect on the sufficiency of equity capital.

We are, nevertheless, inclined to view that in the future, unless additional noninstitutional and noncorporate money is available for venture capital in new construction or in the purchase of existing buildings, this static or diminishing investment demand must ultimately evoke lower investment prices. Much depends on the disposition of owners to sell. Sales activity in New York in 1963 was at a low ebb and showed a declining trend. Similar conditions were reported throughout the country. The primary reason for this has been the lack of a better alternative investment opportunity.

Nevertheless, an increase in the number of property offerings is expected. Many owners and builders who elected to take accelerated depreciation will shortly find themselves running out of the tax shelter they treasure so dearly. In addition, they are finally beginning to perceive that the market has "topped out." As vacancies mount and operating costs rise, rents are not rising sufficiently to cover. Inevitably, some price declines can be anticipated if a declining demand is matched against an increasing supply of investment offerings. The curious factor is that at the moment, we do not see any real change in the equity earnings-price ratio or equity rate of return. Equity yields on good investment real estate are moving within a very narrow range, principally from 7% to 9%. As mortgage debt service has moved downward both in interest and amortization, there has been a corresponding reduction in overall rates of return on a free and clear basis, with equity returns stable.

Much has been said lately concerning the decline in the quality of mortgage credit as a result of relative oversupply of money. The deterioration may manifest itself in four basic ways. First, lenders tend to compromise their principles on the importance of location and consider applications in areas heretofore classified as undesirable. Second, they may be tempted to grant full loans and in many cases justify them with inflated property valuations. Third, they may liberalize amortization payments by extending self-liquidation periods to 30 years on investment property. Another current practice is to waive amortization on new construction for dangerously long periods, say up to five years. Fourth, they become embroiled in an interest rate as a means of getting applications.

Maintaining Equilibrium

The intensification of real estate competition has provoked a need for better real estate market analysis. Heretofore, any reasonably designed and located property could be rented. As the market has attained equilibrium, the question of its capacity to absorb additional units is coming under closer scrutiny. Frankly, the question of marketability in new buildings is to me more important than the appraisal itself. We must improve our techniques of calculating the average annual additions to the inventory that a given area can profitably absorb. Today's equity investor is becoming very conscious of this.

The mortgage lender in today's market has a special responsibility to act as a restraining influence on equity capital investors who seem to be eager to continue the mad building pace without sufficient consideration of market conditions. If the pace of new construction is keyed to realistic estimates of demand capacity, a relative equilibrium will be maintained and the market and equity investment will be protected against the demoralizing effects of an oversupply.

Finally, my basic mood is one of confidence and optimism. A buoying factor is our continuing prosperity. Increasing population and rising personal incomes lend a firm support to the market. Economic forecasts are almost uniformly favorable. When a decline eventually occurs, the built-in stabilizers in our economy and our improved ability in the management of money and credit should act to keep the decline at relatively shallow levels. The various real estate markets can, nevertheless, be affected by recessionary episodes. The best protection against a decline in rents and values that would follow a national recession is a market that is not currently oversupplied, that is, where vacancies currently are not over 5% in the standard type of accommodations.

23
Improving the Quality
of Feasibility Studies

The real estate recession, which appeared dramatically along with the energy crisis in the fourth quarter of 1973, has now been in existence for almost three years and only recently has shown signs of recovery. The tragedy of these years has been expressed in demand retrenchments, bankruptcies, foreclosures, severe capital losses, and the devastation of the real estate investment trust industry. The recession has also brought to light deliberate negligence on the part of many developers, lenders, appraisers, and market analysts. Overfinancing, oversupplying, and overappraising were common. Perhaps the most grievous error in the development planning process was the poor quality of the feasibility study and the use of overly optimistic recommendations to obtain financing that could not be supported. From the vantage point of hindsight, we can now attempt to analyze constructively the methodology used in these studies and suggest how mistakes may be avoided in the future.

Reprinted with permission from *Urban Land,* October 1976, published by the Urban Land Institute, 1090 Vermont Ave. N.W., Washington, D.C. 20005.

What Is Feasibility?

Feasibility is the estimation of the relative profitability of a project arrived at by analyzing the relation between the total development cost and the estimated after-tax net income. The dictionary defines feasibility first as "capable of being done" and second as "capable of being managed, utilized, or dealt with successfully." The second definition is particularly applicable to development planning because it includes the essential ingredients: competence of management, highest land utilization, and success (profits). Frequently the feasibility study is confused with the marketability study. The latter seeks to establish the relative rentability or salability of a project by estimating the rate at which the space will be absorbed by the market over a time period at certain rent or sales levels. The marketability study does not involve consideration of development costs or profitability.

In addition, the feasibility study usually requires the analyst to make suggestions for the improvement of an already devised land use master plan. If such a plan has not yet been physically drawn, the analyst must then decide what the best site utilization would be and recommend an investment land use plan that will set forth the various types of land use, the general location of the uses, the density, the number of units, the coverage or floor area ratio, the parking requirements, the quality and probable cost of the improvements, the utilities, the direct and indirect development costs, and the rent levels or sales price. The investment land use plan is not in any sense a physical site plan. Instead, it represents the investment assumptions by which feasibility is tested. In many instances, land use assumptions are changed because it was determined after analysis that the plan was unprofitable. When a final investment land use plan is decided, it can then be translated into an illustrative physical site plan by a planner or architect.

When no formal plan exists, the developer will usually order a land use and market study (LUMS), which would ordinarily exclude from the scope of services any consideration of development cost. If, however, feasibility is also a requirement, the study should be labeled land use, marketability, and investment feasibility study (LUMIFS) to minimize any confusion over the basic aims. The larger the project the greater the need for a LUMS or LUMIFS. Both studies are an indispensable internal need for development planning and implementation purposes, and they are also used under proper circumstances for mortgage or equity financing.

What Went Wrong with Feasibility Studies?

In retrospect, it is now possible to pinpoint the mistakes made by market analysts, developers, and mortgagees in their treatment of feasibility studies. The blame rests equally on the developer, the mortgagee, and the analyst. The developer treated these studies as a necessary evil required for financing purposes and expected the analyst to deliver the most optimistic forecast possible. The mortgagee did not have the available staff to analyze the feasibility report properly and decide its credibility. The analyst assumed that he had been engaged to support the developer's concepts and often considered himself an advocate rather than an independent observer of the market scene.

It is only fair and reasonable to admit that no one foresaw the depth, the extent, or the duration of the 1974-1976 real estate recession. Thus it is inappropriate to criticize feasibility reports because they too did not foresee the recession. On the other hand, the real estate market had been on a constant upswing since the summer of 1966. Although occasionally set back by tight money and by the very shallow recession of 1970-1971, the market was generally characterized by a boom psychology—a conviction that inflation was a deeply entrenched way of life and that costs would inevitably continue to rise, that growth in population, disposable personal income, and employment was inevitable, and that land development could be calculated solely on a cost basis. These convictions fostered the belief that it mattered little what it cost to produce a commodity. One only had to multiply one's costs by the desired after-tax rate of return and the gullible, money-laden, product-short consumer would readily pay the price. Unsophisticated appraisers and market analysts were particularly misled and became devotees of the philosophy of unlimited demand. No one in the development community had an adequate understanding of market phenomenon.

There are 10 principal reasons for the prevalence of inadequate feasibility studies. These reasons are developed and illustrated below, along with suggestions for constructive remedies.

Faulty or Inadequate Instructions to the Market Analyst

In many instances, the client did not spell out clearly to the consultant the precise nature of the required study. Marketability and feasibility were occasionally confused. The consultant was equally to blame for not eliciting more precise instructions or for not challenging the client's proposed scope of services. For example, often the developer would have a preconceived land use plan and would not want the consultant to suggest any changes. Some consultants bowed to this pressure and refrained from suggesting modifications that might have improved the plan.

Increased independence on the part of the analyst is strongly in the project's favor and the practice of subtly attempting to influence the consultant's findings and recommendations should be dispensed with. A few developers sought to persuade the consultant to present rent or sale levels, absorption, and profitability in their most optimistic light, thus enhancing the financing prospects. The resulting studies were sometimes cynically referred to as opportunity studies rather than objective analyses of profit probabilities.

Essential to the feasibility study is an understanding of the developer's risk and his profit objectives. How much risk is he willing to undertake to obtain larger rewards? What are his profit objectives? What after-tax rate of return does he seek? These goals should be precisely defined at the outset of the report in order to make the findings and recommendations more precise.

Failure to Show a Range of Probable Results

The analyst invariably provided only one projection of revenue, net income, absorption, and profitability, a projection that tended to produce the most optimistic result rather than the most probable because the analyst rarely introduced a conservative estimate. It certainly makes good sense to insist that all reports present at least the highest and lowest range of profitability and state the rationale behind each projection. Sometimes a mid-range figure is indicated, especially if it is not a mean average of the extremes.

Mortgagees, particularly, should insist on a range of probable results. While it doesn't solve completely the problem of the developer coaching the consultant, it does minimize the problem and gives the lender a better grasp of the probabilities and protects him against extending financing on an insupportable basis.

Overstatement of Growth Projections

A growth cult arose in the past decade that believed that growth was inevitable and that nothing stabilized or declined. Chronic optimism was voiced in population, disposable personal income, and employment projections as qualitative demand factors. It must have been quite a shock to this growth cult to see that 1974's disposable real personal income actually declined 2.7% on an adjusted basis.

The real estate market analyst must be more aware of the effect of regional and national economics on local demand. Did the consultant foresee the effects of significant national events on growth? To illustrate, the impact of the energy shortage's creation of a severe real estate demand retrenchment was not widely anticipated nor sufficiently appreciated until the event was upon us. The analyst must also improve his capacity to analyze the local economic base for its effect on real estate demand. He can no longer accept local chamber of commerce figures or similar projections; the meaning of the statistics and the validity of the estimates must be known to him.

Overallocation of the Real Estate Market to the Project

Together with the problems of growth and chronic optimism was the tendency of the market analyst to ascribe too large a share of the total market to the project. Understandably, the consultant felt that systematic land use planning and a carefully controlled environment would attract a disproportionate share of the market. In most cases, this has not proved to be true.

In retrospect, the analyst underestimated the draw of smaller, equally attractive developments and the pull of other geographical areas. Many families will compromise on their housing environment in order to stay within a certain limited physical section where their friends and relatives live. He also learned that many households resist the highly structured, totally planned homogeneous environment of the master plan community, favoring instead a smaller scale and a more spontaneous feeling. Very few projects—even the best—can attract more than 5% of the market. A 7% draw would be considered exceptional.

Insufficient Use of Microeconomics

The developer must, for the most part, accept responsibility for feasibility reports that do not accurately or completely treat market tastes and preferences. Developers historically have been reluctant to pay for the detailed market questionnaires that are often essential to a determination of what the public wants in houses, stores, or offices. A supportable view of the profitability of a project cannot be achieved solely by a macroeconomic approach that depends on statistical market data.

To illustrate, the Charles N. Goodman-designed attractive modern cluster homes in Reston, Virginia, initially sold poorly. These houses were more an expression of developer Robert Simon's personal taste in architecture and design than the public's tastes. The houses were ahead of the times; a well-designed questionnaire to a representative segment of the public might have so indicated. Developers must know more about the public's tastes in housing styles, finishing materials, layout, size, equipment, amenities, and landscaping. Marketing errors that deprive projects of maximum profitability can be avoided, and the costs are miniscule when one considers the benefits.

Developers, however, should not be too wary of innovation. Carefully planned new products, provided they are premarket tested, can be well received, and they offer the developer at least a temporary advantage over his competition. The good feasibility study will be a skillful blend of statistical data, secondary source market evidence, and the human aspects of marketing as reflected in the public's tastes and preferences.

Overappraisal of Land Values

Over the past decade, many developers of master plan communities have paid too much per acre for land, and the burden of excessive carrying charges has deprived most projects of reasonable profitability. Because of the relatively high initial land cost, the developer has not been able to withstand the demand retrenchment which has deflated his sales volume over the past three years. Frankly, land should be written down in many existing projects. Land prices for raw acreage are a casualty of the times. Growing evidence indicates that prices will have to decline even further before developers are attracted to additional purchases. When they do reenter the market, it will probably be on an option series basis in order to avoid excess carrying charges. Because of the weak land market, sellers will have no other alternative than to grant options.

Some appraisers have ascribed too much appreciation to the remaining undeveloped land after the completion of the initial phase of development. A developer is far from making a profit after his initial infrastructure is in place and some sales have occurred, and it is usually premature to assume that his contiguous land is worth far more money. If the value of the appreciated land is used as a basis for increasing financing, an insupportable debt burden is encouraged.

As an example, a Florida appraiser in a large-scale primary home development used a development approach in valuing the land. He calculated sales revenue, subtracted all direct and indirect development costs, and derived an annual net income over a presumed absorption period of 10 years. He next assumed that the land sales would increase 10% annually and would cancel out the discounting of the future receivable income. The result was an indefensibly high valuation on which a major insurance company made an inflated loan. This type of appraising is misleading and does a disservice to the developer and the financial institution.

Failure to Retain a Consultant on a Continuing Basis

The larger the project and the greater the variety of uses, the more urgent it is to have the market analyst periodically update his original study. The usual practice of the developer forgetting his consultant once the crucial study has been completed and the financing arranged is a mistake. Since most large-scale developments represent a 1- to 10-year commitment, the developer must of necessity review annually what he has accomplished and what changes have occurred in the national and local real estate markets. A good market analyst will not depend exclusively on comparison shopping techniques to decide what the public wants, but he will devise questionnaire forms for every purchaser or tenant so that more can be learned about the character of demand. Another invaluable source of planning information is the developer's own sales and rental figures.

Overscaling the Plan in Relation to Market Area

This is a problem that inevitably flows from overstating growth and overallocating the market to the large-scale community development. For example, overscaling caused the development of two very large master plan communities in a metropolitan area the size of Rochester or Syracuse and produced plans for a large-scale community in a metropolitan area of such small size that it would have required 25% of the market to be profitable. No amount of marketing ingenuity will allow overscaled projects to succeed. All are doomed with their current capitalization and must be formally recapitalized through bankruptcy or mortgagee foreclosure or both, or by the willingness of mortgagees to alter drastically debt service terms. A good rule to follow is to be assured that a large-scale community can yield a fair after-tax return with no more than 5% of the total market—if a higher allocation is required, trouble is being courted. The only exceptions to the 5% rule are instances in which the developer is able to attract industry or commerce, thus enlarging his market through increased population.

Overrigidity of the Land Use Plan

In the mutual zeal of the developer, the market analyst, the city planner, and the architect to create a finely honed land use plan, the plan itself may become so rigid in design that it becomes difficult and time-consuming to effect any changes. Even the most artfully conceived plan can be improved in the implementation stage. Changing market conditions over an extended period or pronounced shifts in public tastes may cause the need for plan changes, and when the developer starts to sell retail parcels subject to the plan, he frequently finds that local builders may have different ideas about land use.

The original master plan for the Stamford, Connecticut, urban renewal project provided for low-density industrial uses contiguous to I-95. During the usual urban renewal delays, a demand shift to medium-density office development occurred, arising from corporate relocations from New York. It was then necessary to obtain both federal and local consent to the plan changes, a time-consuming process. Fortunately, in this case, it was a desirable change for the city and no undue problems were encountered, but this can never be assumed.

There are, of course, limitations on the extent to which the developer can build flexibility and latitude into a master plan. Obviously, a change from low to high density or a radical use change will require local planning and zoning approval. To the extent that alternate uses can be built into the plan, the added flexibility will sharply enhance salability for the local builder and avoid an undue extension of permit time with all its associated adverse effects or indirect development costs.

Poor Sequencing and Underestimation of Infrastructure Costs

It is doubtful that there are more than three large-scale communities in the United States that are providing a reasonable after-tax discounted rate of return. One of the major contributors to this disappointing performance has been the disposition to build too extensive a portion of the infrastructure too quickly. Frequently these nonessential up-front costs have been out of proportion to project marketability requirements. This tendency has been particularly evident with recreational facilities. Except in resort communities, the golf course heads the list as a nonessential up-front cost, and all the other amenities should be scaled down or phased better. For example, fewer swimming pools of greater size should be built.

The cost of utility systems has been staggering, especially when heavy off-site costs are mandated, and the problem has been compounded by the installation of roads and utilities long before any demonstrable demand for the land.

Although not directly relevant to this discussion, it must be observed that even with the most economical infrastructure, it is difficult or impossible to obtain a decent after-tax discounted return. The market analyst and the appraiser must recognize and understand the problem of infrastructure costs and take these into consideration in their feasibility studies and valuations, because the infrastructure problem adversely affects the rate of return and land values.

Implementing Feasibility Improvement

The mortgage lender is the key figure in improving the quality of feasibility studies. When a study is required for financing purposes, the lender should select the market analyst, approve the scope of services, and, in some instances, actually order the study directly rather than through the developer. He must insist on a range of results rather than only the most optimistic result, and the lender should force expanded studies where the magnitude of the large-scale community or the nature of the market problems requires it. The lender should also train personnel to review carefully the completed studies to ensure the underwriting process.

The market analyst, in addition to profiting from the deficiencies in feasibility studies previously discussed, must rebuild his staff to include professionals with backgrounds in other than macroeconomics. The well-rounded staff of the future will include marketing specialists, appraisers, cost estimators, financing specialists, and possibly persons with project operational experience. A staff with a skillful blend of these backgrounds will minimize the prospect of gross error and avoid theoretical or impractical findings and recommendations.

The market analyst must retain a distinct position of independence, and he should be neither an advocate nor an apologist for the developer. He must have a professional sense of objectivity and detachment and must resist being coached by the client. This is not to say that the market analyst should effect an arbitrary or capricious attitude; he can be open and receptive to the developer's thinking on land use or even on market considerations. The analyst accepts the developer's observations and conclusions along with other evidence and then arrives at his own professional conclusions.

An absolute necessity even for smaller projects is the inclusion of a sensitivity analysis in the feasibility study. Sensitivity analyses (either computer based or manually based) may be defined as the changing of the variables, namely, the different revenue or expense items, in order to determine the effects of the change on the probable discounted or nondiscounted rate of return. Some computer programs that provide for discounted internal rate of return analyses lack sufficient flexibility to offer the most advanced type of sensitivity study. Quite aside from the technical programming requirements, the variables in the analysis of a large-scale development are so infinite that only the computer can effectively demonstrate all the implications of any changes. In a recent case involving a $75 million urban development, the computer provided such surprising conclusions that, as a result, a radical change in site utilization and marketing was undertaken.

Finally, the developer must recognize the feasibility study as a critical tool for his internal planning purposes and not as something he must endure because a lender insisted on it. He must work closely with the market analyst in achieving the best possible site utilization, but at the same time he must respect the market analyst's professional independence. The developer must understand how important the market analyst's contributions to his profitability can be.

24

Why Real Estate Is Overpriced

Two developments during the past five years have unwittingly conspired to produce what may become an unattractive climate for investment in prime, existing, income-producing real estate. They are the increasing availability of institutional equity financing and mortgage lenders' heightened awareness of inflationary expectations.

The entry of large U.S. pension funds into the equity market, together with the growing disposition of the life insurance companies to invest in real estate equities, have resulted in substantially higher real estate prices. To ensure the stability of their investments, these institutions have been buying properties that have proven records of performance and no problems of deterioration or obsolescence.

Much publicity has been given to the activities of foreign pension funds in U.S. real estate. While their objectives are substantial, the actual dollar volume of foreign investments has only been a fraction of domestic investment.

Reprinted with permission from *The Real Estate Review* 7(3), Fall 1977. Copyright ©1977, Warren, Gorham & Lamont, Inc., 210 South Street, Boston, Mass. All rights reserved.

The American institutions are creating the high prices, and the foreign buyers cannot be blamed for the current low rates of return on investment real estate.

Rising prices resulting from the flood of institutional money vying for the desirable properties have driven down so-called cash on cash rates of return (before subtraction for mortgage debt) to the 8.5% to 9% level. Pension funds tend to buy free of any mortgage to avoid paying income taxes under the unrelated business income tax provisions of the Tax Reform Act of 1969. Since their income is tax-free and their properties are mortgage-free, they can live with a relatively low cash return far more easily than can traditional buyers.

Real Estate Investment Has Become Less Attractive

It is the typical noninstitutional buyer who feels the most disadvantaged in the current market atmosphere. Wealthy individuals and syndicates customarily have relied on mortgage financing to enable them to purchase large properties. They could tolerate initial low returns if mortgage money was available at correspondingly lower rates. Unfortunately, this is not the case at present. Despite an ample supply of mortgage money, interest rates have declined only modestly from their 1976 peaks, and most forecasters expect that rates will rise during the latter half of 1977.

The lender has grown so wary of inflation that he will not lend for extended periods at low interest rates. His expectation of renewed inflation requires him to charge a higher interest rate that compensates for anticipated inflation. As a result, the combination of interest and amortization on a mortgage loan (the debt service constant) at present is higher (about 10.5%), than the overall rate of return (about 9%). The consequences are illustrated in the following example:

Net income, before debt service	$ 9,000
Purchase price at a 9% return	100,000
Obtainable mortgage	75,000
Cash equity	25,000
Debt service on mortgage at 10.5%	7,875
Equity income ($9,000 − $7,875)	1,125
Return on equity ($1,125 ÷ $25,000)	4.5%

This illustrates the advent of negative leveraging, that is, of a mortgage debt service that is higher than the overall rate of return. Negative leveraging is causing many investors to withdraw from the real estate market or, at least, to defer acquisitions. Even when the return is partially or fully tax sheltered in the early years, investors question the wisdom of purchases showing such low return. Alternatives such as tax-free bonds, stocks with capital gain potential, and private purchase of small businesses are looking more attractive these days to the real estate investor.

A Shift to New Real Estate Development

The traditional equity investor is increasingly uncomfortable with negative leveraging. Even the large institutions privately express concern over high real estate prices. Because of discouragement over low returns, it is probable that a portion of the institutional funds will shift into the so-called development properties. In the admittedly riskier field of new construction, there should be perhaps a 200 basis point (2%) improvement in the rate of return.

The probable shift to new development coincides with the emerging real estate recovery. The resumption of a full volume of real estate development activity in 1978 should follow the transitional year of 1977. As more money is diverted to new construction, there may be an easing in the prices of existing real estate. The equity rate of return on existing properties may improve to a sufficient degree that positive leveraging may once again be a reasonable expectation.

Techniques for Reducing the Risks

Both large and small investors can reduce the risks in development investment by insisting on preferred rates of return. The accepted financial technique for doing this is by means of convertible second-mortgage loans, convertible cumulative preferred stock, or other methods of establishing a prior claim against the equity income. Developers will need equity capital to finance the expected expansion since mortgagees are enforcing much more stringent mortgage underwriting requirements. Giving investors a preferred return is an ideal way to raise the required capital while ensuring at least a residual return for the developer as a reward for his entrepreneurship.

Market Changes Ahead

When owners of existing properties realize that investors are shifting either into non-real-estate investments or into development investments because of low, negatively leveraged rates of return, then prices of existing properties will decline. In the interim, the market is in for a profound change as investors begin to avoid overpriced real estate.

25
How Manhattan's Fiscal Problems Have Affected the Office Market

The Prior Boom

The five-year period from 1966 through 1970 witnessed the most intensive, hyperactive office market boom in Manhattan's history. Manhattan's office market was profoundly influenced by the strong national inflation that commenced in the mid-1960s, primarily because of the Johnson administration's unwillingness to finance the Vietnamese War on a more current, conservative basis. In retrospect, the boom was an impressive performance. Absorption of space was at an abnormally high level. Some 28 million square feet were rented between 1966 and 1970, an average of 7.6 million square feet annually, while only 32 million square feet were being completed. Rents rose 50% to the $12- to $14-per-square-foot level. Vacancies were virtually nonexistent. Land values in prime locations such as Park Avenue more than doubled from $300 per square foot to $700 per square foot.

Reprinted with permission from *Real Estate Issues* 2(2), Winter 1977, published by the American Society of Real Estate Counselors of the National Association of Realtors®.

Corporate relocations to the suburbs and elsewhere were lightly regarded and frequently dismissed. The Borden Company, for example, moved its corporate headquarters to Columbus, Ohio. Its Manhattan building was then sold to Condé Nast for $100 per square foot, reportedly the highest price ever paid for a 40-year-old office building. What matter that Pepsico, Continental Oil, American Can, Johns Manville, General Telephone & Electronic, and others had left or planned to leave in this same five years? Internal growth was considered to be so strong that Manhattan could not be affected. Indeed, the office market paid little heed to the rather shallow recession of 1969-1970 even though industrial and other blue collar and service employment declined sharply at the time, presaging a deterioration in local economic conditions. Planning and construction of new office buildings continued in the face of warning signals.

Rising Concern over City Spending

In retrospect, the wildly inflationary boom of the late 1960s masked some disturbing economic and political facts. During this time, New York was sowing the seeds of its own near destruction. Starting with the transit strike on the very first day of the Lindsay administration, the city thereafter appeared to capitulate to strong union demands for wage increases and improved fringe benefits by permitting raises possibly beyond its financial capacity. After all, with assessed valuations in Manhattan increasing $2.4 billion in those five years, why should the city be unduly concerned with its ability to afford these increases?

The city's position was further complicated by the costs associated with the in-migration over many years of culturally and educationally deprived blacks and Hispanics. This forced the essential expansion of programs in welfare, education, and job training. There were also significant related increases in police, fire, sanitation, and other service costs. Taxpayer and business groups became increasingly restless and concerned over what they felt were excessive and poorly structured debt issues to finance these costs. Debatable accounting practices further undermined the confidence of the business community in the city. If prosperity had continued unabated, it might have been possible to carry this financial burden. Events rapidly proved otherwise. While the office market was seemingly riding out the recession of 1969-1970, nonwhite collar job losses were severe. As it subsequently turned out, New York never fully recovered from the 1969-1970 recessionary effects. Coupled with a sharp ensuing retrenchment in office demand and a staggering oversupply, the city moved closer to its own denouement.

A Serious Real Estate Decline

The decline in the real estate market in late 1970 and 1971 was in its own way as unforeseen as the prior five-year boom. It was experienced in diverse ways. Corporate relocation planning intensified. Other companies accommodated their office growth needs simply by decentralizing on a regional and divisional basis. Demand for all practical purposes nearly vanished. The burden of ever-increasing taxes of a wide-ranging nature was the principal motivation in the corporate abandonment of Manhattan. It appeared that crime, congestion, educational problems, deficient commuting, and pollution in themselves were not sufficiently strong reasons for commerce to leave New York City in large numbers. These problems were common to all the older major eastern and midwestern cities and were certainly not peculiar to New York. By 1975, only 1,453,000 square feet of new space was rented, a drop of 65.7% from the 1966-1970 five-year average. An unfortunate complication that further weakened the market was the 42 million square feet of space completed in the five-year period after 1971.

Real estate market indicators told the classical story of demand retrenchment and oversupply. Rents in prime buildings plummeted from the $12 level to $10 or less. Vacancies reached 33 million square feet in 1974, representing a 14% vacancy. Assemblage activity ceased, except to complete assemblages long since previously started. Building plans were shelved. Assembled plots were broken up. Sales activity declined precipitously. Mortgagees quietly re-evaluated their willingness to make mortgage loans on Manhattan property. The once proud, bellwether commercial real estate market of the world was at almost a standstill in 1974-1975.

The Fate of Land Values

Land values really could only be hypothesized or inferred since there was no direct market evidence in the form of land sales made for the purpose of constructing new office buildings. One factor was clear. It was impossible from 1971 through 1976 to find any signs of land value by using so-called land residual capitalization techniques. Although direct building costs had declined under the pressure of high unemployment in the building trades, indirect or "soft" costs, principally construction loan interest, went to new highs.

A combination of high interest, a low level of obtainable rent, high if not excessive building costs, excessive real estate taxes, and inflationary operating expenses theoretically conspired to deprive land of any value whatsoever. Judgment became a major factor. Some degree of eventual recovery had to be anticipated. It was felt that land had fallen between 50% and 60% in the six years of real estate depression that followed the 1966-1970 boom. Fortunately, Manhattan land was in such strong hands that there was no complete demoralization or actual collapse of the land market. Owners, mainly institutional or developmental, doggedly stayed with their investments and hoped for a cyclical recovery.

Land of course is a residual product. It invariably suffered the consequences of demand cutbacks, loss of confidence, oversupply of space, and erosion of the city's economic base. For example, in early 1974 Landauer Associates, Inc., represented the fee owner in a ground lease arbitration for the land underlying the Chrysler Building. The basis for settlement was a land value of $335 per square foot. In 1977, we again represented the fee owner in a ground lease arbitration for the land under 757 Third Avenue, a tall office tower at East 48th Street. The basis for settlement was $140 per square foot. While this location was not as good as the Chrysler Building site, it was nevertheless a very low land value. By way of comparison, at least four comparable sites within six blocks along Third Avenue had been assembled by 1971 in the $300- to $400-per-square-foot range.

To return to our narrative, the recession of 1974-1975 and the widespread public revelation in 1975 of New York's near bankruptcy dealt a cruel double blow to the office market, to land values, and to the city's fortunes. Job losses continued to mount after 1970 until they reached a high near 600,000 by January 1977. The city's financial crisis further eroded the confidence of the business community. Passage of emergency legislation ensuring greater financial control, debt restructuring, and operating economies, supplemented by state and federal loans, averted the bankruptcy but doubts and fears about the city persisted throughout 1975. It was impossible to see any short-term improvement in our predicament.

Turning of the Tide

The gradual national recovery from the 1974-1975 recession subtly influenced the stirrings of a real estate recovery for Manhattan, beginning in 1976. First, the relocation trend abated sharply; the remaining Fortune 500 companies had compelling reasons to stay in New York. Strong internal growth and mergers were gradually creating newly eligible Fortune 500 companies. The corporate advanced services sector, the wide-ranging support services represented by banking, law, accounting, architecture, real estate, public relations, advertising, and other services, was already three times the size of the basic corporate office sector in number of personnel and was growing rapidly in response to national calls for its services. Vacancies in Manhattan by 1976 declined by 10 million to 23 million square feet, or 10% of the total inventory. Rents in prime locations were rising modestly. Suddenly it became apparent that there were no large blocks of space available for very large tenants, except in the historically troubled 1166 Avenue of the Americas Building.

Development activity is about to resume as investors react positively to the recovery signs. For example, Harry Helmsley is scheduled to start construction on the Palace Hotel and residential condominium this fall. The Fisher Brothers-Prudential joint venture is seriously examining the start of an office building west of the Racquet and Tennis Club off Park Avenue. Citicorp has been successful in obtaining $16 per square foot rents in their new 50-story office tower on Lexington Avenue. It is evident that six years of recession are over. The upturn has commenced.

What about the City's Fortunes?

New York's fiscal problems are beginning to come under strong control; a break-even budget has become a realistic prospect despite yet-to-be solved questions about substantial overassessment, widespread tax delinquencies, debt restructuring, and wage increase pressure. Perhaps the most significant and encouraging event has been the closer alignment of the business community with the city. The skills and competence of business management have been used by the city to reorganize its accounting and computer operations. The city has also recognized the importance of retaining industry and commerce by passing various tax abatement statutes designed to induce industry and people to remain. It has also pledged to reduce or eliminate the notorious stock transfer and tenant occupancy taxes which had become symbols of the city's inability to plan and implement a reasonable fiscal program. The present administration has even promised if elected to refrain from increasing the real estate tax rate for four years!

Employment is stabilizing for the first time in seven years. This has been accomplished in the face of severe declines in government employment necessitated by operating economies. Internal employment expansion is beginning to exceed the loss in jobs arising from the decentralization process. Manhattan's population is also expected to stabilize. Youth particularly welcomes the challenges of the city. The major problem of attracting families with children unfortunately remains.

The traditional mix of office tenancy is also changing. For example, five years ago, there were 21 foreign banks licensed in New York. Today there are 117. It is widely recognized that New York is replacing London as the premier international banking center. The foreign multinational corporations invariably have offices in New York and are increasing them at a rapid rate. Currently, over 10% of the space in the Pan Am building is leased to foreign tenants. Heretofore little understood is the fact that corporate relocatees to the suburbs or elsewhere continued to depend on New York companies for their banking, legal, real estate, accounting, engineering, advertising, and other services, thus minimizing the shock impact of office decentralization.

The biggest factor is and will continue to be the restoration of confidence in the political process by the business community. Strong cities uniformly are characterized by a close and respectful relationship between the business and political leadership—witness Chicago, Atlanta, Houston, and Dallas. There is every reason to believe that a closer bond is being forged; it has been amply evident in the mayor's recent key appointments to high positions, in the willingness of business executives to serve, in the state's more extensive involvement in the city's affairs, and in the achievement of a prudent operating budget.

What about the Future for Land?

Although we have been unable to draw any precise mathematical correlation, events of the past seven years conclusively indicated that New York City's fiscal mismanagement contributed heavily to but was by no means the sole reason for the decline in Manhattan real estate land values. Overspending is a pervasive force that finds expression in many ways. Certainly, to the extent that the city lived beyond its means, it has resulted in unnecessarily harsh and regressive taxes, ranging from real estate taxes approaching 30% of gross revenues to city income taxes, occupancy taxes, stock transfer taxes, industrial equipment taxes, franchise taxes, and others. Many in the business community made the judgment that these taxes could no longer be tolerated and that sound alternatives to New York existed where lifestyles could be improved while after-tax income could be increased. A mood of despair and disillusionment with the city prevailed from 1970 through 1975. No amount of jaw-boning by the city's Economic Development Administration could deter many companies from leaving. Many decided the deterioration in the city's affairs was irreversible and that relocation was the sensible solution rather than to stand and fight for prudent fiscal policies.

In the forefront was the abandonment of the city by those companies who sought sylvan suburban retreats while still relying heavily if not exclusively on critical business support services available only in the city, and on the city's cultural, educational, and amusement facilities. Problems typical of all major urban cities such as crime, pollution, education deficiencies, congestion, and high living costs also strongly motivated companies and families to move. Employers complained about the difficulty of inducing rising young executives with families to relocate to New York. With increased leisure time the word *lifestyle* caught on to express the desire of many to live in a smaller, less complicated, and less intensely populated environment, remote from the seamy aspects of urban living found in street crime, drugs, poverty, and prostitution.

Purely as an informed judgment and entirely without pretense as a precisely articulated answer, it appears that overspending not only was the root cause of office relocation, but probably was more than 50% responsible for the loss of the large executive headquarters companies. It must in all fairness be pointed out that the federal government failed to assume enough of the extraordinary welfare and other costs characteristic of New York. Relocation had been occurring since the early 1950s, when General Foods moved to White Plains, New York, and Time and Life and General Electric purchased large tracts in Westchester County in anticipation of doing so. Thus, there were obviously other forces at work to influence decisions to leave New York. Even in earlier times, however, the question of what the business leadership considered to be excessive taxes played some role in shaping corporate relocation decisions. What probably happened is that taxes assumed constantly higher importance as the major reason as the years went by.

At the peak in 1970, assemblage land costs of $400-$500 per square foot were commonplace. Individual key parcels were sold by the Landauer firm for as much as $700 to $1,000 per square foot in order to round out assemblages. It is really difficult to foresee a return to these price levels, at least not for an extended period of time. After all, it took 40 years (from 1930 to 1970) for land prices to begin to recover from the stunning effects of the decade-long depression of the 1930s. Despite increased inflationary pressures, land prices expressed in nominal or so-called inflated dollars will tend to remain lower and lag behind the recovery in rents and occupancy.

This is not to say that nominal land prices will not increase moderately in the next several years. Invariably, they will respond to market forces and an increased level of activity. However, the wild prices paid to obtain possession from tenants with leases and the excessive prices for key parcels will not be quickly seen again. Assuming constant rather than inflated dollars, it is entirely possible that there will be no real increase in land prices within the foreseeable future. In fact, a decline in constant prices is equally likely. Excessive land costs would serve only to drive office space users out of New York because of the higher rents that would have to be charged. In order to continue its progress towards recovery, New York must remain competitive with the suburbs, if not with other sections of the country.

The Future for New York

New York in the 1980s will have a smaller employment base than the 1969 peak. A significant reduction is foreseen in the total inventory of office space from a high of 230 million square feet down to a low of 200-210 million square feet. Much of this reduction will be accompanied by conversion of marginally located office buildings to residential and other uses or by demolition. An innate stability should characterize the 1980s; internal office growth and in-migration together will be equal to or slightly exceed a sharply diminished but always-occurring office and industrial decentralization.

There is nothing catastrophic about the prospects of continuing decentralization. Modern production technology and distribution requirements compel many manufacturers to relocate to outlying areas. There is no denying that all major cities have lost part of their office dominance as well. Improvements in telecommunications, interstate highways, and other technologies have deprived major cities of a part of their raison d'etre, that is, the need to cluster together for ease of personal communication. Personal interaction and relationships are simply not as important as in the past. The agglomeration phenomenon no longer underpins the major cities.

Yet there is convincing evidence that a good proportion of headquarters companies and, more importantly, the advanced corporate service companies that support them still prefer to remain in the central city where the advantages of agglomeration still remain, to say nothing of the advantages of and convenience to cultural activities and sports events, private clubs, restaurants, and friends.

Under these mixed circumstances, in which there have been expressed significantly different views of the viability of central city areas, land values logically have undergone a recapitalization to significantly lower levels. If wise market heads prevail, city land values will be reconstituted as a smaller component of development costs. This will enable the major cities such as New York to compete more effectively with the suburbs and with smaller cities for the favor of office space users.

26
American Real Estate Remains an Attractive Investment

The continuing high cost and relative scarcity of long-term mortgage money is the single most important factor in analyzing the present and prospective real estate market. There are many advantages to the institutional real estate investor in a tight and costly money situation. Just as record interest rates diminish development resolve, the existing inventory of property benefits was accumulated during less competitive conditions. Further, some of the best purchase opportunities exist when the institutional investor can pay all cash in a capital-short market. At the moment, and with some exceptions, there is simply insufficient competition in the real estate market. Rents have risen steadily and, in some cases, spectacularly, while vacancies have been reduced to the vanishing point in such major centers as New York, Boston, Los Angeles, and Washington. The owner of a well-located, modern property is in a unique position, and will be at least for the next three to four years because no general oversupply is expected.

Reprinted from *The Appraisal Journal* (October 1981): 485-93.

Evolving Trends

What are the evolving trends in the American market today? There is a grow-ing number of joint-venture development transactions between the strong na-tional and regional developers and the major life insurance companies. The life insurance companies, anxious in an inflation-plagued economy to increase their rate of earnings on investment portfolios, are eagerly seeking combina-tion mortgage and equity development deals. Their reasoning is that the rate of return will be substantially higher than the best mortgage rate over the same time frame. It is felt, generally, that yields on development investments are running about 200-300 basis points higher than one can reasonably expect from a comparable existing property. This is a strong inducement to many in-stitutional investors and will be a contributing factor to the possibility of an oversupply in the mid-1980s, as will be discussed subsequently.

Another interesting trend is the increase in the number of offerings of property for sale. Probably as a result of the Pan Am Building sale for $400 million, many owners have been attracted to selling. The American investor sees this moment as a good time to sell, while appreciating that the peak may not yet be in sight. The investor sees the market as being in equilibrium at the same time that inflation consciousness is still running high. Indeed, prices paid per square foot for offices and shopping centers are at a record high. In the office building field, the Seagram's Building sold in 1978 for $160 per square foot. In 1980, the Pan Am Building sold for $178 per square foot. Offerings today in central city areas have increased to $200 per square foot and more, compared with development costs for new buildings of $250 per square foot, inclusive of land.

Accompanying the increase in the number of offerings and prices has been an increase in recent years in the size of offerings. For example, large blocks of shopping centers have been sold by the Dayton Hudson Company, a major department store chain, and Monumental Properties Trust for literally hundreds of millions of dollars. In addition to the Pan Am sale, the renowned General Motors Building in New York is being offered for sale, reportedly in the $500 million range. The mammoth World Trade Center may soon be of-fered for $1.6 billion or more. The large-scale properties consistently have been bought by American institutional investors. The properties are too large for the majority of European life insurance companies, pension funds, mer-chant banks, and public investment companies.

The European institutional investor has been slow to form major consor-tiums for the purpose of large-scale American investment. Until they are will-ing to join together, they will be effectively blocked from considering the very large and select properties. Most European institutional investors prefer the direct investment route even though the capital allocation out of total funds may permit them to purchase only smaller and more competitive properties.

This is at distinct variance from the American pension fund viewpoint. Very few American pension funds have made direct purchases for their own account. The overwhelming preference is for open- or closed-end pooled entities. The major life insurance companies, notably Prudential and Equitable, have acted very successfully as investment managers for open-end funds. Of late, Realtor® organizations such as Coldwell Banker & Company and Landauer Associates have begun to compete for the pooled-fund business against the life insurance companies.

Will Discount Rates Rise?

The sustained high cost of mortgage money has raised the question of whether discounted internal rates of return will increase, at least to the presumed extent of the permanent interest rate increase. Until now, as successively higher plateaus of interest rates were reached, the equity investor experienced a corresponding reduction in the equity income component of total yield as the total yield itself tended to remain relatively constant. In other words, the initial so-called cash-on-cash equity rate became smaller and smaller. Real estate investors nevertheless continued to purchase on the theory that a sustained inflation would force significant increases in rents and, hence, in cash flow as leases expired. Even on a discounted basis, the institutional investor reasoned, cash flow would increase to such attractive levels that one could justify paying more and accepting less return at the onset.

Questions have been raised recently of whether or not equity returns are adequate on a discounted basis. The American market appears to be in a testing phase on the question. The outcome in 1981 of the General Motors and possible World Trade Center office building sales, plus other representative, smaller property sales, will provide clarification of whether investors will continue to view inflation as entrenched at a relatively high level. To the extent that inflation is perceived as a continuing plague, equty returns initially may stay low. Perhaps we may take our cue from the British experience, in which the equity investor accepted a lower equity yield with every cyclical rise in interest rates. Apparently at no stage to date has the British investor contested the constant invasion of his equity yield by the higher interest demands of the lender. It will be interesting to learn if the U.S. market will follow the same pattern.

Convertible Mortgages

Another interesting event is the disposition of some lenders to seek convertible mortgages, or mortgages with an option to buy, as a means of improving the discounted internal rate of return. The concept is to make a first or second mortgage loan on which the interest rate may be 200-300 basis points less than the prevailing rate on a straight, intermediate-term mortgage. In return for the lower interest rate, the lender receives the right to convert to, say, a 50% equity interest, or a right for an agreed upon amount to purchase an equity interest subject to its own mortgage. On a discounted basis, the institutional lender's anticipation is that its total yield will exceed the straight interest rate otherwise obtainable on a 10–15-year basis. This is a particularly sage way to consider the purchase of property that is to be developed or that has not reached maturity.

Only time will tell if the lender's judgment in this type of deal will be confirmed. Apparently many lenders are betting on the continuance of inflation at a relatively high rate, say, in excess of 7%. Other lenders, probably in the minority, are opting for 5–10-year mortgages at the highest possible rate but without equity participation. Their rationale is to take current advantage of extremely high rates of 16% or more on prime loans while hedging the future inflation rate by shortening the loan term. This will enable the pure lender to get still higher interest in the intermediate future when the mortgage comes due if conditions so warrant, yet be no worse off than the mortgage-equity investor if inflation moderates to the 4%-5% level and interest rates decline significantly.

Presold Development Deals

Because of low yields on existing properties, we are witnessing a distinct increase in prepackaged and presold development deals. Here, the developer purchases or options land, obtains all necessary zoning and building permits, and preleases to major tenants as much as 50% or more of the space. The institutional investor then issues a written purchase commitment guaranteeing to take title on completion of the construction and occupancy of an agreed percentage of the space. In some cases, the developer will guarantee the rental income for the unleased space, but this is becoming less customary. The developer obtains construction financing on a nonrecourse basis as a result of the purchase commitment and will have little or no cash invested. He or she also receives a fair profit over cost. The institutional purchaser looks for and indeed probably will receive a higher return than for an existing property, at only a slight additional risk. This represents an ideal middle ground between the high prices of existing property and the risk of an outright development deal in which no leasing has been accomplished prior to construction.

Another interesting variant of the previous financing concept is for the lender to make a loan commitment on property to be developed, in which he or she also receives an agreed-upon share interest in the equity. For example, it is possible to obtain a mortgage for 100% of the total hard and soft development costs at an interest rate of 13.5% if the developer is willing to surrender 25% to 33.3% of the equity. Generally, the developer will agree to this because he or she will have little or no capital invested. Needless to say, this type of transaction does not work with marginal development plans. It is reserved for only the finest planned developments.

Sale-Leaseback Credit Deals

The wise American portfolio manager also is seeking a small number of so-called credit deals in which the owner of the property, usually but not always an occupant as well, takes back a long-term net lease with renewal options. Unlike the preinflation days when leases of this type were made at flat rents for 30 years, the new leasebacks provide for some form of graduation in the rent at 5–10-year intervals and at the market on renewals. One such recent sale leaseback was made at 9.5% of the sales price for five years, plus 50% of the intervening increase in the official Consumer Price Index (CPI) adjusted annually for 10 years, plus renewals at the market every 10 years thereafter, plus 50% of the annual increase in the CPI. Depending on the inflation rate, this leaseback should yield at least a 15% discounted return to the buyer.

Best Building Types

What type of real estate represents the current best investment opportunity for the institutional investor? In a forecast of the 1980s made in late 1979, the author suggested a shift in priorities from shopping centers to office buildings as the best choice. Nothing has occurred since to cause me to alter this forecast. Until 1977, the office investor had been burdened with "tenant leases," i.e., with lease provisions favorable to the tenant and unfavorable to the owner. These adverse clauses included flat rent for extended periods, low rent levels in relation to the development cost, ceilings on tenants' reimbursement to the owner for annual increases in real estate taxes and operating expenses, and full sublet rights to the tenant. In the past four years, the office market has completed a significant transition to strong owner leases in which the foregoing provisions have been radically changed to result in graduated or indexed lease rent at short intervals, full reimbursement for intervening real estate tax and operating expenses, and optional recapture of space by the owner from tenants desiring to vacate or constrict their space.

Office rents have increased as much as 300% since mid-1977. The dramatic surge in 1979-1980 was the largest advance in rent levels in the nation's history. Of late, there is some limited and certainly not yet conclusive evidence that tenants are resisting current office rent levels. The largest percentage increases in rent have taken place in New York, Boston, Los Angeles, and Washington. In major metropolitan areas experiencing a higher degree of development activity, such as Denver, Atlanta, Miami, Dallas, and Houston, the rate of rent increase definitely will slow under the pressure of increased competition. Nevertheless, both existing and proposed office buildings continue to offer the promise of the best investment rewards.

A second but very desirable choice would be to purchase a group of leased buildings in a planned light industrial park atmosphere. If capital funds permit, the purchase of an entire industrial park, possibly including the land still remaining for development, affords an even better investment opportunity. Typically, these parks have strict building and environmental controls that give the tenant a sense of comfort and security about the continuance of a controlled environment. Leases are usually of short duration and are conveniently staggered to avoid the possibility of excessive vacancies at one time. Vacancies in planned industrial parks consistently have been far lower than in freestanding, random-located light industrial properties on local highways. The term *industrial park* is somewhat of a misnomer because the overwhelming property use is for warehouse and distribution facilities. Light manufacturing is found only if the product can be produced without noxious odors and sound pollution. The term *light industrial park* would be more appropriate because of the uses.

Light industrial rents have increased steadily but undramatically over the past 20 years. These rents have not experienced, for example, the surge in shopping center rents between 1971 and 1974, or the 1979-1981 office rent surge. Supply and demand tend to remain in a more orderly equilibrium than in other realty markets. Vacancies in the industrial market are currently about 5%, up only about 1.5% over the past two, somewhat troubling, years. U.S. industrial expenditures for new plants, machinery, and equipment have continued at an intense pace. These indicators bode well for the industrial market. The U.S. faces a prolonged period of capital investment in new machine tools, plant modernization and expansion, improved technology, and changes in distribution facilities as the South and West continue to grow in population at the expense of the North and East. In many parks the capital appreciation potential has been enhanced by upgrading parks to a combination of office, research, and light industrial buildings. Coexistence has proved to be completely feasible in the superior planned and restricted parks.

A third favorite is shopping centers. After years of market dominance in the 1965-1979 period, the immensely popular, inflation-sensitive shopping centers of all sizes and types have faltered somewhat in performance. Prior to 1979, there was rarely any local oversupply of shopping center facilities. Success and profitability were a distinct prospect when the major chain stores preleased 50% or more of the space. The real proof of shopping center desirability as an investment occurred in 1974-1976 during our major general and real estate recession. Rents continued to increase in most centers in this period even though the merchants sold a lesser volume of goods. The inflationary price increases then experienced were more than compensatory. Lately, competition has increased significantly for shopping centers in the large to medium metropolitan areas. Since early 1980, retail spending has not been quite so robust. Consequently, percentage rent in some cases has not increased, or the rate of increase has slowed.

Despite these problems, the shopping center remains an excellent purchase, especially in developed areas where an additional competitive supply may be limited by a shortage of sites or lack of zoning. The outlook is good, but a note of caution permeates the atmosphere. If the American family shifts its priorities and saves more and consumes less (a not unlikely event), centers will experience much slower growth. On the other hand, if one believes that inflation will continue at a high rate, say in the 8%-12% range, all centers will benefit. If, as our Federal Reserve Bank firmly believes, inflation can be reduced to the 5% level, percentage rents will not exhibit the same historical rate of increase that has been characteristic since 1965. Developers have turned to the development of community-sized centers in metropolitan areas of smaller population, feeling that the major areas have become saturated.

Rehabilitation and modernization of existing obsolete structures as an alternative to development have attracted much investor interest in the past two years. In many cases, rehabilitation has involved conversion as well. The trend recently has been stunted by costly and scarce money from the commercial banks and thrift institutions, the main sources of financing for these ventures; however, the trend is strongly entrenched. A deeper appreciation of the handsome architecture of other eras has been noticed. Many tenants, both residential and commercial, appreciate both the atmosphere and patina of the older buildings. This is especially the case with service companies. Not all tenants can afford the rents in new buildings. Thus, there is a necessary economic raison d'etre for rehabilitated commercial and residential buildings.

The Next Five Years

Addressing now the prospects for the next five years or so, an intensified volume of real estate development will occur. The major life insurance companies, acting mainly for their own account but occasionally as investment managers for pension funds, will be financing superior development plans by making up to 100% loans on total development cost, for which they will receive as much as 50% of the equity ownership in joint ventures with outstanding developers. If substantial preleasing has taken place, the pension funds will finance these developments on the same basis. Thus, the market will become successively more competitive with each passing year.

The conclusion that we face of a highly competitive market within five years assumes the recovery of the thrift industry in the United States. Its financial problems stem from its need to pay more to depositors on time certificates than it is receiving on the average from its long-term mortgage and bond portfolios. Federal financing assistance may be required to assure solvency of the industry until the ruinous level of interest payable to its depositors is sharply reduced. If and when this happens, added capital will be made available to finance smaller investment properties. Coupled with the propensity of the optimistic American developer to oversupply, it may reasonably be forecast that extremely competitive, probably oversupplied, market conditions could occur in the mid-1980s. Many Cassandra-like statements are now being made about this prospect, but, in all fairness, the prophets appear premature in their anticipation of increasing vacancies and flat rents.

The extent of the difficulties we face by the mid-1980s will be a function mainly of demand. If demand abates because of a general recession, a political crisis, or still another oil shortage, the problem will be exacerbated. If the problem relates solely or mainly to oversupply, a period of reduced development activity could occur, lasting perhaps for three years. Rents in this scenario would remain firm but rental increases temporarily would halt. Vacancies probably would not exceed 10% and conceivably could be less. The initial scenario of both demand abatement and oversupply would provoke moderate-scale reductions in rents and vacancies in the 12%-15% range. If one is to choose the degree of severity, the more moderate scenario is more likely to prevail.

Conclusions

There are far more positive than negative indicators in the American marketplace. Surely, prices and rents have not yet reached the global levels prevailing in London, Tokyo, and other major capital cities; however, the market is tilted to a slight shortage. Tenant demand for all property types has remained strong. Investment interest remains at past highs. There is an ample supply of good properties coming on the market, quite unlike the shortage of offerings that were commonplace up to a year ago.

For the more venturesome, excellent opportunities exist to joint venture with developers the construction of office, light industrial, and shopping center properties. For the less bold, the existing inventory of properties is in a very strong competitive position, and the relative safety of capital investment seems quite assured. The pace and intensity of new development will be somewhat hampered in the near term by costly debt capital. This will tend to protect existing properties from oversupply. Thus, the outlook for the next year and beyond is for increasing rents and prices, albeit at a moderating rate. Cassandra-sounding comments about an overheated market and peak prices seem premature. In some cases, notably in Houston, Chicago, and Atlanta, the peak may be reached earlier.

The key to the intermediate and long-term future lies mainly in what happens to inflation. If inflation abates, as I believe it will, to the 5%-6% level, competition among different forms of investments will increase. Capital demand for real estate could abate as a large allocation of institutional money and personal wealth is diverted into stocks and bonds. This should have the effect of increasing the discounted internal rates of return for real estate. Prices will not decline, because moderate increases in cash flow will more than offset the decline in value occasioned by higher discount rates.

A moderate-scale corrective reaction could occur in the 1984-1986 period. It would be triggered primarily by oversupply brought on by large institutional investment in real estate. Reduction in tenant demand could result from the causes previously cited and create a more serious market dislocation. Chances are that the cyclical downturn, if any, will be mild and brief in the mid-1980s.

For now and probably three more years at least, there will be excellent buying opportunities in American real estate. For larger funds, I would further recommend a dollar-averaging approach, at least to the extent of continuing to purchase even at peak levels when exceptional properties become available at attractive prices. Underpinning any American investment is the strength of our economy and of our political system. There is no better investment climate in the world than in the United States.

27
Real Estate Market Forecast for 1983

General Economic Background

There are as yet few strong signs of a recovery from the general recession that started in the third quarter of 1981. The prevailing wisdom expects a rather weak and extended recovery in 1983. The smokestack industries continue in the doldrums: autos, steel, rubber, chemicals, energy, and others are reporting disappointing sales and low profits. The increasingly important service sector has bulwarked the recession and made a major contribution toward underpinning the economy. Lower inflation and interest rates are a welcome event but carry other somewhat negative implications as well, as will be discussed. On balance, the outlook is guardedly optimistic at best.

The following summary of economic views represents substantially the consensus by experts on the outlook and serves as an essential framework for our own real estate market forecast.

Reprinted with permission from Landauer Associates.

Expectations for the GNP and Interest Rates

Projections for the adjusted GNP range from a low of 1.5% to a high of 5% in 1983. This is in contrast to the adjusted flat GNP figures for the past six months. The consensus points to a 2.5%-3.0% increase which, while not robust, does presage a continuing upward movement in economic activity from the 1982 lows. The major influence in the 1983 economy will be the probable continuance of the significant drop in interest rates that started in August of 1982. All long-term rates may continue to decline through mid-1983. At this writing, the discount rate has dropped to 9%. Obviously the Fed is concerned about the weak economy. Its actions augur especially well for the battered housing market, since even lower interest rates may be expected. The discount rate, considered by many to be a leading psychological indicator, may very well be a better harbinger of current and future rates than the more volatile and less accurate prime rate. The major reservation about the continuance of lower interest rates is the extent to which the awesome federal deficit will soon start to crowd out the private sector in the competitive quest for financing in the capital markets.

What Level of Inflation May Be Anticipated?

Underlying the declining interest rate has been the unusually severe drop in the inflation rate. From a double-digit basis of over 12% in 1981, the economy has witnessed an accelerating decline, particularly in the second half of 1982, to the present annualized level of 5%. Undoubtedly, the Federal Reserve deserves major credit for the containment of inflation. Control of monetary aggregates has provoked wild swings in interest rates, but in the end, it has kept the money supply at sufficiently low rates to ensure lower inflation. The days of the financial roller coaster seem to be over. A companion cause of the deflation has been the weak economy itself. Loan demand has been off sharply, not only in response to the Fed-inspired high interest rates of the past three years, but also because of insufficient vibrancy in the economy.

The Fed's temporary abandonment of the containment of M-1 monetary aggregates as a primary means of reducing inflation should not be interpreted as a basic shift toward excessive monetary ease. The potential instabilities caused by the roll-over of All-Savers Certificates and expanded Keogh and IRA tax benefits does carry inflationary consequences, as these tax savings could distort the money supply unduly upward. In any event, the Fed will be also looking carefully at a combination of interest rate patterns, credit growth behavior, M-2 monetary aggregates, and at financial markets generally as a means of deciding the extent to which an expansion of the money supply is tolerable.

Credibility has become the all-important factor in capital markets. Certainly any expectation of continuing large deficits is an important consideration. For example, interest rates rose 200 basis points when President Carter delivered his January 1980 message in which he advocated virtually a long-term doubling of government expenses. The Fed maintained credibility in 1981-1982 because of its dogged insistence in reducing inflation by maintaining monetary targets. Its recent move to M-2 targets and other measures have not yet adversely affected confidence in its objectives. There is still a basic conviction that Chairman Volcker wishes to prime a weak economy without laying the seeds of a further severe inflationary binge. Monetary targets will indeed be increased by the Fed in 1983, but not to the extent of eroding the purchasing power of the dollar beyond current moderate levels.

Monetary policy alone will not fully contain inflationary forces. The Fed has estimated that a $25 billion drop in the budget deficit has the potential of decreasing interest rates by as much as 1%. Thus, a coordinated fiscal-monetary policy is essential to a stabilized economy. Events in 1983 may indeed be dominated by politics. Pitted against President Reagan will be many congressmen who feel that the budget gap must in some manner be closed, principally by new tax measures and a deferment of some defense spending. We do know that a healthy real estate development industry and real estate ownership in general are heavily dependent on long-term lower inflation and interest rates. The industry generally is divided over the solution to this dilemma. Many doubt the political solution of raising taxes and favor maintenance of or increase in tax incentives as a means of raising government revenues and reducing budgetary deficits.

Closing the Interest-Inflation Spread

The basic problem in a monetary sense is the continuance of an undue spread between interest rates and inflation rates. The real rate of interest at 7% is still far too high and should point to a continued lowering of long-term interest from, say, 13% today to the 10%-12% level within six months. Surely the peak 800 basis point spread between interest and inflation rates of late 1981 and 1982 could not logically have been justified in the face of a sustained low inflation rate at the 5% level. The volatile prime rate is not a good index for long-term rates, but a degree of consonance does exist, again suggesting lower long-term rates. Closing the interest-inflation spread depends on the capital markets' assessment of the extraordinarily high budget deficits. In a sense, the political actions taken in the next six months on taxes and spending will determine how long lower interest rates will last.

Unemployment

An end product of the weak economy is a troublesome unemployment rate of close to 11%. Some 12 million people are unemployed out of a total work force of 100 million. It is difficult to foresee the rate declining to less than 9%

in 1983, and this may be optimistic. Renewed housing construction will help, but the drag in the basic industries will tend to offset the improvement in construction labor employment. Even service sector employment may experience some moderate decline in the rate of its growth or even decline modestly itself in response to low economic activity. Perhaps the brightest note in an otherwise gloomy picture is the 56.5% employment rate. This is down only 2.5% from the 1979 high level of 59%.

Consumer Spending and Saving

The unwillingness or inability of the consumer to spend has hurt the economy and impaired the recovery. Consumers stopped spending in their accustomed volume in the first six months of 1980 and have not resumed as expected. Retail sales for the 1982 fourth quarter are disappointingly low. In many cases, their rate of increase is lagging behind the low inflation rate. Department store sales have been sluggish but have shown fourth quarter 1982 improvement. Poor auto sales have been a major negative in retail sales. Again, fourth quarter increases may enable the industry to achieve its 6 million production level. The outlook is for moderate spending in the first six months with some pickup in the last six months of 1983. Savings as a percent of disposable income have increased from the recession low of 4%-5% to 7% and more in the fourth quarter of 1982. This may be good news for the mortgage-seeker but not necessarily for the retailer. President Reagan's exhortation to save more may have short-term, counterproductive effects on retail markets as savings conceivably rise to the 8%-9% level in 1983, especially with the added inducement of money market rates at the thrift institution level.

The Real Estate Outlook for 1983

Capital Availability

Undoubtedly, the best news for real estate is the combination of increased capital availability for equity and mortgage purposes and the expectation of sustained lower interest rates. After almost three years of money shortages and high interest rates, investors and developers can look forward to a sharply improved monetary climate. The problem is the improvement may be very short-lived. Excessive federal debt requirements from mid-1983 on may crowd capital markets to a point where both inflation and interest rates rise because private and government sector needs cannot both effectively be met.

All sectors of the capital market will have more money for investment in 1983. The thrift industry, buoyed by new and more competitive lending authority and reduced interest costs on deposits, will add to their capital and surplus while having more money to invest. The newly enacted Depository Institutions Act of 1982 gives the thrifts the right to accept ceiling-free money market deposits. Further, it greatly accelerates the deregulation of interest ceilings. It must be regarded as a milestone for the industry. The $600 billion pension fund industry will also allocate more money to real estate as drains abate on their cash flow occasioned by 1982's unexpected retirement fund demands from retirees. Their mood of caution about real estate appears to be diminishing as well. The life insurance companies will sell more whole life policies and increase their cash flow for investment. The prospect for continued low inflation will sharply increase the life insurance companies' net income as families become less immediately concerned about inflation and more about overall savings planning by buying proportionately more ordinary than term insurance. The commercial banks will have ample funds, despite the added competition from the thrift industry. Investment real estate sales will be accomplished mainly by purchase-money mortgage accommodation by sellers and less by all-cash transactions, thus reducing the strain on equity requirements. The outlook for capital supply is distinctly encouraging for 1983. The wry consequence is the lack of development opportunities for the capital, except for housing, as will be discussed. This increased flow of funds will be directed more to the purchase of existing properties, and relatively none will be development capital.

Mortgage Interest Rates

Interest rates will be based on a revised definition of what constitutes *long term*. We do not foresee any 20-to-35-year loans in 1983 without equity ownership or, as a minimum, equity participation in cash flow. Intermediate loans now generally are for three to seven years. *Long term* will be redefined as 10 to 15 years without equity participation or ownership. Very little amortization will be required. Lenders have at least temporarily become more liberal and less restrictive in their mortgage terms.

Yields in December 1982 were 13% for seven- to ten-year unamortized money. It is anticipated that these rates, perhaps disrupted by a temporary increase in early 1983, will eventually decline within the year to the 10%-12% range. This is an exciting prospect for investors and developers. Unfortunately, it comes at a time when many real estate markets are severely oversupplied and when caution dominates institutional thinking.

The 1983 lending focus will be on refinancing of sound, well-rented properties and not on bailing out commercial banks on uncovered loans made on shaky, poorly rented development properties. The mitigation in the bleak office market picture is the knowledge that developers have more cash in their properties now than in the disastrous 1974-1976 period. Many will still find it difficult to avoid foreclosure. There will also be a severe lender clamp down in oversupplied areas, particularly those noted by high vacancies and demand retrenchment.

Renewed interest in rehabilitation and modernization of well-located, structurally sound buildings seems inevitable. Heretofore, institutional financing for rehabilitations and conversions has been inadequate. There will be an increased supply of money for this purpose as lenders have begun to understand that "newness" does not necessarily guarantee a well-finished or desired product. The lender is also recognizing that a strong market exists for a rehabilitated property which can rent for 70% of a new building and has equally satisfactory space. There are significant evidences of this in housing rehabilitation, modernization of shopping centers, and conversion to or refurbishing of office buildings.

Housing Markets

Beleaguered by three years of record high interest rates and a longer-than-expected recession, housing now has the brightest outlook among the real estate markets. Housing starts are expected to recover substantially from 1.0 million in 1982 to 1.25 million in 1983. The volume of housing resales should parallel this upturn.

The decline in interest rates should permit more potential first-time homeowners to enter the market. At the same time, many of the baby-boom cohort will be entering the market for the first time. However, the trend toward reduction in home size should continue. The median living area decreased from 1,655 square feet in 1978 to 1,550 in 1981, but purchasers would not sacrifice amenities. These trends reflect the popularity of condominiums. Although lower than the past few years, interest rates remain at historically high levels, caused by tight monetary policies and capital shortages in the thrift industry. Over the next few years the mortgage-backed securities market should grow, relieving the capital shortage but forcing mortgages to compete with other capital. Nevertheless, 1983 will bring substantially lower rates through the traditional thrift industry sources and an improved supply of mortgage money to finance the expected upturn. A temporizing factor in demand is the tendency for disinflation to reduce the incentive to invest in homeownership as an inflation hedge.

Institutional lending interest in the rental housing mortgage market has been renewed among life insurance companies as well as thrifts. The number of rental units of five or more started in 1982 is less than 150,000 units compared with more than 300,000 in 1979. Also, many rental units were converted to owner-occupied condominiums. This diminished rental unit supply and a strong rental demand have caused the rental apartment vacancy rate to hit a postwar low of 6.3%, compared with 6.6% in 1981. Anticipated escalation of rents, lower nominal interest rates, and new tax incentives, including ACRs, should encourage development of rental housing. Lenders, however, will impose more strict criteria on rental housing. Only well-designed and well-located rentals will win favor from lenders. The units will feature much more closet space and better designed and equipped kitchens and baths, even at the expense of the size of the other rooms. Few loans will be made if the units are not considered desirable for ultimate condominium conversion. The Reagan administration has abandoned Section 8 housing and reduced the federal government's role in other housing programs. The number of federally subsidized housing starts in 1983 will decline to 100,000 units from 155,000 in 1982. A voucher system or block grant or both will be substituted for these housing programs.

Housing market growth is expected to exhibit strong recovery but not to return to the boom levels of prior production peaks. Prices are not expected to increase to any great extent in 1983. It is anticipated that improved housing activity and construction will be a significant factor in the projected economic recovery in 1983.

Office Markets

Offices will generally continue in substantial oversupply throughout the country in 1983. The office boom, which started in 1977, came to a slowdown in 1982, where starts were off 17%. Further sharp reductions in construction activity will take place in 1983. Combined with the recession-induced cutback in demand, the weakness is even more pronounced. In a recent nationwide survey of investment-grade[1] office space, it was found that vacancy rates were frequently two to three times as high in the suburbs than in the central business district. Examples of oversupplied metropolitan markets include Denver, Houston, Dallas, Atlanta, and Los Angeles. New York, San Francisco, and Washington, on the other hand, have fared reasonably well because their problems are seemingly related more to demand reduction than oversupply.

In many metropolitan areas, it will take three to six years to absorb the excess supply, even assuming a resumption of demand to prerecession levels. For those suburbs with especially acute vacancies, two effects will be felt in 1983. First, some properties will be unable to avoid foreclosure. This will especially be true of those undercapitalized developers who simply cannot bear the rent loss and severe soft cost increases as construction loan high interest rates continue to accrue while the buildings remain underrented. Second, there invariably will be a spillover of the market weakness to the CBD. At least some tenants will emigrate in 1983 to the suburbs because of low rent rates and generous other terms. This will have the effect of softening the 1983 CBD rental market in most but not all areas.

Demand retrenchment takes many forms. Current, rather intense resistance to high rents will become more manifest in 1983 through corporate relocation of so-called "back office" clerical and machine operations to less ex-

[1] Office buildings over 50,000 square feet.

pensive areas within the city or in the suburbs. There will be a tendency for the CBD-located typical headquarters tenancy to be comprised of mainly the executive cadre, while less critical functions are performed elsewhere. Resistance to current high rent levels will also be evident in an increase in building population per 1,000 square feet. Architects and space planners will be challenged to accommodate more persons in a given space while still providing a commodious environmental impression.

There is no doubt the office market is hurting. General contractors are anxious for work. Field construction costs are down at least 10%. Materials are especially down in price, including 25% in structural steel. Land prices have ostensibly remained firm but are under downward pressure because liberal mortgage terms at below-market interest rates may be expected from sellers in 1983. Together with the decline in soft costs (principally interest), development costs are down about 15%.

Rents are down 10% to 15%, and somewhat more in some areas, from the mid-1981 highs, reflecting the lack of demand as well as oversupply. The frustration for developers is that even the most cost-effective building planned today will not prove initially to be a good investment because the return on the lowered cost will be inadequate.

As always, the premium locations will fare better than the ordinary locations. Quality projects will be relatively unaffected. One must also place the office market in a relative perspective by remembering the size and quality of the existing well-tenanted inventory of properties. Much of the inventory will be relatively unscathed by the recession, weak demand, and oversupply. Vacancies as a percent of the total inventory vary widely from a low of 3%-5% in Manhattan, 10% in Los Angeles, and 3% in Washington to 16% in Denver and 12% in Houston. Yet they do not necessarily tell the full story. Growth areas will resume growth more quickly and expand more quickly than unsettled or secondary areas. A year of greatly reduced development activity (except to finish what already was started) and weak renting is the most reasonable expectation.

Light Industrial and Warehouse Markets

Light industrial facilities and warehouses will feel the brunt of the existing recession until the recovery takes better hold. The surge in industrial construction starts, which began in 1977 and peaked in 1979, has tapered off since. Currently, owner-occupied industrial plant utilization is at levels below 70%; many operations have become technically obsolete, as corporations choose to close older facilities rather than continue the financial drain.

In a late 1982 nationwide survey of light industrial markets, vacancy rates in most major markets were close to peak levels of 10%. High vacancy rates were experienced particularly in larger buildings and in the heavily industrialized regions of the Northeast and Midwest. These conditions have been accompanied by a 5%-6% decrease in both rent rates and building sales prices from the peak levels of 1980-1981.

The problems in the industrial markets are due more to changing markets, obsolete existing facilities, and recessionary conditions than to the vast overbuilding of newer buildings as is the case with office buildings. Industrial construction starts have been dropping for three years, and any recovery will not have to overcome excessive overbuilding of new facilities.

Another nationwide survey of investment-grade[2] industrial buildings indicated that approximately 500 million square feet of rented buildings larger than 60,000 square feet had been built since 1977. Of these, nearly 70% had been constructed in the South and West regions with significant volumes in Houston, Dallas-Fort Worth, and Greater Los Angeles. Any resumption in economic recovery is expected to result in additional new construction in these same regions. Industrial construction is typically in suburban and outlying locations in sites possessing good access to both highway networks and productive labor forces.

Light industrial and warehouse uses have tended to lag behind the recovery in the general economy following each recession. We tend to feel that the former cyclical experience will change to the extent that any significant resumption of industrial activity will not be restrained by a crippling oversuppy, which would inhibit new construction and limit rents. We forecast 1983 as a year of very low industrial activity, with a continued decline in construction and sales volume. Rents, however, should be close to bottom levels and may represent an encouraging indicator for a recovery in 1984.

Construction starts in investment-grade properties in the principal markets in the U.S. plummeted in 1982 to an estimated 50 million square feet from 1981's 85 million square feet. We see no improvement in this performance in 1983. Too many negatives exist to enable us to be more optimistic, despite the absence of a serious oversupply. The weak industrial economy is the primary deterrent. Uncertainty over the future prospects for Reaganomics is another negative consideration. In the heavy industrial market, plant utilization of 68% is hardly an incentive for new construction, in view of existing plant obsolescence and despite weak industrial demand.

The outlook for warehouse and light industrial use, best exemplified by the ravenous growth of the hi-tech companies, is distinctly more upbeat. Continued but moderating population increases in Sun Belt areas provide a further impetus to recovery of this market sector. On balance, however, 1983 shapes up as a mediocre year in which we just manage to stabilze a fragile situation.

[2] Industrial buildings over 60,000 square feet.

Retail Markets

In the ten-year period from 1967-1976, construction starts of investment-grade[3] retail buildings averaged 92 million square feet per annum. Rents tripled during the same period. However, in the six-year period from 1977-1982, starts averaged only 70 million square feet, with only 1979 considered an especially banner year. In fact, the volume of construction per annum has declined steadily since 1979. Projected 1982 construction starts (not yet available) could be as low as 43 million square feet. Clearly, the shopping center market is not in an expansive phase.

The shopping center market has also been buffeted by a low level of consumer spending since the consumer-induced recession in the first six months of 1980. For example, in the 1979-1981 period, increases in retail sales of about 9% per annum were substantially less than the average corresponding inflation rate of 11.7%. Thus, adjusted for inflation, retail sales averaged a negative 2.7% for the 1979-1981 period. Complete 1982 figures are not yet available, but retail sales are expected to increase about 10% in 1982 against an inflation rate of 5%. Thus, some respite is in prospect for shopping center owners who are dependent for income on percentage leases based on retail sales.

Shopping center vacancies have generally increased from 5% in 1980 to 7.4% in 1982 and are expected to remain between 7% and 8% in 1983. Rents have at best stabilized and at worst are off about 10% from 1980-1981 highs.

Assuming a less-than-robust economic recovery, the shopping center outlook is not especially promising for 1983. The probable increase in auto and housing sales will occur outside shopping center facilities. The shopping goods sector of retail sales, which includes general merchandise, appliances, and furnishings, should increase from 8% to 10%. This will ensure improved rents well over the inflation rate but not necessarily increased income as increased vacancies may offset the increased rent.

The volume of shopping center starts in 1983 will be very low. Some improvement may be noticed in the last six months, but full recovery must await 1984 and 1985. We see 1983 as a holding period for shopping center investment. Much activity will be limited to modernization of existing centers and to the improvement of retail tenant mix. A continued trend to smaller stores further reduces space demand and is an additional negative in foreseeing an upturn. On balance, however, holdings of well-located and well-planned shopping centers will do moderately well in 1983 and face an even brighter future by 1985.

Investment Demand for Real Estate in 1983

After a turbulent year in 1982, the real estate investment market appears to be

[3] Shopping center facilities over 80,000 square feet.

stabilizing. A chief characteristic of the past year was buyer caution in the face of declining rents and uncertain economic prospects. That mood of caution has been tempered by declining interest rates, reduced anticipation of inflation, possible lower required rates of return, and a greater availability of capital from both traditional and new sources.

With the advantage of hindsight, it would appear that the investment market peaked in the third quarter of 1981. As the recession deepened and as rents started to slide, most institutional investors drew back to assess events. The onset of the change in the market, although very significant in terms of its later impact, occurred very subtly. As 1982 unfolded, it became apparent that equity capital was changing its formerly aggressive buying posture. It began to demand higher internal rates of return. There was expressed a growing requirement for a higher initial return on investment. Sellers were expected to provide purchase-money mortgage financing at below-market interest rates to reduce or eliminate negative leveraging. Installment sales and financings with purchase options became more commonplace. Despite softer rents and less inflationary expectations, discount rates tended to remain high.

Much investment confusion, even among experienced institutional buyers, existed in 1982. Demands for higher initial cash-on-cash returns were indiscriminately made. For example, initial cash returns have little valuation significance in cities such as New York where old office rents of $10 to $12 per square foot were renewed as leases expired at $30 to $40 per square foot. By contrast, initial rates of return became significant in shopping centers where percentage rents reflected current rental values at relatively high levels and where somewhat more stabilized future rents could be expected. Directly opposite of existing properties with low existing rents and high rent expectations, in which IRR methodology is the only sensible valuation approach, are the new development properties at current rent levels. Stabilized net income is a reasonable stance for a buyer to assume. Initial cash-on-cash returns indeed have relevance under these circumstances. It seemed, however, that universal condemnation of IRR methodology was being used as a cover by buyers to obtain lower prices.

During 1982, pension funds had either reached their real estate allotment, experienced lower cash flows, or held off as a matter of caution. Even the well-run and highly regarded PRISA open-end funds suffered unexpected demands for cash reimbursement from some of the pension funds in their portfolios. At the same time, the other major institutional investor, the life insurance companies, acting for their own account, had disappointing cash flow amounts for investment as term life insurance sales continued to dominate, despite the gradual easing of the inflation rate. A tight supply of equity capital was very deeply felt in 1982. Nevertheless, there was still considerable domestic and foreign capital available for real estate investment on a more highly selective basis.

The dollar volume of sales slowed in response to softer market conditions and harder investor attitudes. Prices eased slightly as rent expectations were lowered and discount rates held firm. With lowered anticipation of future rent increases, it is felt that discount rates on prime investment properties will decline from 1982's 18% level to the 15%-16% level. This will enable property owners to retain substantially all the property value otherwise lost because of reduced rent levels as leases expire. The capability of sustaining lower discount rates is a reflection in the long run of the trend in the inflation rate and hence the mortgage interest rate. Related market events occur within a reasonable degree of economic consonance. Thus, lower discount rates will only continue if the other related conditions persist as well.

A different investment climate is forming as the new year begins. The reduction in inflation on what is hoped will be a continuing basis and the consequent lowering of interest rates have stabilized an otherwise uncertain market. We cannot cite concrete evidence as yet of firming rents, but our sources tell us that in strong markets such as New York, Washington, and San Francisco, the rent slide has stopped or is about to do so. In oversupplied cities, alas, there will be a tendency for rents to slide further, perhaps 5%-10%, before stabilizing in 1984.

No doubt the investor in 1983 will not be as optimistic about the course of future rents as he was at the market peak in 1981. Some investors are assuming flat rents at current levels for three or four years before assuming a resumption of growth rate thereafter. However, there is an important offsetting factor which gives the seller a substantial opportunity for an excellent price in 1983. With the significant decline in interest rates and the prospect for a further drop to the 10%-12% level by mid-1983, there are signs in current negotiations that discount rates have declined in consonance. Thus, if a future income stream is forecast at a lesser inflation rate, the value may not fall at all because discount rates have declined correspondingly or more.

Proportionately more investment capital will enter the 1983 market, especially the life insurance companies and pension funds, but also foreign institutions and investors. We expect an increase in private and public syndications, reaching large as well as medium-sized properties. Institutions will maintain their criteria on quality. Syndications will not be quite as selective, but they will carefully avoid marginal situations. The Economic Recovery Tax Act of 1981 will act as a magnet in drawing together wealthy investors to take advantage of the 15-year depreciation allowances on a straight-line or accelerated basis as well as investment tax credits. We anticipate many private syndications with units of $100,000 to $1 million will be created, as SEC regulations have been eased to eliminate under defined circumstances the 35-person limitation before the syndication must become a public issue.

We expect real estate investment demands to rebound somewhat from the depressed levels of 1982. Transactions will take place, but the true catalyst for more intense activity will be a stronger economy without a concomitant return of higher inflation.

Summary

Despite the severe oversupply in the office market, the CBD-located office building in those central areas least affected by oversupply should be the favorite institutional investment. Most suburban office investments should be avoided because of the general weakness in the suburbs. However, if suburban offices are well tenanted with decent lease terms, then on a selective basis these may be good investments as well. Otherwise the office outlook in 1983 is bleak, with vacancies and reduced activity dominating the market.

The well-located, well-tenanted planned industrial park remains a superior long-term investment, despite the prospect of a moderate increase in current vacancies of 8% to the 10% level in 1983. The shadow of overbuilding does not overhang the industrial market as in the office market. The problem is that a large amount of capital is pursuing industrial parks. Unfortunately, the entire investment-grade industrial market is only 13% of the total nonresidential market. Opportunities for investment are thus more limited.

Shopping centers have been feeling the effects of the prolonged recession, at year end in its sixteenth month. Consumers reduced their spending early in 1980 and have not since resumed a normal pace. There are brighter prospects ahead. The general economic recovery in 1983 will motivate increased retail sales while the inflation rate remains low. The ample supply of retail facilities presages an extremely competitive market for shopping centers in 1983. Net operating income should not in general increase, as higher vacancies offset higher rents. We remain confident of a very substantial recovery in shopping center performance in the 1984-1985 period and would advise investors to buy now if the price is reasonable, that is, with returns of 8% to 12%, depending on the long-range outlook in the market area.

While we made no general presentation of the land market, we can summarize by saying that land prices have remained firm on the surface only in the past two years after surging in 1977 from the mid-1970 lows. In fact, land sellers have become more liberal in granting below-market interest rates on purchase-money mortgages and in subordinating these mortgages in whole or in part to development financing. In dealing with the hard realities of all-cash equivalents, it would be fair to say that land values have been down as much as 20%. Stabilization is the best prospect for 1983 in land prices.

The amount of institutional capital committed to real estate in 1983 will in part depend on institutional attitudes about stock market performance. Pension funds and life insurance companies have a choice between real estate and securities. Our best estimate is that there will be no diminution of capital for real estate. Most of it will be invested in existing properties. Little if any will go into development properties, except to finish what has already been started.

A quiet year ahead? Definitely! Nothing will be built in commercial real estate except for developments in which there are substantial prior lease commitments, or those being completed. The existing inventory of prime properties will not be unduly hurt by the recession. Only those leases expiring in 1983 will be adversely affected by lower renewal rates than originally expected. Investment interest will continue strong although on a highly selective basis. Transactions will take place, but the real thrust must await a far stronger economy and an absorption of the oversupply.

28

Trends in American Real Estate

One need not spend undue time on the past to grasp the trends in American
real estate but to me there is a key base year from which all recent economic
events in the United States have sprung. The year 1965 marked the end of an
era of relative economic tranquility following the devastation of World War II.
The immediate postwar years were characterized by population and industrial
growth, which were remarkably achieved with low interest and inflation rates.
For example, long-term bond rates increased from 2.39% in 1950 to 4.14% in
1964. Inflation increased from 1.0% to 2.6%, averaging less than 2%. So-
called G.I. home mortgages were readily available in 1950 at 4% interest on a
30-year, self-liquidating basis. The Pan Am Building was financed in 1963 by a
loan from New York Life Insurance Company at 5⅝% interest.

All this changed after 1965. The next year, President Lyndon Johnson,
under mounting political pressure, yielded to his party's entreaties and decided
to finance the rapidly escalating Vietnamese War with government borrowings

This article is based on a paper the author presented at the Building Owners and Managers Association of Australia's National Congress, in Sydney, Australia, September
27, 1983.

rather than additional taxes. As a result, our first credit squeeze occurred in 1966. Economic events have been radically different ever since. American financial markets have been dominated by recurrent financial crises, marked by volatile changes in interest and inflation rates and by wide swings in the availability of money and credit. More distressing was an obvious secular trend to successively higher interest and inflation rates with each economic cycle. Alas, the relative tranquility of the Eisenhower and early Kennedy years was lost, and volatility became the dominant theme.

Why must these earlier events be stressed in regarding trends in American real estate? Probably the primary reason is to point out the increased risk that volatility provokes. Market behavior is not as easy to predict as it might have been prior to 1965. We have witnessed the temporary undermining of the real estate market by the profound erosion of demand occasioned by the general economic recessions of 1969-1970, but with increased negative effect in 1974-1976 and 1981-1982. The real estate market simply could not withstand the depth of the later two recessions and failed badly during these periods.

The Higher Yield of Real Estate

Despite the increased risk and volatility, real estate has fared better than stock or bond investments over an extended time frame. Precise statistical comparisons for the comparable years are not available, but from later indexes starting in 1970, even the Wall Street investment firms would concede that through 1982, real estate had enjoyed a higher yield (defined as a combination of income and capital gain) throughout most selected time frames of 10 years.

Yes, on the whole, inflation has treated real estate kindly over the years. So well in fact that many real estate investors became quite well adjusted to inflationary consequences since yields tended to be very substantially higher than inflation and interest rates. In 1966 inflation was only 2.80%. It went to 10.77% in 1974, then receded somewhat, and by 1980 had risen to 13.16%. At this very moment, inflation has again receded to 4%-5%. Hopes are high that lower inflation rates will be sustained. The Federal Reserve Bank supports this notion, but others, of course, disagree.

A significant respite is now evident. However, there is little long-term assurance that it will stay at a low level. The present Republican administration's fiscal policy of incurring huge budgetary deficits will inevitably create, in the view of many economists, a substantial inflation and interest rate rise as the private capital market competes with the public sector over their respective financing needs. Some very credible economists demur, feeling that our enormous increase in capital plus a policy of continued monetary ease by the Federal Reserve Bank will enable the country to handle both public and private financing without provoking the classical consequences. However, both the private and institutional real estate investor have an unsettled feeling about the somewhat murky future. Some inquiring minds are asking whether real estate's ascendancy may be over for a time. I for one doubt it, but the question nags many of us.

By referring to Figure 28.1, one can trace the performance of the Prudential mutual real estate pension fund (PRISA) from 1970 to year's end 1982. Compared with such standard measures as common stock indexes, long-term bonds, short-term U.S. Treasury bills, and the consumer price index, real estate greatly outperformed all other investments and far exceeded the consumer price index. In the 1970-1977 period, real estate was grouped at the same approximate level with all other indexes except the volatile stock market. Starting in 1977, however, the rate of capital appreciation accelerated unbelievably until it flattened in 1982. While real estate significantly increased, bonds sank deeply until the 1981-1982 run-up, which was prompted by economic outlook projections of lower interest rates and by the Federal Reserve's more moderate monetary policy.

Figure 28.2 also demonstrates that real estate in the PRISA fund outperformed all other indexes as measured by rate of return through the same period, after adjustment into real from nominal dollars. From 1979 through 1982, the real rate of return was close to 5%, while common stocks were at about a 1% return and bonds were sharply negative from 1979 on. If we were able to project the 1983 figures, one would probably see a decline in real estate rates of return up to 20%, a sharp increase in real stock market returns (since the Standard & Poor Index rose over 50% from August 1982 to August 1983), and a decline in inflation, from 13% in 1981 to 5% in 1983. There is still considerable confidence that as the current oversupplied market will begin to attain equilibrium once again in 1985-1986, the dominance of real estate over other investments will reassert itself. The stock market could sustain further growth in the intervening 1984-1985 period but may very well be overtaken by real estate thereafter, thus preserving a higher historical comparative return for real estate than stocks.

Supply Factors of Recent Years (1967-1983)

Since 1968 our company, together with Data Resources, Inc., has maintained a database of historical post-1966 supply trends in investment-grade American real estate.

Investment grade is generally defined as nonresidential and nonhotel buildings of a minimum of 50,000 square feet. This considerable sample plus an estimate of construction prior to 1967 has a current replacement cost of $380 billion. Interestingly, 60% of the volume is office buildings; 27% is retail, and 13% is industrial. These properties have been further subdivided into four national regions and 20 major metropolitan markets. Some 66% of the sample

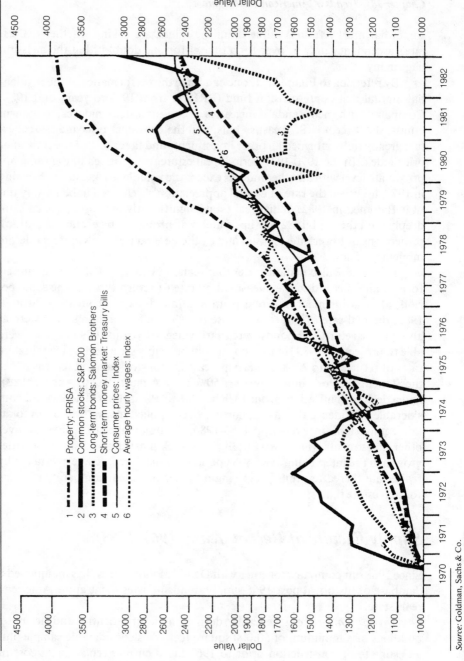

Figure 28.1 Value of a Single $1,000 Investment Including Reinvested Income, 7/31/70–12/31/82

1 Property: PRISA
2 Common stocks: S&P 500
3 Long-term bonds: Salomon Brothers
4 Short-term money market: Treasury bills
5 Consumer prices: Index
6 Average hourly wages: Index

Source: Goldman, Sachs & Co.

Figure 28.2   Effective Annual Total Return on a Series of $1,000 Investments Quarterly, 7/31/70–12/31/82 (real dollars)

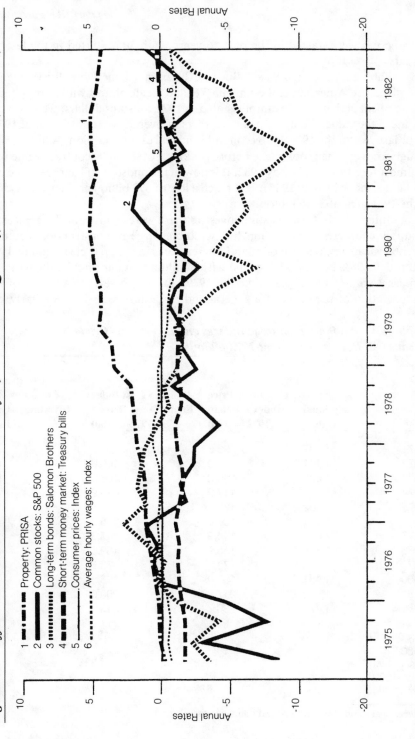

1 Property: PRISA
2 Common stocks: S&P 500
3 Long-term bonds: Salomon Brothers
4 Short-term money market: Treasury bills
5 Consumer prices: Index
6 Average hourly wages: Index

Source: Goldman, Sachs & Co.

properties were started in the past 16 years, with 30% started in the last six years.

Table 28.1 and Figure 28.3 illustrate the extraordinary volatility that tends to affect the American real estate market and create almost wild swings in development activity. For example, stated in 1972 constant dollars, we saw a decline in the value of construction contracts of over 55% from 1972 until 1976, the last year of the 1974-1976 economic and real estate recession. A historically high recovery then took place before peaking in 1981. The contract value was almost four times higher by 1982. It is now in the midst of still another spectacular decline, which by 1985 might reach a low of $75 billion or even less against the 1981 high of $156 billion.

Interestingly for the astute investor, there were significant differences in supply characteristics during the incredible surge in construction volume, rents, vacancies, and discount and interest rates in the up cycle period of 1977 through 1981. For the 13% of industrial buildings in our sample, the national market volume of supply peaked in 1979, about two years in advance of the recognition of the onset of a general and real estate recession. Similarly, the

Table 28.1   National Economic Indexes and Investment-Grade Real Estate Trends (All figures in constant 1972 billion$)

Year	Gross National Product	Consumer Price Index—Urban (1972 = 100)	Building Cost Index Engin. News Record (1972 = 100)	Construction Contracts Value Investment-Grade Real Estate
1971	1,107	96.8	90.5	95.5
1972	1,171	100.0	100.0	100.0
1973	1,235	106.2	108.5	97.5
1974	1,218	117.9	114.9	82.8
1975	1,202	128.7	124.5	52.2
1976	1,271	136.1	135.9	44.5
1977	1,333	144.9	147.3	52.7
1978	1,386	155.9	159.6	87.3
1979	1,483	173.5	173.5	111.6
1980	1,481	197.0	185.3	114.8
1981	1,510	217.4	200.0	156.4
1982	1,477	230.7	213.5	111.1
11-year % growth	33%	138%	136%	16%
1980-81 % growth	2%	10%	8%	36%
1981-1982 % change	-2%	6%	7%	-29%

Source: Engineering News Record and Landauer Associates, Inc.

27% of retail buildings in the sample reached a construction volume high in 1979. Because of the relative absence, until lately, of credible national figures, it was little realized that shopping center construction was in such a pronounced down phase. In fact, construction starts declined by two-thirds from 1979 through 1982. At least some sanity prevailed in both the industrial and shopping center markets as construction declined after 1979 in the face of fair economic conditions. We do not see an excessive overhang of surplus industrial and retail space in the American market today.

**Figure 28.3   National Economic Indexes and I.G.R.E.
(Investment-Grade Real Estate) Trends**

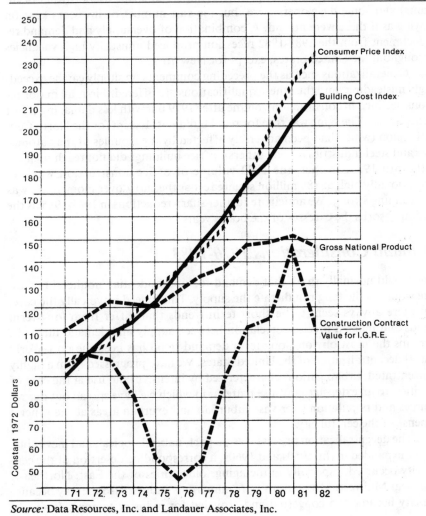

Source: Data Resources, Inc. and Landauer Associates, Inc.

The American office market has by far been the area of greatest weakness and, hence, concern in recent years. Fueled by various economic forecasts of an ever-expanding white collar employment growth, and by an institutional investment preference for office buildings, the investment-grade office market rocketed off in 1977 and continued in an ever-increasing, almost hysterical orbit through 1981 before an abrupt reentry into reality in 1982, which will undoubtedly be followed by further declines in construction starts in the 1983-1984 period. From a 1972-1976 base of an average of 66 million square feet of annual starts, the starts in our sample built to 247 million square feet in 1981. Why were not lenders and investors more acutely aware that the office market was becoming saturated? Surely, the commercial space users (owner-occupants) and some developers were, but the vast number of investors kept on buying as if there were no end. A combination of oversupply and demand retrenchment from the 1981-1982 recession produced unusually high vacancies throughout the United States, except for New York.

Generalizations such as the preceding comments on supply can be exceedingly misleading, and thus these qualifications are offered. First, all major regions declined in construction volume after 1979 but with less damaging effect in the South. The same was true for retail buildings. Except for the North Central region (which had been adversely affected by the troubles of the automotive and steel industries among others), office buildings did not reach their zenith until 1981. In fact, the 1982 volume of office construction was still exceptionally high at 185 million square feet as the carry-over momentum was still running strong. We anticipate further sharp reductions in 1983-1985 as the nation absorbs the excesses of the boom years.

Demand Considerations 1970-1983

One would normally think that demand for nonresidential, nonhotel real estate would in the long run dictate the supply. This indeed is typically the case, but there always seem to be short-term trends that differ from long-term trends and make a precise correlation between supply and demand difficult. Perhaps the most obvious long-term demand trend has been the post-World War II decentralization of the United States. We have progressed from a highly concentrated, urban nation, characterized by intensive land use at the core of all cities, to an extensive land-use pattern, in which we have spread out our resources and population over vast suburban and exurban areas at the general expense of the central city.

The decentralization process was, in part, natural, logical, and inevitable. As we expanded in the 1950s and 1960s, a corresponding desertion of the center city occurred, especially in the aging, older cities of the East, Northeast, and Near Midwest. Motivations were numerous. Industry led the way because the city became too congested and crowded for industry to cope. It sought open space for horizontal production and proximity to highways and growing airports. It sought as well a respite from the strident unionism of the immediate postwar years, recognizing that there was no ultimate refuge from the disposition of working people to organize for their own welfare and protection. As our interstate highway system grew, our distribution patterns followed suit and major warehousing and distribution facilities were constructed at every strategic location.

Population and Climate as Factors

Population followed the demand for industrial and service workers. The cities' numbers dropped moderately from 1960 to 1980, but at an increased rate between 1970 and 1980. Cities such as Boston lost as much as 21% in that 20-year period. New York lost 11% and Chicago 17%. Families with children especially wanted to move not only for the job opportunities, but because of a growing perception that our central city's educational system was declining in quality with the influx of disproportionately greater numbers of blacks from the South and Hispanics from South America and the Caribbean region.

Climate also significantly contributed to population shifts. The mild climates of the South or the Southwest proved a magnet in drawing both business and families from the heavily populated North and Midwest, where freezing cold winters were considered particularly difficult despite almost 100% central heating. Mild weather was particularly attractive, as a sharply improved standard of living for most families focused new attention on such recreational pursuits as biking, boating, swimming, and camping. Leisure time became ingrained as a way of life. It also became an important factor in corporate relocation studies as large-scale corporations advanced the thesis of the "quality of life" as a reason for leaving the central business districts in favor of suburban locations.

The Suburban Boom

Consequently, all suburbs, especially in the South and Southwest, experienced an unprecedented boom, broken only by the deep recessionary episode of 1974-1976 and, again, as a consequence of oversupply and demand retrenchment in 1982-1983, following the 1981-1982 economic recession. The central business districts of the nation weakened through the early- to mid-1970s, as the corporate exodus continued. It seemed that no amount of infusion of federal monies could stem the tide. Those older cities with established rapid transit systems and the new systems installed in San Francisco, Washington, and Atlanta were a major element in the eventual renaissance of the central business district, as we shall later recount. Of course, one city's loss is another's gain. The devastation that relocation together with in-migration of culturally deprived families wreaked on the aging cities of the industrial North and Midwest was truly significant.

Increase in White Collar Employment

Another major demand factor influencing the enormous increase in the office inventory has been the significant surge in white collar employment in the United States. The service industries have had unusual growth. Led by banking, accounting, law, real estate, engineering, advertising, and computer services, the annual growth rate over the 1970s has averaged 3.3%. After a 1981-1982 reduction to the 1.5% annual growth rate level, it is expected that the growth rate will moderate to 2% annually, still an impressive number. The relative decline in jobs per 100,000 square feet of manufacturing space has been somewhat made up by the large increase in the production of high technology goods and by the white collar jobs created by the shift. However, our economy is maturing. Our gross national product expressed in constant 1972 dollars has had an average annual increase of only 3.3%, hardly indicative of a high-growth economy. However, our high rate of industrial obsolescence makes always for activity from which the Realtor® can benefit.

Inflation as a Factor

Unfortunately, at the expense of the aged, the disadvantaged, those on fixed incomes, and the young, inflation until recently has been rampant and has fueled demand for real estate. Many on inflation-sensitive incomes, or owning inflation-sensitive investments, have been beneficiaries of a long-term monetary and fiscal policy that permitted the excesses to which we have been exposed. So-called Reaganomics, although novel and a seemingly better alternative than the tax-and-spend philosophy of prior Democratic regimes, is still largely untested and indeed very vulnerable to the awesome budget deficits we are now facing. So, our financial volatility and the risk it entails continue for the real estate investor and occupant. A seeming conflict exists between the fiscal policy of the government, with its high budget deficits, and the rather strict monetary policy of the Federal Reserve. Everyone appears a loser at the moment unless coordination is achieved.

The Resurgence of the Central Business District

One last secular trend is of special interest and significance. In the late 1970s and since, a remarkable renaissance has occurred in the central business districts of the older major cities, but to some extent in all cities, old or new. No one is quite sure why this phenomenon has occurred. Surely, a hedge against the possible but unlikely energy shortages of 1973-1974 and 1979-1980 may be one reason. Some disillusionment with the suburbs and their problems could be another. Suburbs have sustained traffic, congestion, education, in-migration, and pollution problems similar to those in the central cities. Continued growth and the increasing importance of advanced corporate and professional services as distinguished from and at a faster rate than corporate headquarters growth is undoubtedly a further factor.

The distinct improvement in rapid transit to the suburbs has also influenced many corporate decision makers to remain in the central business district because train and bus riding has become faster, more convenient, reliable, and comfortable. The more subtle phenomenon of social, economic, and cultural agglomeration seems to have returned to our collective consciousness. With the surge of the up cycle of the late 1970s has come a resurgence of the concept of clustering, or togetherness. The dramatic improvement in the real estate fortunes of the central city cannot only be explained in terms of the up cycle. Speaking of agglomeration, convenience to every urban need is appreciated more than ever. The intensity of American land use has been once again turned to an advantage while overly extensive land use leaves one frequently with a feeling of insularity and economic debilitation. Sadly, while not appropriate to this article, one must point out that the so-called gray physical areas, that is, the land uses generally extending from the vibrant central business and living districts to the suburbs, have undergone a profound deterioration and appalling population loss that tends to be obscured by the wealth of the central business district and the suburbs.

A Closer Look at Current Events

Our interest now switches to the post-1977 period. As if by some magical order from a superior being, the real estate market began the most extensive and intensive recovery from the 1974-1976 recession one could possibly imagine. Frankly, no one foresaw the depth and length of the up cycle in the next five years. Fortunes were made in real estate as institutional investment became successively more disillusioned with stock market performance. Rents in New York surged from $12 per square foot to $35-$45 per square foot.

> *If one is willing to accept somewhat arbitrary dates, the real estate cycle commenced its upward movement on or about January 1, 1977, and that rising phase reached its peak by December 31, 1981. Our view, with the benefit of hindsight, is the market attained its zenith in the third quarter of 1981. Up until that time, prices were at record highs. Surely IRRs were at their lowest. But cracks in the market foundation were forming. Interestingly, some of the cracks came from other than hard market evidence. Managers of pension funds became increasingly concerned and cautious. There was much discussion of the overheated market. Concurrently, vacancies were rising and rents peaking. Capital markets suddenly [sustained an increasing degree] of unavailability of equity and debt capital.*

The change became strikingly evident early in 1982. Demands for redemptions on open-end real estate funds increased. Rents started to fall. In New York City, for example, midtown office rents fell as much as 15% from their theoretical peak during 1982, while downtown rents stabilized and did not either rise or fall. Oddly, there was still equity capital for investment, but that capital became increasingly independent by discounting futures to a far greater extent than in the up cycle and by demanding higher IRRs. Suddenly the all-cash, institutionally dominated market changed to a "terms" market, dominated by syndicators who introduced such novel concepts as guaranteed up-front returns; installment purchases; purchase money mortgage financing; and by financings rather than purchases, sometimes linked to purchase options. Developers progressively lost their sales independence in 1982. Many had short-term commercial bank financing and were forced to sell to pay off construction loans and recapture as much equity as possible.[1]

More evident than any other real estate market event was the enormous glut of office space that developed in late 1981 and has continued to date. Cities such as Houston and Washington, D.C., which heretofore had been considered almost invulnerable to economic downturns and oversupply, suddenly developed vacancies as high as 20% in the suburbs and 10% in the central city. Strong cities such as Chicago and Los Angeles were feeling the consequences of oversupply. The shopping center and industrial oversupply has not been as severe as in offices because, as previously pointed out, the supply volume peaked in 1979 and the consequences have not been as dire. We are nevertheless in a slump of somewhat major proportions in the nonresidential markets. It will be 1985 before the first significant stirrings of renewed demand for a new supply will occur. In the interim, there are plenty of buildings with all manner of space to satisfy the gradually accelerating demand as our economy continues to improve.

Financial and Investment Considerations

While the spotlight was on institutional investment during the up cycle, in the late 1970s, there also occurred an increasing volume of tax sheltered public and private syndications, mainly of existing properties. The syndicators, acting as general partners in limited partnerships, were originally local investors and developers. The properties consisted mainly of

---

[1]John Robert White, "How the Institution Looks at Portfolio Management," *National Real Estate Investor,* September 1983, p. 56. Reprinted with permission from Communication Channels, Inc., 6255 Barfield Road, Atlanta, GA 30328.

apartment houses and small office buildings in the under-$10-million price category. In the early 1980s, however, many Wall Street investment companies assumed the role of general partner, together with the syndication specialists, such as Integrated Resources, Inc., and JMB Realty Corporation, which significantly increased their volume of transactions. So did they increase the size of the syndication for each property. Suddenly a $50 million transaction was not beyond the syndicator's reach. Recently, the prestigious Boca Raton Hotel was purchased by VMS Realty, Inc., a syndicator, for $100 million. Merrill Lynch & Company has raised $250 million in a single blind pool real estate offering. Suddenly, the institutions are confronted with real competition.

In 1982, according to a survey by Strategic Real Estate (formerly Questor Associates), an information service of Kenneth Leventhal & Company, there was a total of $3.7 billion real estate syndication dollars raised, of which $2.9 billion were public issues while the balance was privately financed. It appears the public has jumped once again into real estate with both feet. General and limited partners alike are ignoring the negative indicators in the down side of the cycle in their fervor to own real estate. The emergence of the major Wall Street firms as syndication sponsors, such as Merrill Lynch and Balcor/American Express, Inc., could conceivably lead to $5 billion in capital raised in 1983, according to Strategic Real Estate. The implications of this will be subsequently discussed.

The 1982 circumstances were especially wry. There were plenty of properties on the market at relatively high IRRs. Unfortunately, there was not the same amount of institutional matching capital to purchase them. Many unusual investment opportunities were lost in 1982 because of investor caution or capital shortages. Only the syndicators were smart enough to continue buying. Starting in the late third quarter of 1982, however, as concrete evidence of substantially lower interest rates became evident, owners of new properties withdrew their properties from sale or arranged extended mortgage financing. Still others did nothing, assuming that interest rates might fall to the 10%-11% level by year's end 1983. Most if not all available properties under $20 million were eagerly snatched up by the syndicators at prices and terms that the stodgy institutional buyer could not understand or would not compete for. [No price is now beyond the reach of the syndicator.] So, as we face the third quarter of 1983, [there are more properties on the market as owners respond to the generous prices paid by syndicators.]

[Clearly,] 1982 was a declining year in most respects. Rents surely declined, vacancies increased, and forward development planning virtually ceased as the oversupply and recession really took effect. For example, office starts were off 25% in 1982. 1983 will not be any better in

terms of the investment market. There will be little new construction because of generally oversupplied conditions. The only buildings started will be those with prior substantial renting commitments. Rents may also continue to decline in most metropolitan areas under the pressure of oversupply. Vacancies will continue high as the economy undergoes an extended recovery. The first stirrings of real estate recovery will really not even begin to take place until 1984. What, if anything, have we learned from our five-year rising phase of the cycle and the probable three years of decline since? [2]

Where Do We Stand Now?

- *The large institutional buyers, principally the top 100 pension funds but also the major life insurance companies, have become direct buyers of investment real estate. At the moment, they are using investment managers. Eventually some will build their own staff to do it themselves. They will be forced to purchase [mainly] large properties because the syndicators have swept the cupboard bare of smaller properties. This may force institutional syndication [among the larger syndicators] similar to the traditional institutional syndication that financed the General Motors Building.*

- *The large, experienced [pension funds] have started the process of dollar averaging for many reasons. The foremost reason is the pressure of annual accretion of funds at extraordinary levels. A second [reason] is a growing confidence in the institution's capacity to take advantage of market conditions, as in the 1982 episode that has been discussed. A third is the constant ERISA pressure of diversification. A fourth is an improved understanding of the need for a long-range view of real estate as an investment. The only limitation the investment manager places on his dollar averaging is the basic sense of each deal. To the extent that criteria must be compromised, or the deal has insufficient supportable rationale at a given moment, the manager will refrain, even if he does not fully invest all his allocated monies.*

- *The open-end fund is now somewhat in disfavor because of valuation problems and philosophical differences between client and appraiser over what constitutes a peak. Investment managers generally want the peak to be recognized and the valley to be somewhat elevated. Appraisers with a sense of perspective tend to discount the extreme peaks and extreme valleys. Yet at a given moment, who is to say when a peak or valley is reached, or indeed, is approaching? Meanwhile, the controversy continues.*

- *The closed-end fund has gained significantly in popularity in the past few years. The success of the RREEF funds is dramatic evidence of this. There is something comforting about raising a specific amount of money on a ten-year period of ownership basis. Once the funds are totally committed, another fund may be formed. Meanwhile, the fully invested, closed-end fund is not under the annual appraisal pressure of an open-end fund.*

- *There is an obvious need to improve commercial bank construction [loan-]lending practice. While the defaulted and uncovered construction loan situation is by no means as acute as it was in the mid-1970s, many of the poor lending policies of the mid-1970s have resurfaced in the form of inadequate market analysis; failure to insist on minimum lease commitments; and absence of take-outs. Commercial bankers are not inept. Their problems have mainly arisen because of competition among the banks and local developers. If the construction loan is courted, it may lead to compromising loan standards. I must ask, though, is that type of lending really sound in the long run?*

- *The [1977-1981] up cycle and the current state of the down cycle have confirmed one fact: The institution does not really want to dominate the joint venture development process. In fact, the opposite is the case. Recent events have confirmed the reemergence of the developer as the major force and general partner. [Mortgage] institutions, on the other hand, are rapidly retreating from a posture of independence to their more traditional passive role, in which reliance is placed mainly on the developer to produce the final product.*

- *At the moment, we are advocating some basic changes in the general definitions of mortgage terms. As the amount of mortgage capital has significantly increased, we [are now lamentably witnessing the gradual] return to the old definitions, based on a 35-year, self-liquidating term. The short-term loan should [ideally] be redefined as up to seven years in length, usually with [little or] no amortization. Ten to 15 years should become commonplace as medium- to long-term mortgages. Anything over 15 years should be substantially amortized, especially for the extension period, and should be subject to interest rate review.*

- *During most of 1982, discount rates remained stubbornly high in spite of the drop in inflation and interest charges. Too few investors took advantage of the opportunity. A drop in IRRs [of approximately 300 basis points] is now taking place as we see prices responding to investor acceptance of lower rates of return. In themselves, lower rates of return do not necessarily suggest higher prices. There are many other factors involved. For example, rent projections must now reflect lowered inflationary expectations and a still far from ro-*

bust economy. It will undoubtedly be essential to reduce the basic rent levels from the peak in many metropolitan areas as inevitable adjustments must be made to reflect the oversupply. Vacancy allowances must be increased as well. Forecasting in general will have a less rosy hue.

Of late, we have seen a resurgence of interest of unusual intensity in prime quality real estate. Thus, despite the caution I have expressed, institutions and syndicators want real estate because they anticipate similar lower rates on all other alternate forms of investment. What then is better than real estate under these circumstances? Certainly John Q. Public believes it, as evidenced by the volume of syndicate sales.

One fact is sure: There is no more "pie in the sky." While our declining phase will be shorter and more shallow, the fact is, with the possible exception of Manhattan, we have been and will be in the doldrums for the 1982-1983 period, inclusive. This is not to imply that transfers will not take place. On the contrary, there will be a lot of transactions, but the heady days are over. A new realism has permeated the market. Rents and vacancy factors will be adjusted to reflect actual market conditions rather than unattainable projections. Futures will be more substantially discounted by conservative forecasting. On the other hand, prices will remain high because buyers will accept lower rates of return in view of the increased popularity of real estate. The only long-term reservation in the outlook is a genuine concern that the syndicators will compromise standards on investment criteria by overpayment and injudicious selection. This would reflect poorly on the entire industry and provoke the scorn experienced in the REIT days and previously as well. [3]

The Outlook

Reduced capital spending in offices, shopping centers, and light industrials is anticipated in 1984, with some carry-over into 1985 in the dearth of office construction. Although the general economy has been stronger than expected in 1983, the rate of increase is expected to slacken and real estate's improvement will be tempered by the distinct possibility of higher interest rates and perhaps lower capital availability by mid-1984.

The year 1984 is viewed as one of relative quietude in terms of construction activity, leasing demand, and institutional (life insurance companies and pension funds) investment in real estate. It will take at least two and, in aggravated cases, three years to attain a reasonable balance between supply and demand in office buildings and probably two years in shopping centers.

[3]*Ibid,* pp. 58 and 60.

Of the various types of nonresidential properties, we feel strongly that the shopping center will be the best investment opportunity in 1984 and for at least two years beyond. This arises from a combination of factors. First, there is no real glut of shopping center space since the construction and development market peaked in 1979 and has been at a relatively low level since. Second, disposable personal income, particularly the consumer portion, has increased significantly with the economic recovery. Third, savings have increased from a low of 3% of disposable personal income to the 8% level today. Increases in consumer spending are very evident in autos, general merchandise, and apparel. Economists point out that the consumer stopped exceptional purchasing early in 1980 and has only recently resumed. This presages well for additional net income from increased retail sales as most leases have percentage of gross receipt clauses.

The question of capital availability and interest rates really is central to the 1984 outlook and beyond. The conventional view is that interest rates after the recent 150 basis points run-up to 13.5% will again recede before year's end and into at least the first part of 1984. Whether rates decline to the 10%-11% level is somewhat speculative to judge, but certainly 11% seems a reasonable expectation. The developers, however, will not be able to respond to lower interest costs because the glut of space is a distinct disincentive.

From the investor viewpoint, we see a mixed investment market developing with the life insurance companies and pension funds mainly sticking to all-cash purchases. The institutional syndicators, mostly life insurance companies and specialty companies such as Integrated Resources, will continue to pay a higher price than the all-cash equivalent because their investors prefer depreciation-originated tax shelters rather than income in a market swollen with cash from a 50% increase in the stock averages. It is the fervent wish of calm industry heads that syndication does not get out of hand and that prudent standards be maintained, as compared with the REIT debacle of the 1970s.

Beyond 1984, the real estate pace of recovery will intensify as more development activity is created and more capital moves into real estate investment. We expect a prosperous five-year period from 1985-1989 or so, which will permit real estate to remain in the forefront against the principal investment competitors.